Microsoft®

VISUAL BASIC® 4

Other titles in the *Step by Step* series:

For Microsoft Windows 95
(available in Fall 1995)

Integrating Microsoft Office Applications Step by Step, for Windows 95
Microsoft Access for Windows 95 Step by Step
Microsoft Access/Visual Basic Step by Step, for Windows 95
Microsoft Excel for Windows 95 Step by Step
Microsoft Excel/Visual Basic Step by Step, for Windows 95
Microsoft PowerPoint for Windows 95 Step by Step
Microsoft Project for Windows 95 Step by Step
Microsoft Windows 95 Step by Step
Microsoft Word for Windows 95 Step by Step
Microsoft Works for Windows 95 Step by Step
More Microsoft Windows 95 Step by Step
Upgrading to Microsoft Windows 95 Step by Step

For Microsoft Windows 3.1
(available now)

Microsoft Access 2 for Windows Step by Step
Microsoft Excel 5 for Windows Step by Step
Microsoft Excel 5 Visual Basic for Applications Step by Step, for Windows
Microsoft Visual FoxPro 3 for Windows Step by Step
Microsoft Mail for Windows Step by Step, versions 3.0b and later
Microsoft Office for Windows Step by Step, version 4
Microsoft PowerPoint 4 for Windows Step by Step
Microsoft Project 4 for Windows Step by Step
Microsoft Word 6 for Windows Step by Step
Microsoft Works 3 for Windows Step by Step

Microsoft® Visual Basic® 4

Step by Step

Michael Halvorson

Microsoft Press

PUBLISHED BY
Microsoft Press
A Division of Microsoft Corporation
One Microsoft Way
Redmond, Washington 98052-6399

Library of Congress Cataloging-in-Publication Data
Halvorson, Michael.
Microsoft visual basic 4 step by step / Michael Halvorson.
p. cm.
ISBN 1-55615-694-4
1. BASIC (Computer program language) 2. Microsoft Visual BASIC.
3. Microsoft Windows 95. I. Title.
QA76.73.B3H336 1995
005.265--dc20 95-23105
CIP

Printed and bound in the United States of America.

1 2 3 4 5 6 7 8 9 QMQM 9 8 7 6 5

Distributed to the book trade in Canada by Macmillan of Canada, a division of Canada Publishing Corporation.

A CIP catalogue record for this book is available from the British Library.

Microsoft Press books are available through booksellers and distributors worldwide. For further information about international editions, contact your local Microsoft Corporation office. Or contact Microsoft Press International directly at fax (206) 936-7329.

Acquisitions Editor: Casey D. Doyle
Project Editor: Laura Sackerman
Technical Editor: Marc Young

Acknowledgments

This book reflects the skill of many dedicated professionals. I would like to thank Casey Doyle for initiating the project and answering many questions; Dean Holmes for his humor and encouragement; Kim Eggleston for creating an exciting new design; Michael Victor for creating the illustrations; Bill Teel for preparing the electronic images; Peggy Herman, Elisabeth Thébaud, and Dick Carter for their elegant composition; and Sally Anderson, Patrick Forgette, Wendy Maier, and Stephanie Marr for their careful proofreading and copy editing. Extra special thanks go to project editor Laura Sackerman, who managed the schedule expertly and worked tirelessly to improve each draft of the manuscript, and to technical editor Marc Young, for poring over the program listings, smoothing out my mistakes, and sharing graduate school stories.

I would also like to thank Eric Peterson, Lisa Holcomb, Steve Johnson, and Steve Traut of the Microsoft Visual Basic development team for reviewing the manuscript and for providing useful feedback. Microsoft Solution Provider marketing manager Erick Alexander Cody visited with me about authentic Enterprise Information Systems, and you'll see his influence in Lesson 10. Finally, thanks to my Magnolia softball teammates, who entertain me on and off the field each summer, in spite of themselves.

Contents at a Glance

Table of Contents

Part 2 Programming Fundamentals

Running a program and creating a Windows 95 executable file, see "Building an Executable File," page 29 (Lesson 1)

Creating objects by using the interface design tools, see "The Toolbox," page 7 (Lesson 1)

Creating a user interface, see "The User Interface Form," page 7 (Lesson 1)

Adding artwork, see "The Shape Control," page 210 (Lesson 8)

Setting object properties, see "The Properties Window," page 7 (Lesson 1)

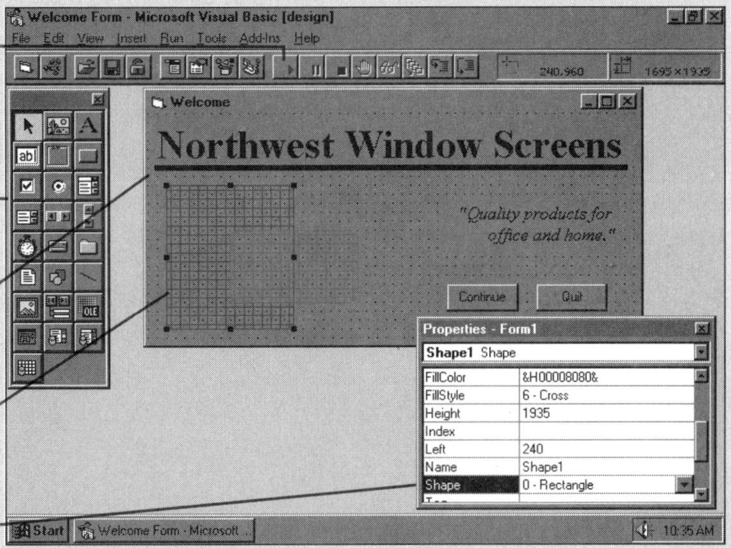

Adding pictures and animation, see "Adding Animation to Your Programs," page 228 (Lesson 8)

Creating clocks and timers, see "Using Timer Objects," page 169 (Lesson 6)

Creating a file browser, see "Using File System Objects," page 39 (Lesson 2)

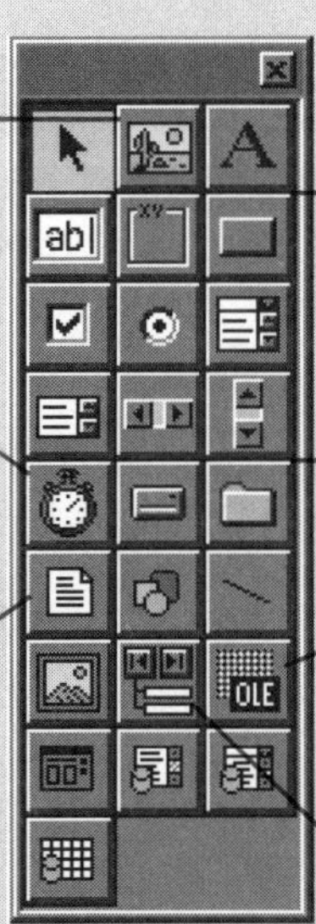

Creating custom forms and dialog boxes, see "Objects for Gathering Input," page 45 (Lesson 2)

Controlling Microsoft Office applications, see "Using the OLE Control," page 284 (Lesson 10)

Viewing and modifying databases, see "Managing Databases," page 263 (Lesson 9)

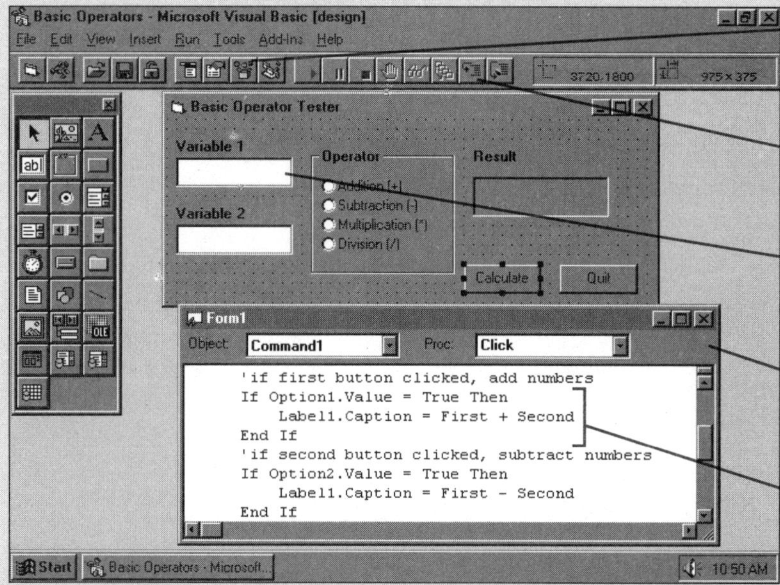

Examining the objects in your program, see "The Visual Basic Object Browser," page 294 (Lesson 10)

Debugging your application, see "Finding and Correcting Errors," page 143 (Lesson 5)

Working with data in programs, see "Using Variables to Store Information," page 104 (Lesson 4)

Entering and editing Visual Basic program statements, see "Writing the Code," page 22 (Lesson 1)

Adding program logic, see "If...Then Decision Structures," page 132 (Lesson 5)

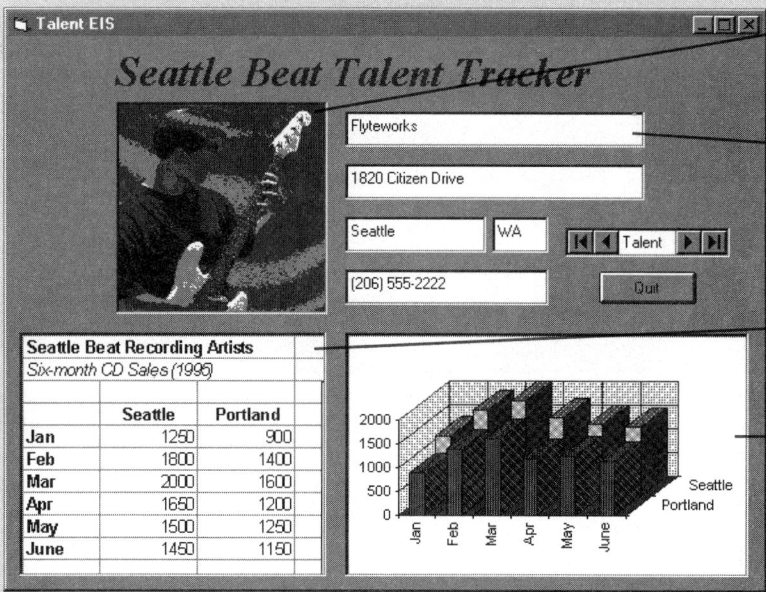

Integrating corporate data, see "Creating an Enterprise Information System," page 283 (Lesson 10)

Displaying database fields, see "Using Text Box Objects to Display Data," page 265 (Lesson 9)

Creating a link to an Excel worksheet, see "Using the OLE Control," page 284 (Lesson 10)

Inserting charts that can be updated automatically, see "Insert application objects," page 287 (Lesson 10)

About This Book

In "About This Book" you will learn:

- How to find your best path through the lessons in this book, based on your experience.
- How to use this book to teach a class, if you're an instructor.
- What the terms and notational conventions used in this book mean.
- Where to find additional information about Visual Basic.

This book teaches you how to use the Microsoft Visual Basic Version 4 Programming System to write useful and interesting applications for the Microsoft Windows 95 operating system. If you've wanted to learn Visual Basic programming but haven't known how to get started, this is the book for you. Visual Basic contains carefully integrated programming tools that will help you design, build, and test real, working applications. Best of all, you can use your existing artwork, databases, and Windows-based applications to create custom solutions for your workgroup, school, or small business. Visual Basic is easy to learn, and your time investment will pay off quickly.

Microsoft Visual Basic 4 Step by Step introduces programming concepts one at a time—starting at the *beginning*—and reinforces them with step-by-step exercises, practice files, and Review & Practice sections. A specially prepared disk containing all the sample applications and practice files in the book is included to jump-start your programming efforts. Instructions for copying the practice files to your computer's hard disk are in "Getting Ready," the next section in this book.

Finding the Best Starting Point for You

This book is designed for new programmers who are learning Visual Basic for the first time and for programmers who are moving to Visual Basic from another programming language, such as Microsoft C or MS-DOS QBasic. In this book, it is assumed that you're using Visual Basic Standard Edition, but the instructions apply equally to Visual Basic Professional Edition. Visual Basic Professional Edition simply has some extra, advanced features that aren't illustrated or discussed in this book. The readers who will benefit most from this book are application and database users who have had previous experience with Microsoft Windows and Windows-based applications such as Microsoft Word, Microsoft Excel, and Microsoft Access. The graphical applications you'll create in this book will look similar to these products. If you want to create applications and utilities that make Windows 95 and Windows-based applications easier to use, you're in the right place.

This book is divided into four major parts, each containing several related lessons. At the end of each part is a Review & Practice section that gives you the opportunity to practice the skills you learned in that part. Part 1 introduces you to the Visual Basic programming environment and teaches you how to create a functional user interface by creating objects, setting properties, and writing program code. Part 2 discusses how to build Visual Basic program statements, with an emphasis on variables and operators, decision structures, and debugging. Part 3 covers how to add printer support, error handling, artwork, and animation to a user interface. Part 4 covers working with text files and databases and using the OLE control to incorporate the functionality of other Windows-based applications into your Visual Basic programs.

Start by reading "Getting Ready," the next section in this book, and follow the instructions for installing the practice files. Then find where you fit in the following table to determine where to start in the main body of the book.

If you are	Follow these steps
New to Visual Basic and new to programming	Be sure to read "How to Think Like a Programmer," in the "Getting Ready" section. Then work through the lessons in order, starting with Lesson 1.
Experienced with Visual Basic for Applications	Work through the lessons in Part 1, skim the lessons in Part 2, and work through the lessons in Parts 3 and 4.
Experienced with QuickBasic or MS-DOS QBasic	Work through the lessons in Part 1, skim the lessons in Part 2, and work through the lessons in Parts 3 and 4.
Experienced with Microsoft C or Microsoft Visual C	Skim through the lessons in Parts 1 and 2, and then work through the lessons in Parts 3 and 4. For specific information about creating a user interface by using Visual Basic, read Lessons 2, 3, 7, and 8.

Using This Book as a Classroom Aid

If you are an instructor, you can use *Microsoft Visual Basic 4 Step by Step* for teaching Visual Basic to beginning programmers and for teaching specific Windows programming techniques to application developers. You might want to select certain lessons that meet your students' needs and you might want to incorporate your own demonstration programs into the lessons. The Review & Practice sections make good programming assignments, and you can extend them for self-study and evaluation purposes.

If you plan to teach the entire contents of this book, you should set aside at least five days of classroom time to allow for discussion, questions, and any customized lessons you might create. The book is also well suited to quarter-long courses, extended training programs, and self-study. The bulleted list at the beginning of each lesson offers good lecture and homework topics.

Conventions Used in This Book

Before you start the lessons, you should take a look at the terms and conventions I'll use throughout the book.

Typographic Conventions

- Characters for you to type appear in **boldface**.
- New terms and the titles of books appear in *italic*.
- Names of keyboard keys for you to press appear in SMALL CAPITAL LETTERS.
- Program code appears in monospace type:

  ```
  Label1.Caption = "Welcome!"
  ```

- In *syntax statements,* which are generic program statements that show you the structure of program code, placeholders appear in monospace italic type:

  ```
  Print expression
  ```

  Here, when you created a real program, you would replace *expression* with a real expression.
- Optional parts of syntax statements appear inside square brackets:

  ```
  Dim variable [As type]
  ```

Procedural Conventions

- Numbered lists (1, 2, 3, and so on) indicate steps you should follow.
- A triangular bullet (➤) indicates a single task for you to do.

Other Features of This Book

Open Project button

- You can perform many operations in Visual Basic by clicking a button on the toolbar or a control in the toolbox. When the instructions in this book tell you to click a tool-bar button or a toolbox control, a picture of the button or control will be shown in the left margin of the book, next to the instructions. The Open Project button in the margin next to this paragraph is an example.
- Text in the left margin provides tips and summary notes for the information being discussed. It also lists instructions for using the keyboard instead of the mouse to perform an action.
- Sidebars introduce special programming techniques, background information, or features related to the information being discussed.
- Screen capture illustrations show sample user interfaces and the results of your completed steps.
- The One Step Further exercise at the end of each lesson introduces new options or techniques that build on the skills you used in the lesson.
- The Lesson Summary table at the end of each lesson provides a comprehensive listing of all the commands and programming techniques introduced in the lesson.

How to Find Out More About Visual Basic

References to the Visual Basic *Programmer's Guide* at the end of each lesson direct you to specific chapters in the documentation for additional information. Use these materials to take full advantage of the features in Visual Basic.

Online Help

The Help system in Visual Basic provides a complete online reference to the programming environment, statements, and features of Visual Basic. You'll learn more about the Help system in "Getting Ready," the next section in this book.

Visual Basic *Programmer's Guide*

This manual includes information about setting up and starting Visual Basic, using the programming environment to build programs, and exploring a variety of intermediate and advanced programming topics.

Visual Basic *Language Reference*

This manual contains an alphabetic reference to the objects, functions, statements, methods, properties, and events in the Visual Basic programming language. The same information can be found under the Programming Language Summary topic in the Contents section of the Visual Basic online Help.

Visual Basic *Guide to Data Access Objects*

This manual contains advanced information about creating and modifying databases by using Visual Basic. It is supplied only with Visual Basic Professional Edition.

Getting Ready

In "Getting Ready" you will learn how to:

- Install and use the Step by Step practice files.
- Use the Visual Basic online Help system.
- Think like a programmer.

This section of the book prepares you for your first steps using Microsoft Visual Basic. You will learn how to install the *Microsoft Visual Basic 4 Step by Step* practice files, how to use the Visual Basic online Help system, and how to begin thinking like a Visual Basic programmer.

Using the Practice Files Disk

The disk attached to the inside of the back cover of this book contains practice files that you'll use as you work through the lessons in the book. Some of the files on the disk are partially completed programming projects that you'll work on to learn programming techniques. Other files are the finished results of the projects in the book, for your reference. In the following exercise, you'll install the Step by Step practice files on your hard disk. Install the practice files in the default installation folder (C:\Vb\Practice), if possible, so that your installation matches that shown in the lessons in this book.

NOTE In the instructions and exercises in this book, it is assumed that your Step by Step practice files are installed in the default C:\Vb\Practice folder on your hard disk. If your practice files are not in this folder, adjust the pathnames for the practice files as necessary when you work through the exercises in the book.

Install the practice files

Follow these steps to copy the practice files to your computer hard disk so that you can use them with the lessons.

1. Start Microsoft Windows 95.
2. Remove the disk from the package inside the back cover of this book, and put the disk in drive A or drive B of your computer.
3. On the taskbar's Start menu, click the Run command.
4. In the Run dialog box, type **a:\setup.exe** (or **b:\setup.exe**, if you put the disk in drive B), and press ENTER.

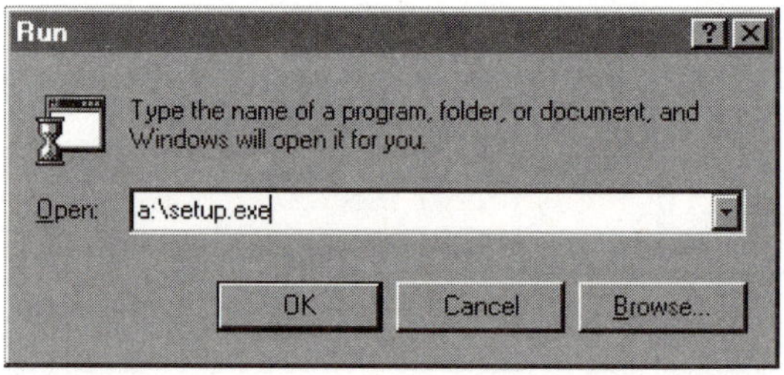

5. Follow the instructions on screen to complete the installation process. Install your practice files in the recommended folder (C:\Vb\Practice), if possible.

   The installation program copies the practice files from the floppy disk to your hard disk. The practice files will take up a little over 1 megabyte of disk space.
6. Remove the disk from the disk drive and replace it in the package inside the back cover of the book. Because the practice files are now on your computer's hard disk, you won't need the practice files disk again as you work through the lessons unless you want to reinstall some or all of the practice files later.

The text in each lesson in this book explains when and how to use any practice files for that lesson. The installation doesn't create any application programs—the practice files are project files and code modules that you open and run in Visual Basic 4. When it's time to use a practice file in a lesson, the book will give instructions for how to open the file.

In the step-by-step instructions for each lesson, you will be directed to rename your practice files by using the *My* prefix. Be sure to follow these directions for saving the files and giving them new names. Renaming the practice files allows you to use the renamed copy of a file to complete a lesson while leaving the original file intact. That way, if you want to start a lesson over or repeat a lesson later, you can reuse the original file. When you've finished with this book, you'll be able to review your progress by loading the practice files that have the *My* prefix into Visual Basic and examining them. If you read a lesson and choose not to create the demonstration programs on your own, you can open the completed practice files in Visual Basic to see how the programs work.

In version 4 of Visual Basic, project files have the .vbp filename extension.

The practice files are called *projects* and have the .vbp (Visual Basic project) filename extension. Each practice file is located in its corresponding lesson subfolder inside the Practice folder. For example, the practice files for Lesson 1 are in the \Vb\Practice\Lesson 1 subfolder. You will learn how to open and run Visual Basic projects in Lesson 1.

Different Versions of Visual Basic

Visual Basic 4 is sold in three versions: Standard Edition, Professional Edition, and Enterprise Edition. All three versions of Visual Basic have the same base set of features, so the exercises in this book apply equally to all three products. Visual Basic Standard Edition is the foundation product. It has full support for 32-bit programming under Windows 95 and Microsoft Windows NT. Visual Basic Professional Edition includes additional features related to the Microsoft Jet Data Access Engine, creating OLE Automation servers, and compiling 16-bit applications for Windows version 3.1. It also includes a larger collection of Windows metafiles and bit maps, which you can use to add colorful artwork to your programs. Visual Basic Enterprise Edition is the high-end, client-server version of Visual Basic. It includes all the features of Professional Edition plus special components that support team development, remote automation, code profiling, and source control for remote data access.

If you are using Professional Edition or Enterprise Edition and you want more information about the advanced features of that version, consult your documentation set for the details. If you are running Visual Basic under Windows NT, consult your Windows NT user guide for information about how Windows-based applications run in that environment.

Using Visual Basic to Create 32-Bit Applications

Visual Basic 4 has been specifically designed to create 32-bit applications for Microsoft's 32-bit operating systems, Windows 95 and Windows NT. 32-bit applications take advantage of the larger address space and memory management capabilities of Windows 95 and Windows NT, so they are faster, they are more robust, and they are easier to work with in a multitasking environment than traditional 16-bit applications are.

When you compile Visual Basic programs under Windows 95 or Windows NT, you get the advanced 32-bit application features automatically because your program is built by a 32-bit compiler intimately familiar with the features of the Windows 95 and Windows NT operating systems and the Microsoft Win32 application programming interface (API).

32-bit Visual Basic applications provide the following benefits under Windows 95 and Windows NT:

- Access to the full 32-bit address space of the Intel 386, 486, and Pentium microprocessors. A 32-bit Visual Basic application can use up to 2 gigabytes of system memory.
- Enhanced performance because of 32-bit computations and memory operations.
- Increased protection against system crashes that result from the inappropriate actions of other programs. Each Visual Basic application runs in its own protected memory region and is protected from the bugs of other programs.
- Fully preemptive multitasking, or the ability to switch from one program to another at any time. Users can now switch to and from Visual Basic applications as they wish, giving them more control over how they do their work.
- Access to the Win32 API, which experienced programmers can use to add advanced capabilities to their programs.

For compatibility with previous versions of Windows, Visual Basic Professional Edition includes a separate 16-bit version of Visual Basic 4 that allows you to compile programs as 16-bit applications so that they can run under Windows 3.1. (Projects that you create by using the 16-bit version of Visual Basic 4 are fully compatible with the 32-bit version of Visual Basic 4.) This feature allows you to create one core program for all recent versions of Windows—an advantage for programmers who need to support users running older versions.

The Visual Basic Help System

Visual Basic includes an online reference that you can use to learn more about the programming environment, development tools, and programming language in the Visual Basic Programming System. You can access Help information in several ways.

To get Help information	Do this
By topic or activity	On the Visual Basic Help menu, click Contents.
While working in a window or a dialog box	Press F1, or click the Help button in the dialog box.
About a specific programming tool, property, or language element	On the Help menu, click Search For Help On, click the Index tab, and type the word you're looking for in the text box.
About how to program	On the Help menu, click Learning Microsoft Visual Basic, and then click a lesson or click Instructions.

You use the following steps to get help on a specific topic in Visual Basic. This practice exercise instructs you to search for information about the Project window, but you can substitute your own topic.

Get help on a specific topic

The Help menu is your door to the Visual Basic Help system.

1. Start Visual Basic if it is not already running.

   If you're not sure how to start Visual Basic or how to use the Visual Basic menu bar, see "Start Visual Basic" in Lesson 1.

2. Click the Help menu on the menu bar.

   The contents of the Help menu appear.

3. On the Help menu, click the Search For Help On command.
4. Make sure the Index tab is selected, and type **project** (or another search topic) in the text box.

   As you type the word *project,* Help topics beginning with "p," then "pr," and so on, appear in the list box until your screen looks like the illustration on the following page.

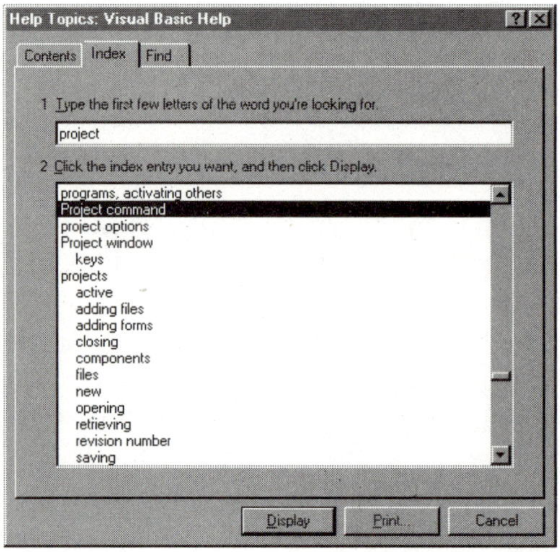

5 Double-click the Project Window topic in the list box.

The Project Window topic appears in a list box in the Topics Found dialog box.

6 Click Project Window (Visual Basic Help) and click the Display button.

The Help window displays information about the Visual Basic Project window. If all the information doesn't fit in your window, the window will have scroll bars that you can use to see the rest of the text.

7 Click See Also, which is near the top of the window and is underlined by a dotted green line.

A See Also pop-up window opens. Click any of the listed topics to learn about any features related to the Project window that you are interested in right now.

8 Press ESC to close the See Also pop-up window.

9 On the File menu, click Exit to exit the Help system.

You can also click the Close button on the Help window title bar to exit the Help system.

The Visual Basic Help system is a useful resource for learning about the programming environment or any topic related to Visual Basic programming. Be sure to use it if you have a question.

Thinking Like a Programmer

If you haven't written a program before, you might be wondering just what a program is and how you go about creating one in Visual Basic. This section provides an overview of the programming process.

A Visual Basic program is an application for Windows.

A *program* is a set of instructions that collectively cause a computer to perform a useful task, such as processing electronic artwork or managing files on a network. A program can be a tiny utility, such as a program that calculates a home mortgage, or it can be a large application program, such as Microsoft Excel. A *Visual Basic program* is an application written specifically for Windows by using the Visual Basic Programming System. To write a Visual Basic program, you determine what you want your program to do, design the screen—or *user interface*—for the program, and then build the program by using the Visual Basic Programming System. Let's examine each of these steps in detail.

Planning the Program

The first step in programming is planning.

The first step in programming is determining exactly what you want your program to accomplish. This sounds simple (isn't it obvious?), but without a mission statement, even the best programmer can have trouble building an application he or she is happy with. Planning a program is a little like planning a barbecue. For a barbecue to go off smoothly, you need to prepare for it ahead of time. You need to organize the menu, invite your friends, buy the food, and (most likely) clean your house. Although a barbecue can be entertaining if friends just happen to drop by and bring stuff, programs usually don't turn out the best if they're built with the "stone soup" mentality.

When you're learning to program, you should spend some time thinking about the programming problem you are trying to solve well before you sit down in front of your computer. Up-front planning will save you development time down the road, and you'll probably be much happier with the result. One part of planning might be creating an ordered list of programming steps called an *algorithm*. An algorithm for a barbecue might look like the illustration on the following page.

Creating an algorithm, or an ordered list of programming steps, is often an important part of preparing to write a program.

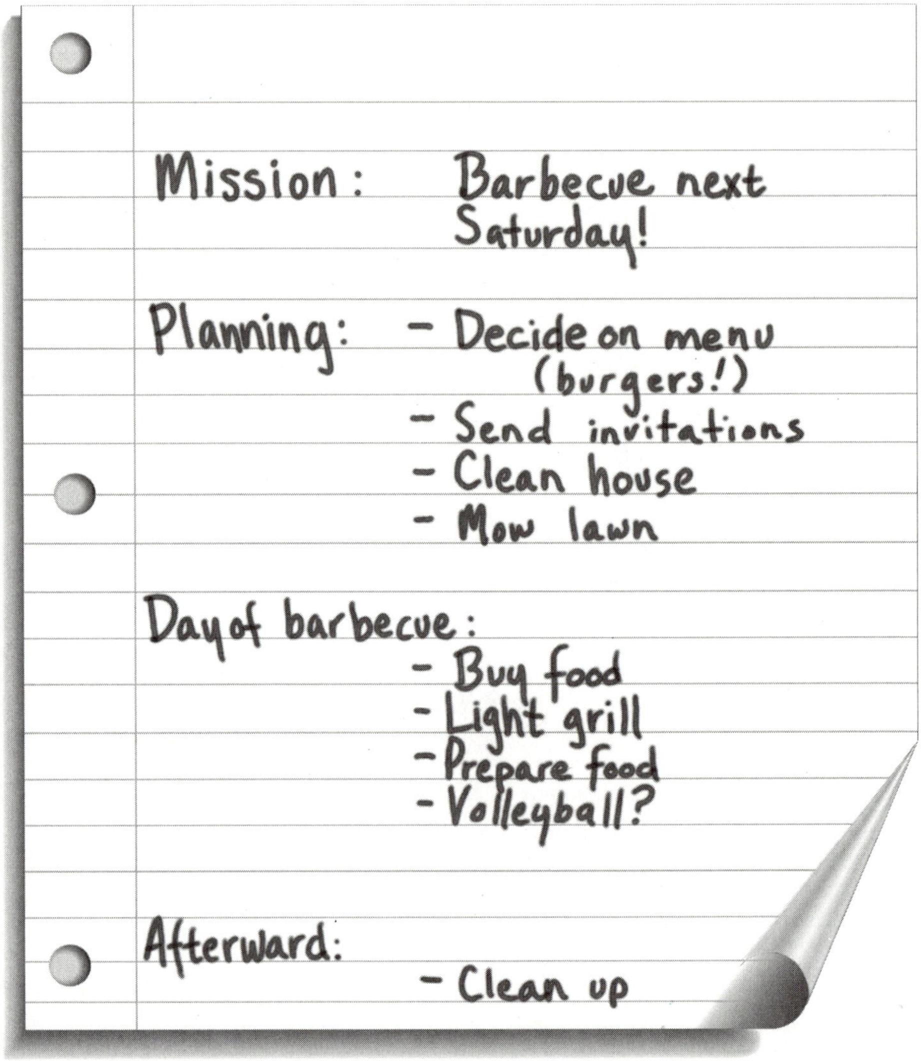

Designing the User Interface

The user interface comprises all the screens and images used in the program.

After you have established a clear goal for your program, it is important to think generally about how it will look and how it will process information. The complete set of screens and images used in a program is called the program's *user interface*. The user interface includes all the menus, dialog boxes, buttons, objects, and pictures that users see while they operate the application. The Visual Basic Programming System lets you create all the components of a professional Windows-based application quickly and efficiently. Several of these elements are visible in the following Windows 95 program, which I created by using Visual Basic:

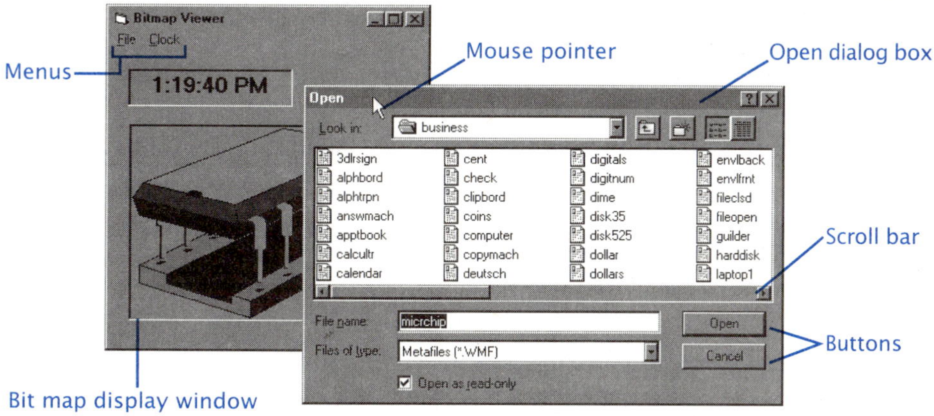

If you're familiar with Windows-based applications, you'll recognize most of the user interface elements. *Menus* contain many of the *commands* available in a Windows-based application; *dialog boxes, buttons,* and the *mouse pointer* help the user supply information to the program; and *windows* and *scroll bars* allow the user to view and navigate information displayed on the screen. To maximize the usability of your Visual Basic program, it is important that you use the Windows user interface elements in a standard and predictable way. Microsoft has published a set of design guidelines for Windows-based applications, and you'll learn about the most important interface guidelines as you read this book. Because most Windows-based applications are used by people other than the original programmer, it is important that you design them so that they have as many familiar features as possible.

NOTE If you would like to read the official interface design guidelines for Windows 95, see *The Windows Interface Guidelines for Software Design* (Microsoft Press, 1995).

Ask Yourself Questions

Lessons 1 and 2 discuss how to build an effective user interface.

When you plan Visual Basic programming projects, you might find it useful to draw a rough sketch of the user interface you'd like to present to your users. Doing this will not only help you design the interface, it will also help you think about how your program should work. It might be useful to ask yourself the following questions about your program:

These questions will help you plan your program.

- What is the goal, or mission, of the program I am writing?
- Who will use the program?
- What will the program look like when it starts?
- What information will the user enter in the program?
- How will the program process the input?
- What information (output) will the program produce?

Even before you know *how* the program will do what you want it to, you should have a good idea of *what* it should do and how it should look. After you have finished this preliminary work, you're ready to start building the program by using Visual Basic.

Building a Program by Using Visual Basic

NOTE After reading this section, turn to Lesson 1 and create your first Visual Basic program!

Building a Windows application by using Visual Basic involves three programming steps:

1. Creating the user interface by using Visual Basic controls
2. Setting the characteristics, or *properties,* of elements in the user interface, as needed
3. Writing the program code for one or more user interface elements, as needed

Creating a Windows program by using Visual Basic is surprisingly easy, as you'll see in Lesson 1. If you've used a drawing program such as Paint, you have many of the skills you need to create an effective user interface. To build the interface elements, you click an interface control in the Visual Basic toolbox, and then you "draw" the user interface element by dragging and clicking with the mouse. This is usually a simple matter of clicking to position one corner of the element and then dragging to create a rectangle that's the size you want. After you create the element—a text box, for example—you can refine it by setting properties for the element. For a text box, you can set properties to make text in the text box boldface, italic, or underlined, for example.

You complete your program by typing code for one or more user interface elements in a special window called the Code window. Writing program code gives you more control over how your program works than you can get by using the design controls alone. By using program code, you completely express your thoughts about how your application will process data, input, and output. The Visual Basic programming language contains several hundred statements, functions, and special characters, but most of your programming tasks will be handled by a few dozen easy-to-remember keywords. The Visual Basic programming language is not unique to the Visual Basic software you're using; Microsoft Visual Basic for Applications is included in Excel, Microsoft Access, Microsoft Project, and other applications for Windows. If you've used the most recent version of one of these applications, or if you've had some experience with Basic in the past, you'll recognize most of the keywords, statements, and functions in Visual Basic 4.

NOTE The rules governing the structure and content of the Visual Basic programming language are called its *syntax*. The word *syntax* comes from the Greek verb *syntattein,* which means to draw up an army in an orderly way. When you write Visual Basic program code, you will be marshaling keywords for the compiler.

The Origins of Basic

The original Basic language was created by John G. Kemeny and Thomas E. Kurtz in 1963 at Dartmouth College. It quickly became popular as a teaching language in universities and schools and was adapted for use on personal computers by Bill Gates in the mid-1970s. Since those early days there have been several updated versions of Basic created for personal computers, including Microsoft QuickBasic and MS-DOS QBasic. Although Visual Basic's fully graphical development environment and programming language are a far cry from the early Basic interpreters, the elegance and simplicity of the original Basic has, to a great extent, remained in the language. Visual Basic's power and ease of use are the primary reasons it was chosen as the programming language for Windows applications such as Excel.

Testing, Compiling, and Distributing the Program

The complete programming process is often called the software development life cycle.

After you create a working version of your program, you need to test it carefully, compile it into an executable program (that is, a stand-alone Windows program), and distribute it to your users. If you decide to revise the program later, you repeat the process, beginning with planning and an analysis of any new goals. These steps complete the software development life cycle, which is illustrated in the following diagram:

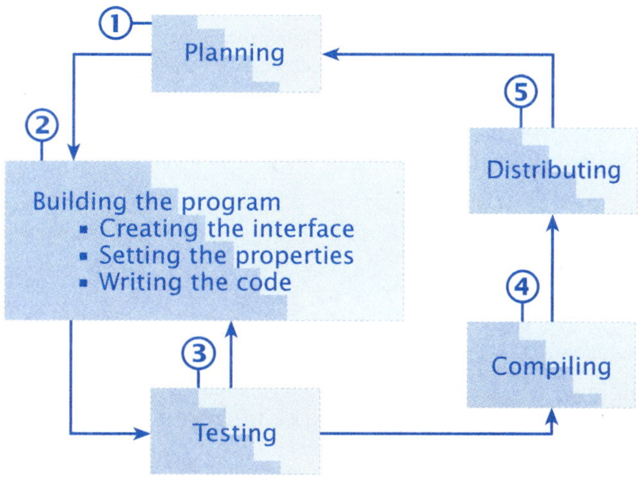

Testing the Program

A software defect is called a bug.

Testing a program involves checking it against a variety of real-life operating conditions to determine whether it is working correctly. A problem that stops the program from running or from producing the expected results is called a software defect, or *bug*. If you've used software for any length of time, you've probably run into your share of computer glitches caused by faulty software. Now that *you* are the programmer, it's your job to stamp out these problems *before* they reach the end user. Fortunately for all of us, Visual Basic provides some excellent debugging tools to catch bugs. You'll learn how to find and correct bugs in Lesson 5.

Compiling the Program

Executable files have the .exe filename extension.

When you've finished creating and testing your program, you can compile it into an executable (.exe) file that will run under Windows 95 or Windows NT. Creating an executable file in Visual Basic is as simple as clicking the Make EXE File command on the File menu, as you'll learn in Lesson 1. If you plan to run your new Visual Basic application only on your own system, creating the executable file will be your final step for the program. Simply double-click the program's .exe file in Windows Explorer when you want to run your new program, or create a shortcut icon for the file to place on your Windows desktop.

Distributing the Program

Visual Basic programs require dynamic-link library (DLL) files in order to run.

If you want to share your new program with friends or colleagues, or if you want to sell your program, you'll need to put the program and a few necessary support files on a disk (or the network), where your users or customers can get at them. All Visual Basic programs require one or more dynamic-link library (DLL) files in order to run, so you'll need to copy the necessary files from your hard disk to a distribution disk to get your users up and running. The exact DLL files needed depend on the operating system your users are running and the Visual Basic features used by your program. Chapter 30 in the Visual Basic *Programmer's Guide* documents the files you need for your distribution disks and discusses how you can write a custom setup program to install your software if you want to. For now, be assured that when you create Visual Basic programs, you and your users will immediately be able to enjoy the benefits of the new software. Let's get started!

Part

1

Getting Started with Visual Basic

Lesson

1

Writing Your First Program

Estimated time
55 min.

In this lesson you will learn how to:

- Start Visual Basic.
- Use the Visual Basic programming environment.
- Construct and run your first Visual Basic program.
- Save your program and exit Visual Basic.

It's easy to write powerful Microsoft Windows–based programs by using Microsoft Visual Basic. You might not believe this now, but after a few lessons I think you'll agree. Visual Basic's ability to perform some impressive tasks rests on key fundamentals we'll cover carefully in the first part of this book. Even if you haven't written a program before, you'll find that programming uses many of the same reasoning abilities and computer skills you use every day. In this lesson, you'll learn how to start Visual Basic and how to use the Visual Basic Programming System to write and run programs. You'll learn the essential Visual Basic menu commands and programming procedures, run a simple Visual Basic program called Step Up, and get your feet wet by constructing a new program called Lucky Seven. You'll also learn how to modify a program, store it safely on disk, and exit Visual Basic.

The Visual Basic Programming Environment

The Visual Basic programming environment contains all the tools you need to build powerful programs for Windows quickly and efficiently. Use the following procedures to start Visual Basic now.

NOTE If you haven't yet installed Visual Basic or the practice files that came with this book, work through "Getting Ready," earlier in this book. Then return to this lesson.

Start Visual Basic

1 In Windows 95, click the Start button, point to Programs, and point to the Visual Basic 4.0 folder.

The icons in the Visual Basic 4.0 folder appear in a list.

2 Click the Visual Basic 4.0 program icon.

The Visual Basic programming environment appears, as shown in the following illustration:

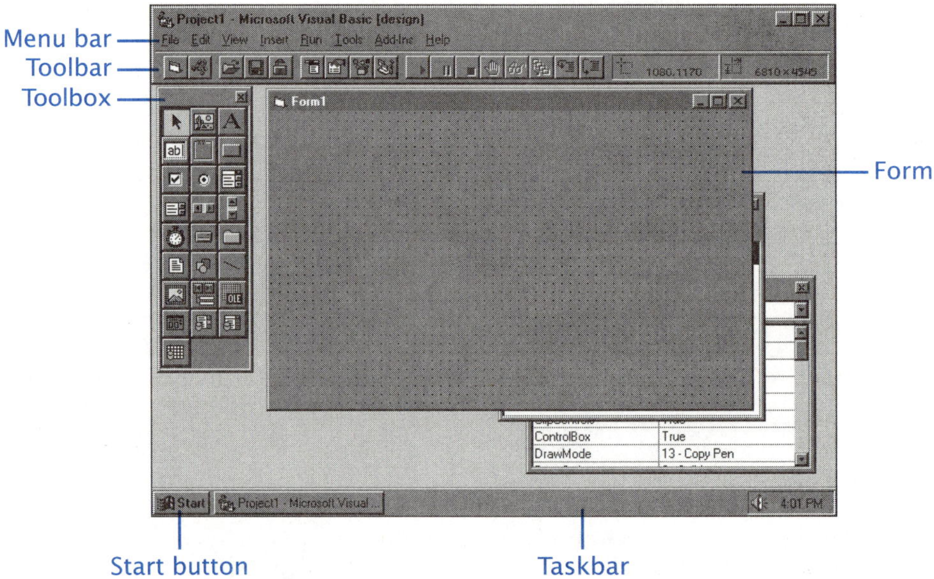

To display the function of a toolbar button, position the mouse pointer over the button for a few moments.

The Visual Basic programming environment contains programming tools to help you construct your Visual Basic programs. The *menu bar* provides access to most of the commands that control the programming environment. Menus and commands work according to standard conventions used in all Windows-based programs, and you can access them by using the keyboard or the mouse. Located below the menu bar is the *toolbar,* a collection of buttons that serve as shortcuts for executing commands and controlling the Visual Basic programming environment. If you've used Microsoft Excel or Microsoft Word, the toolbar should be a familiar concept. To activate a button on the toolbar, you click the button by using the mouse. Along the bottom of the screen is the Windows 95 taskbar. You can use the taskbar to switch between various Visual Basic components and to activate other Windows programs.

In the following exercise, practice using the menu bar and toolbar to load and run a sample Visual Basic program called Step Up.

Use the menu bar to open an existing programming project

1 Click the File menu by using the mouse.

The contents of the File menu appear.

2 On the File menu, click the Open Project command.

Visual Basic project files are distinguished by the .vbp or the .mak filename extension.

The Open Project dialog box appears. This dialog box allows you to open any existing Visual Basic program on your hard disk, attached network drive, CD-ROM, or floppy disk.

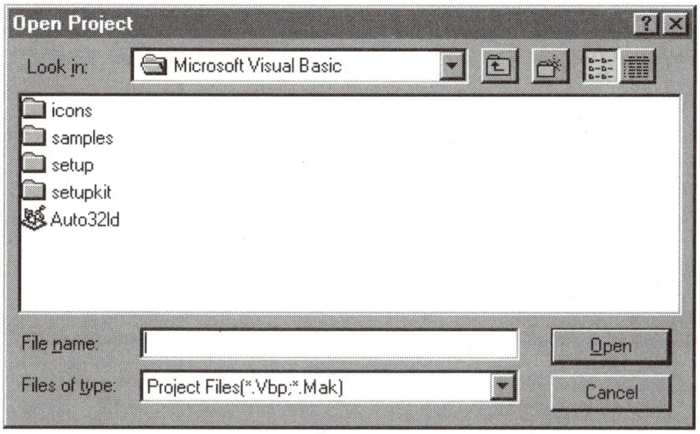

Up One Level button

3 Click the Up One Level button twice, and then double-click the Vb folder.

4 Double-click the Practice folder, and then double-click the Lesson 1 folder.

The \Vb\Practice folder (the default folder created by the Visual Basic 4 Step by Step Practice Files installation program) contains all the practice and sample files for the book. You'll use the Lesson *xx* folder corresponding to each lesson as you work your way through this book.

5 Select the Step Up project, and then click Open.

The Step Up project file loads the user interface form, the properties, the program code, and the standard module of the Step Up program.

6 Click the View Form button to take a look at the program's user interface.

The program form appears, as shown in the illustration on the following page.

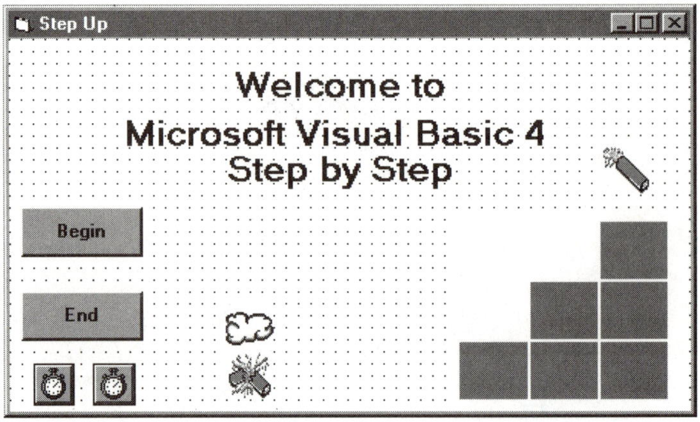

Step Up is just a simple Visual Basic program designed to get you in the swing of things. Since Step Up contains several of the elements found in a typical Visual Basic program, you'll be able to use it to explore the programming environment a little. When you run Step Up, it displays some animation and a message welcoming you to this book.

Start button

7 Click the Start button on the Visual Basic toolbar to run the Step Up program in the Visual Basic environment.

The toolbox and the Properties window disappear, and the Step Up program starts to run.

8 Click the Begin button to see some simple animation. Your screen will look like this:

9 Click the End button to quit the program and return to the programming environment. That's all there is to it—you've just run your first program in Visual Basic!

The User Interface Form

To maximize a form, click the Maximize button in the upper right corner of the form.

In Visual Basic, a *form* is a window you customize to create the user interface of your program. In the Step Up program, the form is the window you saw while the program was running. A form can contain menus, buttons, list boxes, scroll bars, and any of the other items you've seen in a typical Windows-based program. When you start the Visual Basic programming environment, a default form, called Form1, appears with a standard grid (a group of regularly spaced dots) on it that you can use to create your program's user interface and line up interface elements. You can adjust the size of the form by using the mouse; the form can take up part or all of the screen. In the Step Up program, a background graphic, a welcome message, and two buttons were added to the form to create the user interface. A Visual Basic program can contain one form or several forms.

The Toolbox

You can move the toolbox to another location on the screen by pointing to the toolbox title bar, holding down the left mouse button, and dragging the toolbox.

You add the elements of a program's user interface to a form by using the tools, or *controls*, in the toolbox, which is typically located along the left side of the screen. After controls have been added to a form they become *objects,* or programmable user interface elements, in the program. The toolbox contains controls that you can use to add artwork, labels, buttons, list boxes, scroll bars, grids, menus, and geometric shapes to a user interface. These elements will be visible to the user of your program when the program runs and will operate like the standard objects in any Windows-based application. The toolbox also contains controls that you can use to create objects that perform special "behind the scenes" operations in a Visual Basic program. These powerful objects do useful work but are not visible to the user when the program is running; they include objects for manipulating information in databases, working with Windows-based applications, and tracking the passage of time in your programs.

You can display the name of a control in the toolbox by placing the mouse pointer over the control for a few moments. You'll start using the controls in the toolbox later in this lesson.

The Properties Window

The Properties window lets you change the characteristics, or *property settings,* of the user interface elements on a form. A property setting is a quality of one of the objects in your user interface. For example, the welcome message the Step Up program displayed can be modified to appear in a different font or font size or with a different alignment. (With Visual Basic, you can display text in any font installed on your system, just like with Excel or Word.) You can change property settings by using the Properties window while you are creating your user interface or via program code while your program is running. The Properties window contains an object drop-down list box, which lists all the user interface elements (objects) on the form; the Properties window also lists the property settings that can be changed for each object. Practice changing the Caption property of the End button in the Step Up program now.

Change a property

1 Verify that the Step Up program has stopped running (you'll see the word *design* in the title bar when the program has stopped), and then click the End object on the form.

The End object (a command button) is surrounded by rectangles, or is *selected*. To work with an object on a Visual Basic form, you must select the object first.

Properties button

2 Click the Properties button on the toolbar.

The Properties window appears, as shown in the following illustration:

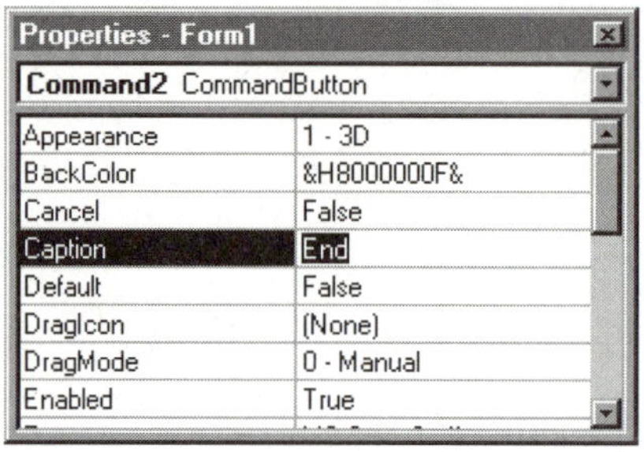

The Properties window lists all the property settings for the second command button on the form. (There are 23 properties in all.) The command button properties are listed in the left column of the window, and the current setting for each property is listed in the right column. The properties are listed in alphabetical order.

Thinking About Properties

In Visual Basic, each user interface element in a program (including the form itself) has a set of definable properties. You can set properties at design time by using the Properties window, and properties can be referenced in code as the program runs to do meaningful work. (User interface elements that receive input often use properties to transmit the information.) When you're first starting, however, properties can be a difficult concept to grasp. Putting them in terms of something from everyday life can help. Consider this bicycle analogy.

A bicycle is an object you use to ride from one place to another. Since a bicycle is a physical object, it has several inherent characteristics. It has a brand name, a color, gears, brakes, and wheels, and it is built in a particular style. (It could be a touring bike, a mountain bike, or a bicycle built for two.) In Visual Basic terminology, these characteristics are the *properties* of the bicycle object. The mold that created the bicycle frame would be called the bicycle control. Most of the bicycle's characteristics would be defined while the bicycle was being built, but a few additional ones (such as speed and age) could be properties that change as the bicycle is used. As you work with Visual Basic, you'll find object properties of both types.

3 Scroll in the list box until the Caption property is visible.

The Properties window scrolls like a regular list box.

4 Double-click the Caption property (the property name in the left column).

The current caption ("End") is highlighted in the right column, and a cursor blinks to the right of it.

5 Press DEL, type **Quit**, and then press ENTER.

The setting of the Caption property is changed from "End" to "Quit". The caption changes on the form, and the next time you run the program, the command button will have *Quit* in it.

The Project Window

A Visual Basic program is made up of several files that are assembled together, or *compiled*, when a program is complete. To help you switch back and forth between these components as you work on a project, the designers of Visual Basic have included a *Project window* in the programming environment. The Project window lists all the files used in the programming process and provides access to them via two special buttons: View Form and View Code. You can add, remove, and save individual files to a project by using commands on the File menu. As changes are made in a project, they are reflected in the Project window. The project file that maintains the list of all the supporting files in a programming project is called the Visual Basic project (.vbp) file. (In Visual Basic versions 1 through 3, project files had the .mak filename extension.) In the next exercise, you'll display the Project window for the Step Up program.

Display the Project window

Project button

➤ Click the Project button on the toolbar.

The Project window appears on top of the other windows in the programming environment.

To review what a program is and how Visual Basic programs are created, see "Thinking Like a Programmer" in the "Getting Ready" section earlier in this book.

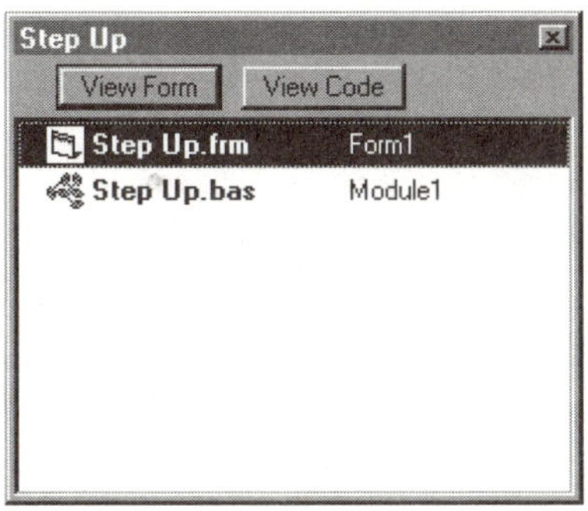

The project file in this programming project is named Step Up. In the Step Up project, the files Step Up.frm and Step Up.bas are listed. The Step Up.frm file contains the user interface form and any program code associated with the objects on the form. The Step Up.bas file contains code shared by all parts of the program. When the program is compiled into an executable file, or prepared so that it can run under Windows, these files will be combined to form a single .exe file.

Lucky Seven: Your First Visual Basic Program

Now that you've had some experience using the Visual Basic programming environment, it's time to build your first Visual Basic program. The Windows-based application you're going to construct is Lucky Seven, a game program that simulates a lucky number slot machine. Lucky Seven has a simple user interface and can be created and compiled in just a few minutes by using Visual Basic. Here's what your program will look like when it's finished. (If you'd like to run Lucky.exe before you start, you can find it in the \Vb\Practice\Lesson 1 folder on your hard disk.)

Programming Steps

The Lucky Seven user interface contains two command buttons, three lucky number windows, a graphic of a stack of coins, and the label Lucky Seven. These elements were produced in the program by creating seven objects on the Lucky Seven form and then changing several properties for each object. After the interface was designed, program code for the Spin and End command buttons was added to the program to process the button clicks and produce the random numbers. To re-create Lucky Seven, you'll follow the three construction steps I discussed in the "Getting Ready" section: creating the user interface, setting the properties, and writing the program code. The process for Lucky Seven is summarized in the following table:

Programming step	**Number of items**
1. Create the user interface.	7 objects
2. Set the properties.	10 properties
3. Write the program code.	2 objects

Another way to think about the Lucky Seven program is by using the following algorithm, or list of programming steps. Creating an algorithm can be a useful starting point when developing a program.

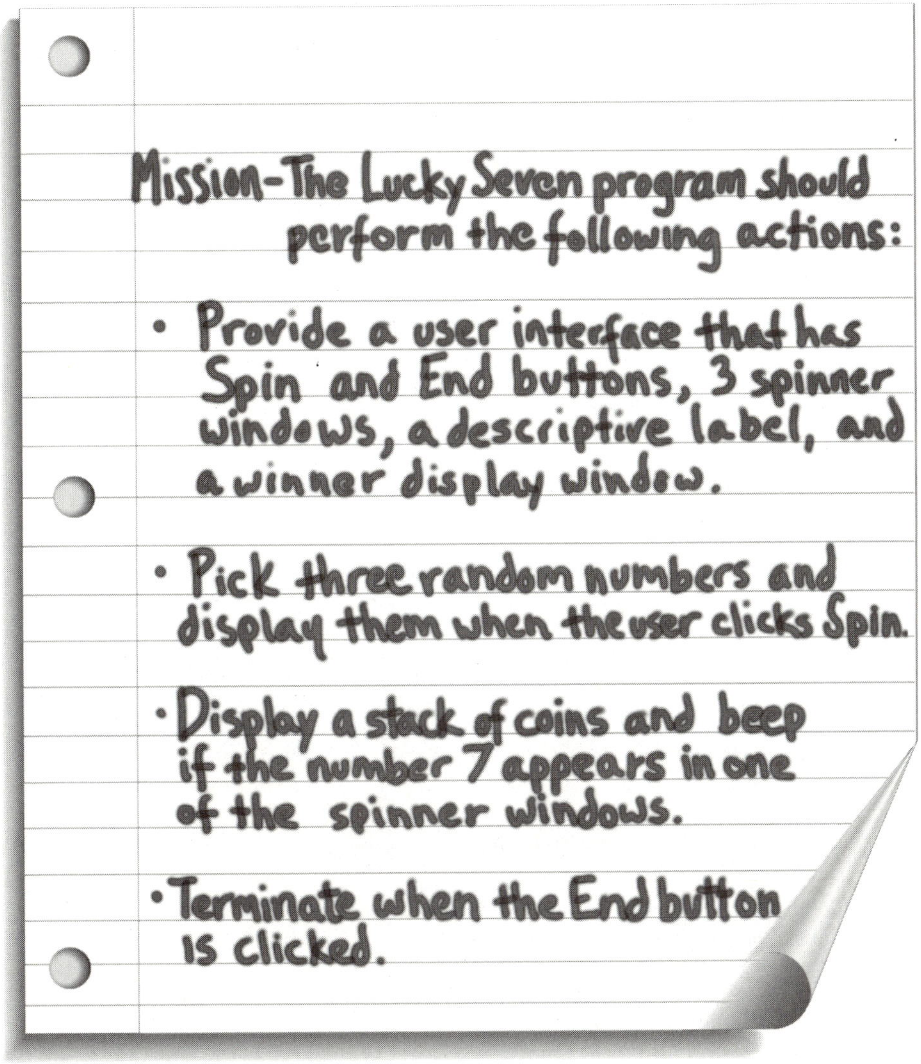

Creating the User Interface

Start building Lucky Seven by creating a new project and then constructing the user interface by using controls in the toolbox.

Create the user interface

You start a new programming project by clicking the New Project command on the File menu.

1 On the File menu, click the New Project command.

Click No if you are asked whether you want to save any changes to the Step Up program. The Step Up program is removed from memory, and Visual Basic cleans the slate for a new programming project. Visual Basic displays a blank form in the center of the screen for you to use for building your user interface. You'll create the two buttons in the interface first.

CommandButton control

2 Click the CommandButton control in the toolbox, and then place the mouse pointer over the form.

The CommandButton control is selected, and the mouse pointer changes to crosshairs when it rests on the form. The crosshairs are designed to help you draw the rectangular shape of a command button. When you hold down the left mouse button and drag, the command button object takes shape and snaps to the grid formed by the intersection of dots on the form. Try creating your first command button now.

3 Move the mouse pointer close to the upper left corner of the form, hold down the left mouse button, and then drag down and to the right. Stop dragging and release the mouse button when you have a command button similar to the one shown here:

The name of the command button is Command1.

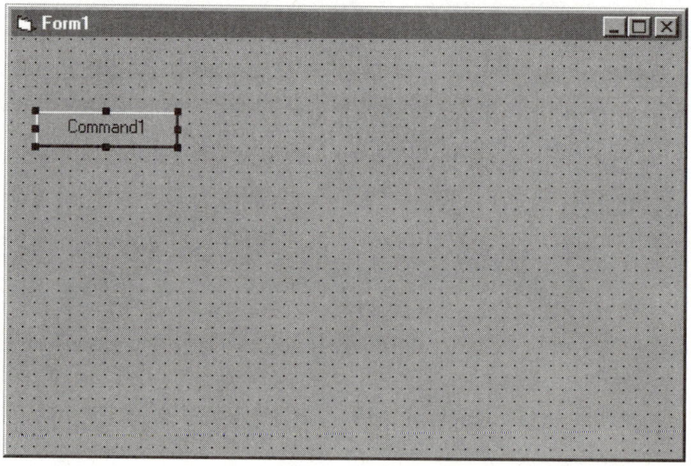

A command button with selection handles appears on the form. The button is named Command1, the first command button in the program. (You might make a mental note of this button name—you'll see it again later when you write your program code.)

You can move command buttons by using the mouse and resize them by using the selection handles whenever Visual Basic is in *design mode* (whenever the Visual Basic programming environment is active). When a program is running, however, the user will not be able to move interface elements unless you have changed a special property in the program to allow this. Practice moving and resizing the command button now.

Move and resize a command button

The grid helps you design your user interface.

1. Drag the command button to the right by using the mouse.

   The button snaps to the grid when you release the mouse button. The form grid is designed to help you edit and align different user interface elements. You can change the size of the grid by using the Environment Options command on the Tools menu.

2. Position the mouse pointer on the lower right corner of the command button.

   When the mouse pointer rests on a corner or a side of a selected object, it changes into a sizing pointer. You can use the sizing pointer to change the shape of an object.

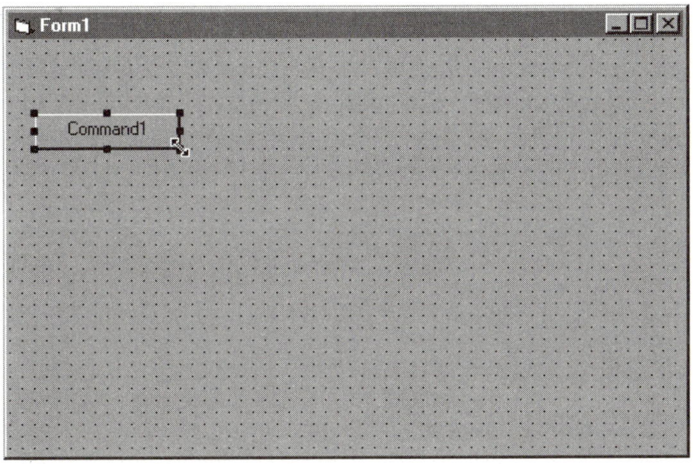

3. Enlarge the object by holding down the left mouse button and dragging the pointer down and to the right.

   The command button changes size and snaps to the grid.

4. Use the sizing pointer to return the command button to its original size, and then move the button back to its original location on the form.

Now add a second command button to the form, below the first button.

Add a second command button

CommandButton control

1. Click the CommandButton control in the toolbox.
2. Draw a command button below the first button on the form. (For consistency, create a command button of the same size.)

You can delete an object by selecting the object on the form and then pressing DEL.

3 Move or resize the button as necessary after you place it. If you make a mistake, feel free to delete the command button and start over again.

Add the number labels

Now add the labels used to display the numbers in the program. When the user clicks the Spin button, three random numbers appear in label boxes. If one of the numbers is a seven, the user hits the jackpot.

Label control

1 Click the Label control in the toolbox, and then place the mouse pointer over the form.

The Label control is selected, and the mouse pointer changes to crosshairs when it rests on the form.

2 Create a small, rectangular box like the one shown here:

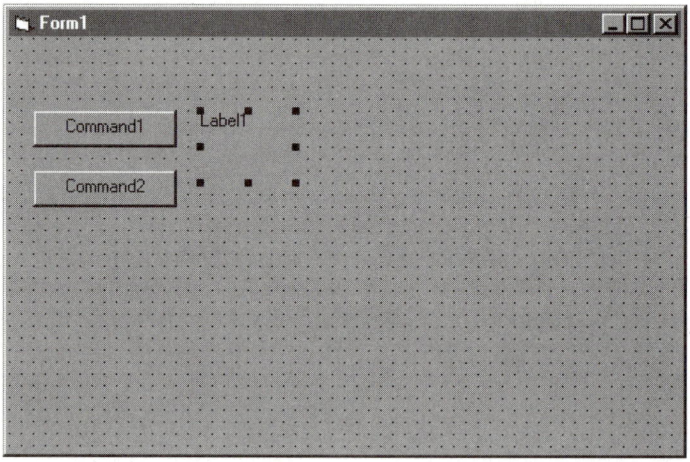

The label object you have created is called Label1, the first label in the program. A label is a special user interface element designed to display text, numbers, or symbols when a program runs. Now create two more labels, named Label2 and Label3, on the form.

NOTE As you create labels in this exercise, take a look at the two boxes on the right side of the toolbar. These boxes, which both contain horizontal and vertical measurements, are called *sizing boxes*. The left box gives the location of the upper left corner of the selected object, and the right box gives the dimensions of the object. The numbers in the boxes are in a unit of measure called *twips;* a twip is one-twentieth of a point. (A point is 1/72 inch, so a twip is 1/1440 inch.) You can use the sizing boxes to position objects on the form, and you can compare the relative sizes of objects you're creating.

---

3 Click the Label control, and then draw a label box to the right of the first label.

Create a label that is the same size as the first. The caption "Label2" will appear in the label.

4 Click the Label control again and add a third label to the form, to the right of the second label.

The caption "Label3" will appear in the label. Now you'll use the Label control to add a descriptive label to your form. This will be the fourth and final label in the program.

5 Click the Label control in the toolbox.

6 Create a larger rectangle directly below the two command buttons.

When you've finished, your four labels should look like the following. (You can resize the label objects if they don't look quite right.)

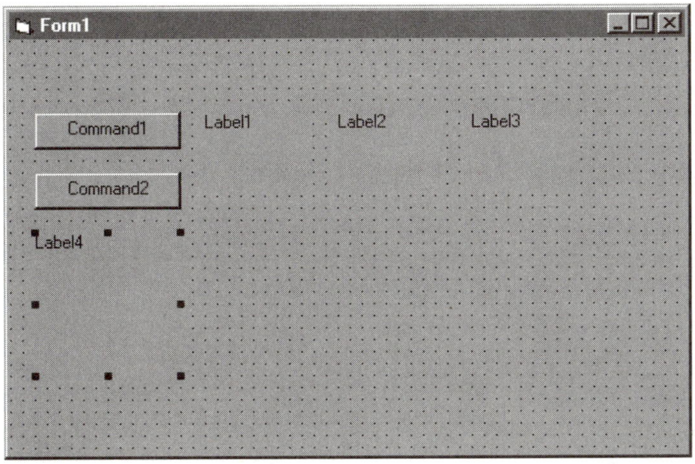

Now add a picture box to the form to display the stack of coins the user wins when he or she draws a seven and hits the jackpot. A picture box is designed to display bit maps, icons, and other artwork in a program. One of the best uses for a picture box is to display a piece of Visual Basic clip art.

Add a picture

PictureBox control

1 Click the PictureBox control in the toolbox.

2 Using the PictureBox control, create a large, rectangular box directly beneath the three number labels.

When you've finished, your picture box object should look like the following:

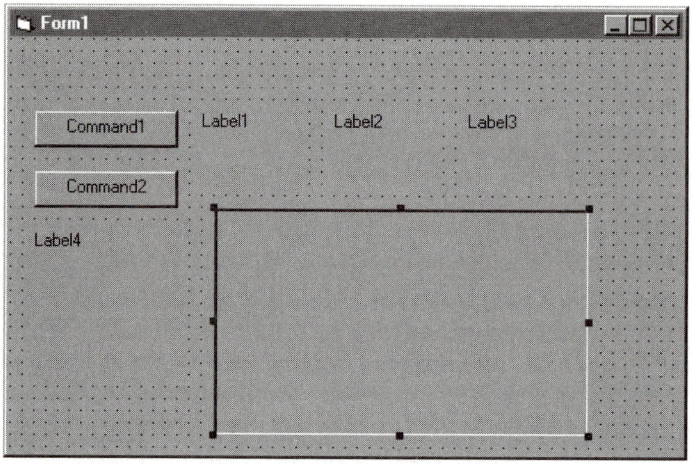

This object will be called Picture1 in your program; you'll use this name later in the program code.

Now resize the form a bit. All that extra space on the right is not necessary.

Resize the form

- Drag the right edge of the form window to the left to within one grid column of the picture box object.

That's it! When your program is run, the program window will be this size. You're ready to customize your interface by setting a few properties.

Setting the Properties

As you discovered earlier, in the Step Up program, you can change properties by selecting objects on the form and changing settings in the Properties window. Start setting the properties in this program by changing the caption settings for the two command buttons.

Set the command button properties

1. Click the first command button (Command1) on the form.

   The command button is surrounded by selection handles.

2. Click the Properties button on the toolbar.

Properties button

The Properties window appears, as shown in the following illustration:

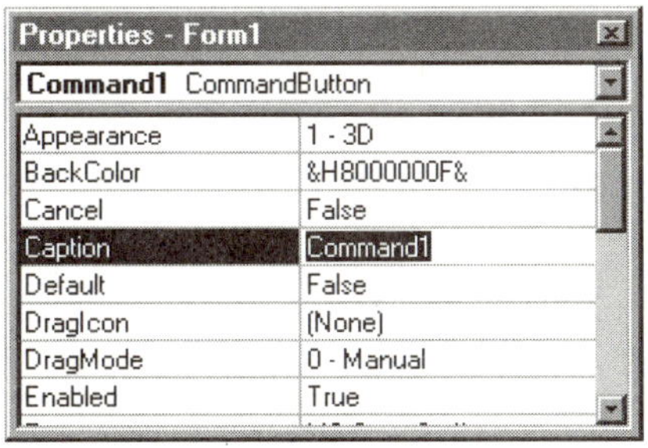

The Properties window lists the settings for the first command button. These include settings for the background color, caption, height, width, and font of the command button.

3 Double-click the Caption property in the left column of the Properties window.

The current Caption setting ("Command1") is highlighted in the Properties window.

4 Type **Spin** and press ENTER.

The Caption property changes to "Spin" in the Properties window and on the form. Now change the caption of the second button to "End". (You'll select the second button in a new way this time.)

5 Open the object drop-down list box at the top of the Properties window.

A list of the interface objects in your program appears in the list box:

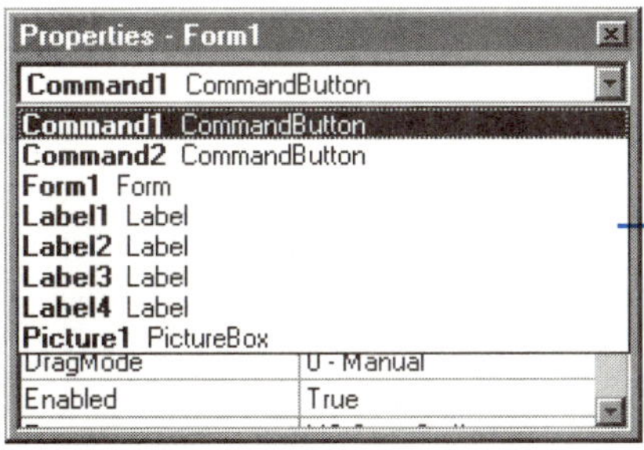

Object drop-down list box

6 Click Command2 (the second command button) in the list box.

The property settings for the second command button appear in the Properties window.

7 Double-click the current Caption property ("Command2"), type **End**, and then press ENTER.

The caption of the second command button is changed to "End".

NOTE Using the object drop-down list box is a handy way to switch between objects in your program. You can also switch between objects by clicking each object on the form individually.

Now set the properties for the labels in the program. The first three labels will hold the random numbers in the program and will have identical property settings. (You'll set most of them as a group.) The descriptive label settings will be slightly different.

Set the number label properties

To select more than one object on a form, hold down the SHIFT key while clicking the objects.

1. Click the first number label, and then hold down the SHIFT key while clicking the second and third number labels.

   A selection rectangle appears around each label as you click it. When you've selected all three labels, release the SHIFT key.
2. Click the Properties button on the toolbar.

   The Properties window appears. Since more than one object has been selected, only the properties that can be changed as a group are displayed in the Properties window. You'll change the BorderStyle, Alignment, and Font properties now so that the numbers that appear in the labels will be centered, boxed, and in an appropriate font and point size.
3. Click the Alignment property, and then click the drop-down list box arrow that appears to the right.

   A list of alignment options appears in the list box.
4. Click the 2 - Center option.

   The Alignment property for each of the selected labels is changed to 2 - Center. Now change the BorderStyle property.
5. Click the BorderStyle property, and then click the drop-down list box arrow that appears to the right.

   A list of the valid property settings (0 - None and 1 - Fixed Single) appears in the list box.
6. Click 1 - Fixed Single in the list box to add a thin border around each label.

   Now change the font for the labels by changing settings for the Font property.
7. Double-click the Font property in the Properties window.

The Font dialog box appears, as shown here:

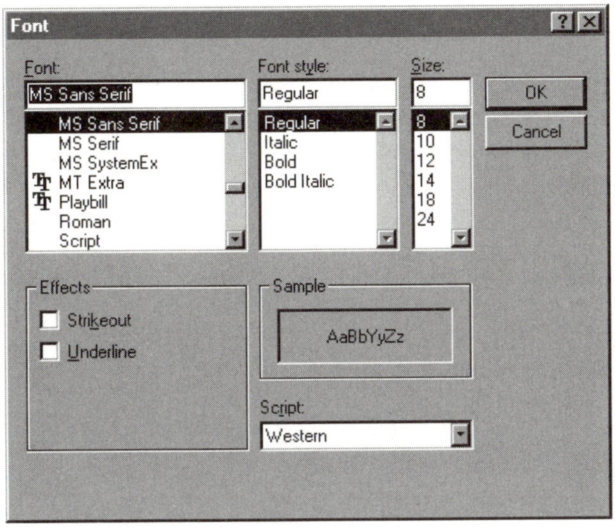

8 Change the font to Times New Roman, the font style to Bold, and the point size to 24, and then click OK.

The label captions appear in the font, style, and size you specified. Now delete the three captions so that the boxes will be empty when the program starts. (Your font selections will remain with the labels since they are stored as separate properties.) To complete this operation, you first need to select each of the labels individually.

9 Click the form to remove the selection handles from the three labels, and then click the first label.

10 Click the Properties button on the toolbar, and then double-click the Caption property and press DEL.

The caption of the Label1 object is deleted. You'll use program code to put a number in this property later in this lesson.

11 Delete the captions in the second and third labels on the form.

You've finished with the first three labels. Now you'll change the Font, ForeColor, and Caption properties of the last label.

Set the descriptive label properties

1 Click the fourth label object on the form.

2 Click the Properties button on the toolbar.

3 Change the Caption property to "Lucky Seven".

Now use the Font dialog box to change the Font property.

4 Double-click the Font property, and use the Font dialog box to change the font to Arial, the font style to Bold, and the point size to 24. Click OK.

The font in the label box is updated. Notice that the text in the box wrapped to two lines since it no longer fits on one. This is an important concept: the contents of an object must fit inside the object. If they don't, the contents will wrap or be truncated. Now change the foreground color of the text.

5 Double-click the ForeColor property in the Properties window.

A palette of available font colors appears on the screen.

6 Click the box containing dark purple.

The text in the label box changes to dark purple. The color you have selected is translated into a hexadecimal (base 16) number in the Properties window. Most programmers won't have to deal with this format often, but it is interesting to see how Visual Basic actually records such information inside the program. Now you're ready to set the properties for the last object.

The Picture Box Properties

The picture box object will contain the graphic of the stack of coins in your program. This graphic will appear when the user hits the jackpot (that is, when at least one seven appears in the number labels). You need to set the Picture property, which specifies the name of the graphics file to be loaded into the picture box, and the Visible property, which specifies the picture state at the beginning of the program.

Set the picture box properties

1 Click the picture box object on the form.

2 Click the Properties button on the toolbar.

3 Double-click the Picture property in the Properties window.

The Load Picture dialog box appears, as shown in the following illustration:

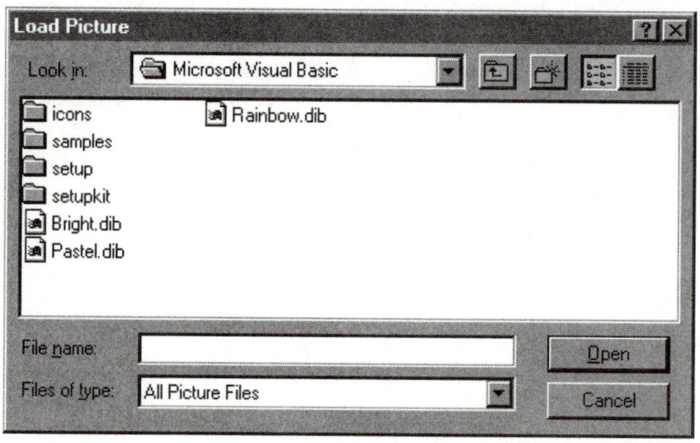

4 Navigate to the \Vb\Practice folder in the Load Picture dialog box.

The subfolders in the \Vb\Practice folder appear.

5 Double-click the Lesson 1 folder.

The Windows metafile Coins.wmf appears in the Load Picture dialog box. Windows metafiles contain graphics objects that can be rendered in a variety of different sizes, so they look equally good in small and large boxes.

6 Select the file Coins.wmf in the dialog box, and then click Open.

The Coins Windows metafile is loaded into the picture box on the form:

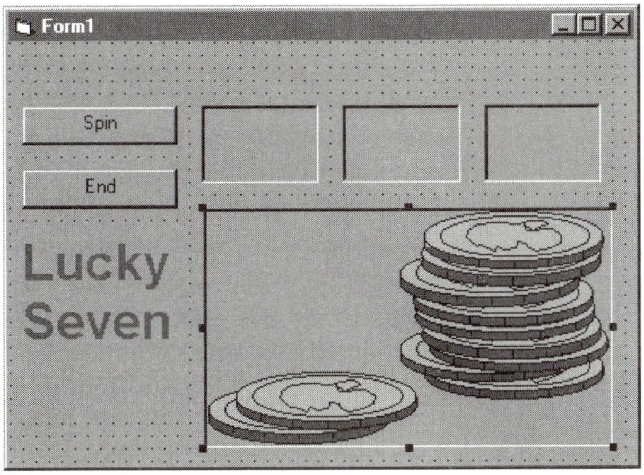

NOTE If you're using Visual Basic Professional Edition, you can also find the Coins Windows metafile in the \Program Files\Microsoft Visual Basic\Metafile\Business folder, along with many other useful images.

The Lucky Seven program will hide this picture by changing the Visible property of the picture box object to False until a jackpot occurs. Change the Visible property to False now so that the coins will be invisible when the program starts.

7 Click the Visible property, and then click the Visible drop-down list box arrow.

The valid settings for the Visible property appear in a list box.

8 Click False to make the picture invisible when the program starts.

The Visible property is set to False. This affects the picture box when the program runs but not now while you are designing it.

Reading Properties in Tables

In this lesson, you've set the properties for the Lucky Seven program step by step. In future lessons, the instructions to set properties will be presented in table format unless a setting is especially tricky. Here are the properties you've set so far in the Lucky Seven program in table format, as they'd look later in the book.

Object	Property	Setting
Command1	Caption	"Spin"
Command2	Caption	"End"
Label1, Label2, Label3	BorderStyle Alignment Font Caption	1 - Fixed Single 2 - Center Times New Roman, Bold, 24-point (Empty)
Label4	Caption Font ForeColor	"Lucky Seven" Arial, Bold, 24-point Dark purple (&H008000808)
Picture1	Picture Visible	"\vb\practice\lesson 1\coins.wmf" False

Writing the Code

Program code is entered in the Code window.

Now you're ready to write the code for the Lucky Seven program. Since most of the objects you've created already "know" how to work when the program runs, they're ready to receive input from the user and process it automatically. The inherent functionality of objects is one of the great strengths of Visual Basic—once objects are placed on a form and their properties are set, they're ready to run without any additional programming. However, the "meat" of the Lucky Seven game—the code that actually calculates random numbers, displays them in boxes, and detects a jackpot—is still missing from the program. This computing logic can be built into the application only by using program statements—code that clearly spells out what the program should do each step of the way. Since the program is driven by the Spin and End buttons, you'll associate the code for the game with those buttons. The *Code window* is a special window in the programming environment that you use to enter and edit Visual Basic program statements.

In the following steps, you'll enter the program code for Lucky Seven in the Code window.

Use the Code window

1. Double-click the End command button on the form.

When you double-click the object, the Code window appears, as follows:

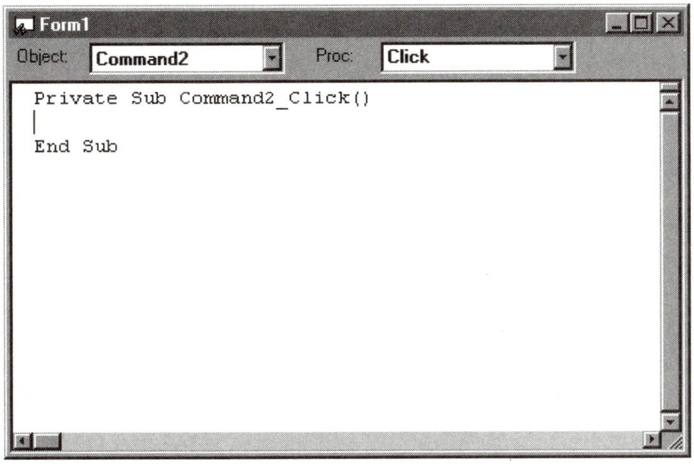

The Code window displays program statements that mark the beginning and the end of a Visual Basic subroutine, or *procedure*, a block of code associated with a particular interface object or program task:

```
Private Sub Command2_Click()

End Sub
```

The body of a procedure always fits between these lines and is executed whenever a user activates the interface element associated with the procedure. In this case, the event is a mouse click, but as you'll see later in the book, it could also be an event of a different type.

2 Type **End**, and press the DOWN ARROW key.

The End statement stops the execution of a program.

As you type the statement, the letters appear in black type in the Code window. When you press the DOWN ARROW key (you could also press ENTER or simply click a different line), the program statement turns blue, indicating that Visual Basic recognizes it as a valid statement, or *keyword,* in the program. End is the program statement you use to stop your program and remove it from the screen. The Visual Basic programming system contains several hundred unique keywords such as this, complete with their associated operators and symbols. The spelling of and spacing between these items is critical in program code to allow them to be accurately recognized by the Visual Basic compiler.

NOTE Another name for the exact spelling, order, and spacing of keywords in a program is statement *syntax*.

3 Move the cursor to the beginning of the line with the End statement in it, and press SPACEBAR four times.

The indent moves the End statement four spaces to the right to set the statement apart from the Private Sub and End Sub statements. This indenting scheme is one of the programming conventions you'll use throughout this book to keep your programs clear and readable. The group of conventions regarding how program code is organized in a program is often referred to as program *style*.

Now that you have written the code associated with the End button, you'll write code for the Spin button. These programming statements will be a little more extensive and will give you a chance to learn more about program syntax and style. You'll study each of the program statements later in the book, so you don't need to know everything about them now. Just focus on the general structure of the program code and on typing the program statements exactly as they are printed. (Visual Basic is fussy about spelling and the order in which keywords and operators appear.)

Write code for the Spin button

1 Open the Object drop-down list box in the Code window.

The Lucky Seven interface objects appear in the list box.

2 Click Command1 in the list box.

A procedure associated with the Command1 button appears.

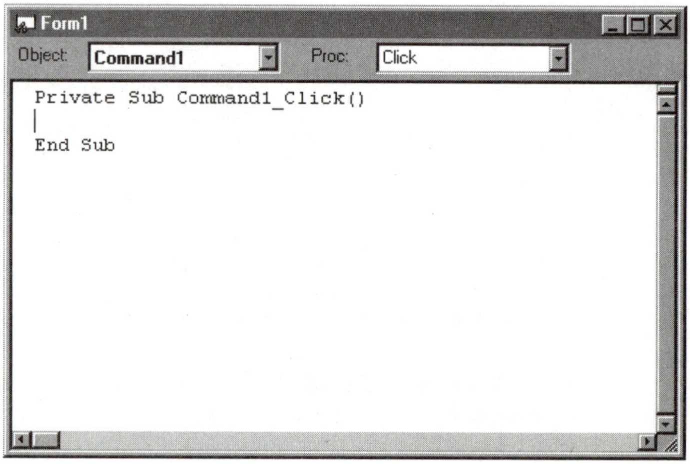

You can maximize the Code window to view more of your program code at one time.

Although you changed the caption of this button to "Spin", its name in the program is still Command1. (The name and the caption of an interface element can be different to suit the needs of the programmer.) Each object can have several procedures associated with it, one for each event it recognizes. The click event is the one we're interested in now because users will click the Spin and End buttons when they operate the program.

3 Type the following program lines between the Private Sub and End Sub statements, pressing ENTER after each line and taking care to type the program statements exactly as they appear here. If you make a mistake, delete the incorrect statements and try again.

```
Picture1.Visible = False       ' hide coins
Label1.Caption = Int(Rnd * 10) ' pick numbers
Label2.Caption = Int(Rnd * 10)
Label3.Caption = Int(Rnd * 10)
'if any caption is 7 display coin stack and beep
If (Label1.Caption = 7) Or (Label2.Caption = 7) _
  Or (Label3.Caption = 7) Then
    Picture1.Visible = True
    Beep
End If
```

When you've finished, the Code window should look like the following:

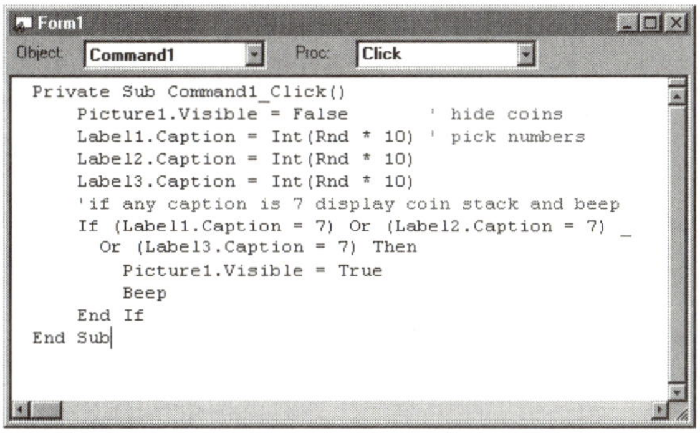

NOTE As you enter the program code, Visual Basic formats the text and displays different parts of the program in color to help you identify the various elements. If Visual Basic displays an error message, you may have mistyped a program statement. Check the line against the text in this book, make the necessary correction, and continue typing. (You can also delete a line and type it from scratch.) The menu commands and editing keys you use in Visual Basic are similar to the editing commands you use in other applications for Windows. For more information, consult the Visual Basic online Help.

A Look at the Command1_Click Procedure

The Command1_Click procedure is the heart of the Lucky Seven program.

The Command1_Click procedure is executed when the user clicks the Spin button on the form. The procedure uses some pretty complicated statements, and since I haven't formally introduced them yet, the whole thing might look a little confusing. However, if you take a closer look you'll probably see a few things that look familiar. Taking a peek at the contents of the procedures will give you a feel for the type of program code you'll be creating later in this book. (If you'd rather not, feel free to skip to the following section, "Saving the Program.")

The Command1_Click procedure performs three tasks: it hides the coin stack, creates three random numbers for the label windows, and displays the coin stack when the number seven appears. Let's look at each of these steps individually.

The first task in the procedure is accomplished by the line

```
Picture1.Visible = False       ' hide coins
```

This line is made up of two parts: a program statement and a comment. The program statement (Picture1.Visible = False) sets the Visible property of the first picture box object (Picture1) to False (one of two possible settings). You might remember that you set this property to False once before by using the Properties window. You're doing it again now in the program code because the first task is a spin and you need to clear away any coins that may have been displayed in a previous game. Since the property will be changed at runtime and not at design time, the property needs to be set by using program code. This is a handy feature of Visual Basic, and we'll talk about it more in Lesson 2.

Comments describe what program statements do.

The second part of the first line (the part displayed in green type on your screen) is called a *comment*. Comments are explanatory notes included in program code following a single quotation mark ('). Programmers use comments to describe how important statements work in a program. These notes aren't processed by Visual Basic when the program runs; they exist only as documentation describing what the program does. You'll want to use comments often when you write Visual Basic programs to leave a "plain English" record of what you're doing.

The next three lines handle the random number computations. The Rnd function in each line creates a random number between 0 and 1 (a number with a decimal point), and the Int function multiplies the numbers by 10 and rounds them to the nearest decimal place. This computation creates random numbers between 0 and 9 in the program. The numbers are then assigned to the Caption properties of the first three labels on the form, and the assignment causes the numbers to be displayed in boldface, 24-point Times New Roman type in the three label windows.

The last group of statements in the program checks whether any of the random numbers is seven. If one or more of them is, the stack of coins is made visible on the form and a beep announces a jackpot. Each time the user clicks the Spin button, the Command1_Click procedure is called and the program statements in the procedure are executed.

Saving the Program

You can save your program at any time during the programming process.

Now that you've completed the Lucky Seven program, you should save it to disk. Visual Basic saves your form's code and objects in one file and the "packing list" of project components in another file. (The project components are listed in the Project window.) You can use these component files individually in other programming projects by using the Add File command on the File menu. To save a program in Visual Basic, click Save Project As on the File menu or click the Save Project button on the toolbar.

Save the Lucky Seven program

1 On the File menu, click the Save Project As command.

2 Click Yes when Visual Basic asks whether you want to save changes to Form1.

The Save File As dialog box appears, as follows:

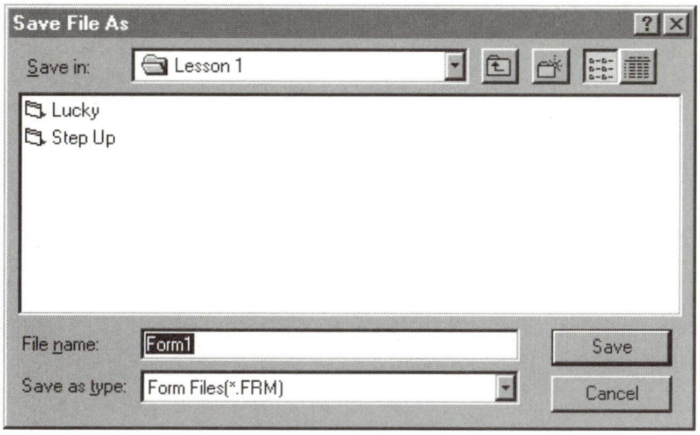

3 Select the Lesson 1 folder in the dialog box, if it's not already selected.

You'll save your project in the practice folder that the Microsoft Visual Basic 4 Step by Step Practice Files installation program created on your hard disk. (You can specify a different folder if you like.)

4 Type **My Lucky** in the File Name text box, and press ENTER.

The Lucky Seven form is saved under the name My Lucky.frm. The Save Project As dialog box then appears.

NOTE I recommend that you save each project you create in this book by using the *My* prefix to keep a record of your progress and to preserve the original practice files. That way you can check the original files if you have any problems.

---

5 Type **My Lucky** and press ENTER.

The Lucky Seven project is saved under the name My Lucky.vbp. To load this project again later, you would click the Open Project command on the File menu and click My Lucky in the Open Project dialog box. You can also load a recently used project by clicking the project name at the bottom of the Visual Basic File menu.

Congratulations! You're ready to run your first real program. To run a Visual Basic program from the programming environment, you can click Start on the Run menu, click the Start button on the toolbar, or press F5. Try running the Lucky Seven program now.

The complete Lucky program is located on disk in the \Vb\Practice\Lesson 1 folder.

If Visual Basic displays an error message, you may still have a typing mistake or two in your program code. Try to fix it by comparing the printed version in this book with the one you typed, or load Lucky from your hard disk and run it.

Run the program

Start button

1. Click the Start button on the toolbar.

   The Lucky Seven program runs in the programming environment. The user interface appears, just as you designed it.

2. Click the Spin button.

   The program picks three random numbers and displays them in the labels on the form, as follows:

   Since a seven appears in the first label box, the stack of coins appears and the computer beeps. (The sound depends on your Windows 95 Control Panel setting.) You win!

3. Click the Spin button 15 or 16 more times, watching the results of the spins in the number windows.

   About half the time you spin, you hit the jackpot—pretty easy odds. (The actual odds are 3 times out of 10; you're just lucky at first.) Later on you might want to make the game tougher by displaying the coins only when two or three sevens appear. (You'll learn how to do this when you learn more about variables, operators, and decision structures in Part 2.)

4. When you've finished experimenting with your new creation, click the End button.

   The program stops, and the programming environment reappears on your screen.

Building an Executable File

A .exe file can run under Windows.

Your last task in this lesson is to complete the development process and create an application for Windows, or an *executable* file. Applications for Windows created by using Visual Basic have the filename extension .exe and can be run on any system that contains Windows 95 and the necessary support files. (Visual Basic installs these support files—including dynamic-link libraries and custom controls—automatically. If you plan to distribute your applications, see Chapter 29 in the Visual Basic *Programmer's Guide* for more information.) Try creating My Lucky.exe now.

Create an executable file

1 On the File menu, click the Make EXE File command.

The Make EXE File dialog box appears, as follows:

The dialog box contains text boxes and list boxes that you can use to specify the name and location of your executable file on disk. It also contains an Options button that you can use to control the program icon and version information associated with the file. By default, Visual Basic suggests the Lesson 1 folder for the location.

2 Click OK to accept the default filename and location for the file.

Visual Basic creates an executable file on disk in the specified location.

To run this program later under Windows 95, use the Run command on the Start menu or double-click the filename in Windows Explorer. You can also create a shortcut icon for Lucky Seven on the Windows desktop by using the right mouse button to click the Windows desktop, pointing to New, and then clicking Shortcut. When Windows asks you for the location of your application file, click Browse and select the My Lucky executable file in the \Vb\Practice\Lesson 1 folder. Click the Open, Next, and Finish buttons, and

Windows will place an icon on the desktop that you can double-click to run your program. The shortcut icon will look like this:

You've finished with Visual Basic for now. You'll exit the programming environment in the following exercise.

Exit Visual Basic

1 Save any changes you have made to your program.

2 On the File menu, click the Exit command.

The Visual Basic program exits.

One Step Further: Adding to a Program

You can restart Visual Basic at any time and work on a programming project you have stored on disk. Try restarting Visual Basic now and adding a special statement named Randomize to the Lucky Seven program.

Reload Lucky Seven

1 Click the Start button, point to Programs, point to Visual Basic 4.0, and then click the Visual Basic 4.0 program icon.

2 Click the File menu.

The commands on the File menu appear. Near the bottom of the menu is a list of project files that have recently been used on your computer. Since you just finished working with Lucky Seven, My Lucky.vbp should be first on the list.

3 Click My Lucky to load the Lucky Seven program from disk.

The Lucky Seven program loads from disk, and the Project window appears on the right side of the screen.

4 Click the View Form button in the Project window to display the Lucky Seven form.

The Lucky Seven form appears. Now add the Randomize statement to the Form_Load procedure, a special procedure that is associated with the form and that is executed each time the program is started.

5 Double-click the form (but not one of the objects) to display the Form_Load procedure.

The Form_Load procedure appears in the Code window, as shown in the following illustration:

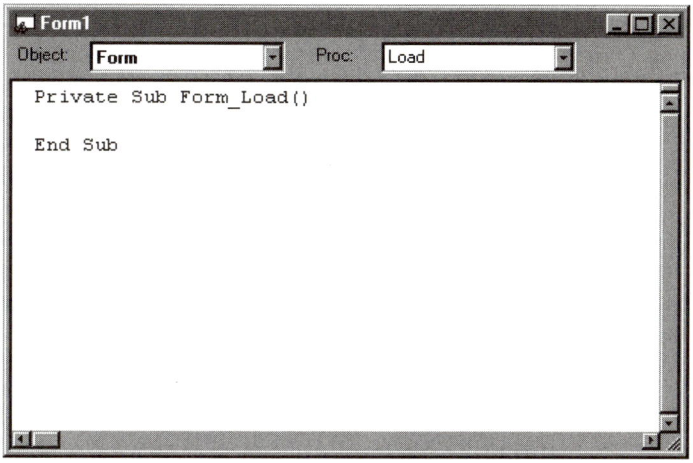

6 Press SPACEBAR four times, type **Randomize**, and press the DOWN ARROW key.

The Randomize statement is added to the program and will be executed each time the program starts. Randomize uses the system clock to create a truly random starting point, or "seed," for the Rnd statement used in the Command1_Click procedure. You may not have noticed, but without Randomize the Lucky Seven program produces the same string of random spins every time you restart the program. With Randomize in place, the program will spin randomly every time it runs. The numbers won't follow a recognizable pattern.

7 Run the new version of Lucky Seven, and then save the project to disk. If you plan to use the new version a lot, you may want to create a new .exe file too. Visual Basic does not update executable files automatically when you change the source code.

If you want to continue to the next lesson

➤ Keep Visual Basic running, and turn to Lesson 2.

If you want to exit Visual Basic for now

➤ On the File menu, click Exit.

If you see a Save dialog box, click Yes.

Lesson Summary

To	Do this	Button
Start Visual Basic	Click the Start button on the taskbar, point to Programs, point to the Visual Basic 4.0 folder, and then click the Visual Basic 4.0 program icon.	
Display a button's function	Place the mouse pointer over the button on the toolbar or in the toolbox.	
Open an existing project	On the File menu, click the Open Project command.	
Start a new project	On the File menu, click the New Project command.	
Run a program	Click the Start button on the toolbar. *or* Press F5.	
Move the toolbox	Drag the toolbox by using the mouse.	
Set properties	Click the Properties button on the toolbar to display the Properties window. Open the object drop-down list box to display the user interface elements on your form, click the object you want to set properties for, and then click the property settings you want in the Properties list box.	
Display the Project window	Click the Project button on the toolbar.	
Create a user interface	Use toolbox controls to place objects on your form, and then set the necessary properties. Resize the form and the objects as appropriate.	
Move an object	Drag the object on the form by using the mouse.	
Resize an object	Select the object, and then drag the selection handle attached to the part of the object you want to resize.	
Delete an object	Select the object, and then press DEL.	
Open the Code window	Double-click an object on the form (or the form itself). *or* Click the View Code button.	

To	Do this	Button
Write program code	Type Visual Basic program statements associated with the object you want to program in the Code window.	
Save a program	On the File menu, click the Save Project As command. *or* Click the Save Project button on the toolbar.	
Create a .exe file	On the File menu, click Make EXE File.	
Quit Visual Basic	On the File menu, click Exit.	
Reload a project	On the File menu, click the Open Project command. *or* Click the file in the recently used file section of the File menu	

For online information about	On the Visual Basic Help menu, click Contents. In the Help Topics dialog box, click the Contents tab, double-click Visual Basic Help, double-click Using Visual Basic, and then
Creating a user interface	Select the topic "Creating the Interface"
Setting properties	Select the topic "Setting Properties"
Writing program code	Select the topic "Writing and Debugging Code"

For more information on	In the Visual Basic *Programmer's Guide,* see
Installing Visual Basic	Chapter 1, "Introduction"
Writing a Visual Basic program	Chapter 2, "Your First Visual Basic Application"
Saving project files, creating executable files, and setting programming environment options	Chapter 4, "Managing Projects"

Preview of the Next Lesson

In the next lesson, "Working with Controls," you'll explore in detail the user interface controls in the toolbox. You'll learn how to create user interface objects on forms, how to reference them in program code, and how to use them effectively in programs.

Lesson

2

Working with Controls

Estimated time
55 min.

In this lesson you will learn how to:

- Use text box and command button objects to create a "Hello World" program.
- Use file system objects and an image object to browse artwork on disk.
- Use option button, check box, and list box objects to process user input.
- Use an OLE object to launch Windows-based applications on your system.
- Use a data object to view records in a Microsoft Access database.
- Install custom controls.

As you learned in Lesson 1, Microsoft Visual Basic controls are the graphical tools you use to build the user interface of a Visual Basic program. Controls are located in the toolbox in the programming environment, and you use them to create objects on a form with a simple series of mouse clicks and dragging motions. In this lesson, you'll learn how to display information in a text box, browse drives and folders on your system, process user input, launch Microsoft Windows–based applications, and view database records. The exercises in this lesson will help you design your own Visual Basic applications and will teach you more about objects, properties, and program code. You'll also learn how to add custom controls to the toolbox so that you can extend the functionality of Visual Basic.

The Basic Use of Controls: The "Hello World" Program

A great tradition in introductory programming books is the "Hello World" program. "Hello World" is the name given to a short program that demonstrates how the simplest utility can be built and run in a given programming language. In the days of character-based programming, Hello World was usually a two-line or three-line program typed in a program editor and assembled with a stand-alone compiler. With the advent of graphical programming tools, however, the typical Hello World has grown into a complex program containing dozens of lines and requiring several programming tools for its construction. Fortunately, creating a Hello World program is still quite simple with Visual Basic. You can construct a complete user interface by creating two objects, setting two properties, and entering one line of code. Give it a try.

Create a Hello World program

1 Start Visual Basic.

The Visual Basic programming environment appears, as shown in the following illustration. The two controls you'll use in this exercise, TextBox and CommandButton, are labeled in the toolbox.

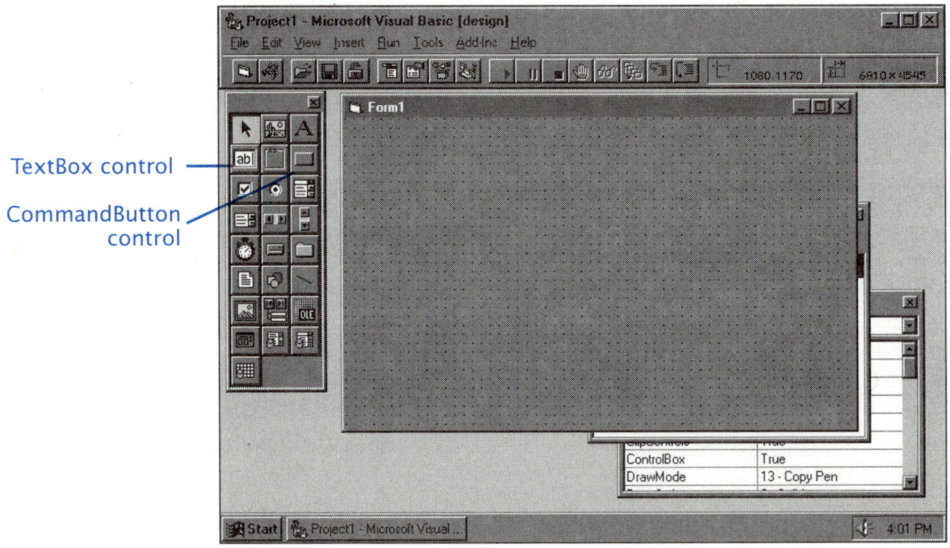

2 Click the TextBox control in the toolbox.

TextBox control

3 Move the mouse pointer to the center of the form (the pointer turns into crosshairs when over the form), and then draw a text box similar to the following:

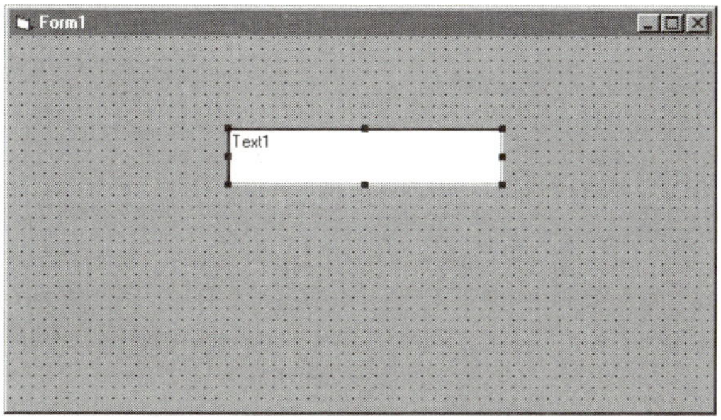

A text box object is used to display text on a form or to get input from a user while a Visual Basic program is running. How a text box works depends on how you set its properties and how you reference the text box in the program code. In this simple program, a text box object will be used to display the message "Hello, world!" when you click a command button on the form.

Now try adding the command button.

CommandButton control

4 Click the CommandButton control in the toolbox.

5 Move the mouse pointer below the text box on the form, and draw a command button.

Your screen should look like the following:

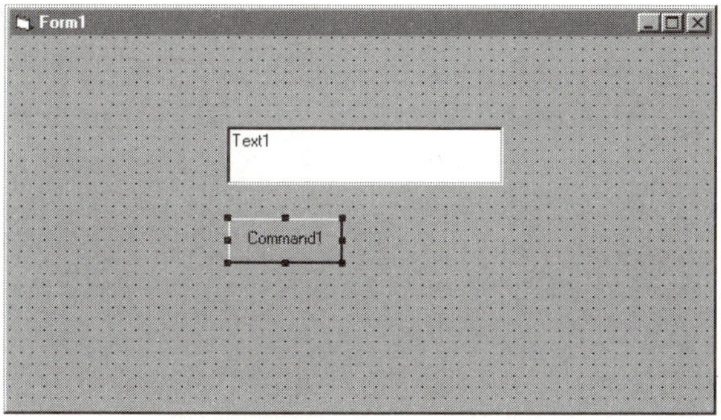

A command button object is used to get the most basic input from a user. When a user clicks a command button, he or she is requesting that a specific action be taken in the program immediately. In Visual Basic terms, the user is using the command button to create an *event* that needs to be processed in the program. Typical command buttons in a program are the OK button, which a user clicks to accept a list of options and indicate that he or she is ready to proceed; the Cancel button, which a user clicks to discard a list of options; and the Quit button, which a user clicks to exit the program. In each case, the designer of the program needs to create the buttons so that they work as expected when they are clicked.

A command button's characteristics are modified (like those of all objects) with property settings and references to the object in program code.

For more information about setting properties, see the section "Setting the Properties" in Lesson 1.

6 Set the following properties for the text box and command button objects, using the Properties window. The setting (Empty) means that you should erase the current setting and leave the property blank. Settings you need to type in are shown in quotation marks. You shouldn't type the quotation marks.

Control	Property	Setting
Text1	Text	(Empty)
Command1	Caption	"OK"

7 Double-click the OK command button, and type the following program statement between the Private Sub and End Sub statements in the Code window:

```
Text1.Text = "Hello, world!"
```

This statement changes the Text property of the text box to "Hello, world!" when the user clicks the command button at runtime. (The equal sign assigns everything between the quotation marks to the Text property of the Text1 object.) This is an example of changing a property at runtime—one of the most common uses of program code in a Visual Basic program. Since the statement is in an *event procedure* that is executed when the Command1 command button is clicked, the property setting (and therefore the text box contents) will change immediately after the user clicks the command button.

The complete Hello.vbp program is located on disk in the \Vb\Practice\Lesson 2 folder.

Now you're ready to run the Hello World program and save it to disk.

Run the Hello World program

Start button

1 Click the Start button on the toolbar.

The Hello World program runs in the Visual Basic programming environment.

2 Click the OK command button.

The program displays the greeting "Hello, world!" in the text box, as shown here:

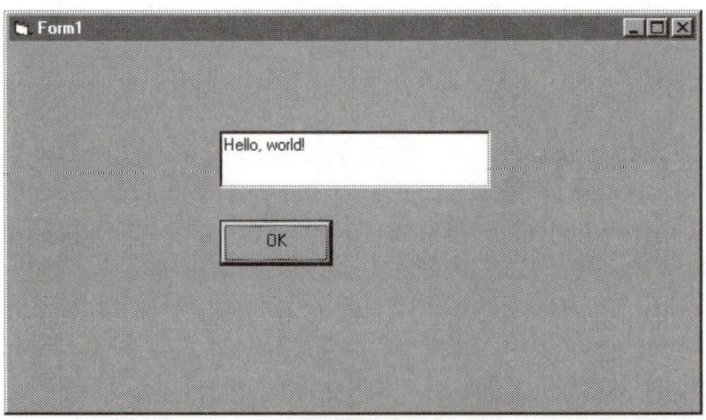

When you clicked the OK command button, the program code changed the Text property of the Text1 text box to "Hello, world!" and the "Hello, world!" text was displayed in the box. If you didn't get this result, repeat the steps in the previous section, "Create a Hello World program," and build the program again. You might have set a property incorrectly or made a typing mistake in the program code.

End button

3. Click the End button on the toolbar to stop the program.

   You could also have clicked the Close button on the program form to stop the program.

4. On the File menu, click the Save Project As command.

   Visual Basic asks you if you want to save the changes to your form (Form1).

5. Click Yes, and then navigate to the \Vb\Practice\Lesson 2 folder. Delete the name in the File Name text box, and then type **My Hello World** and click Save.

   Visual Basic saves your form to disk with the name My Hello World.frm. Visual Basic saves forms separately from project files, so you can reuse forms and procedures in future programming projects without rebuilding them from scratch.

   After you enter the form name, you are prompted for a project file name (a name for the file that Visual Basic uses to build your program). This is called a Visual Basic project file, and it has a .vbp filename extension.

6. Type **My Hello World** again, and click Save.

   Visual Basic saves your project to disk under the name My Hello World.vbp. When you want to open the program again later, you select this file by using the Open Project command on the File menu. Visual Basic then loads each of the files in the project list.

Congratulations—you've joined the ranks of programmers who have written a Hello World program. Now let's move on to some other objects.

Using File System Objects

Visual Basic provides three very useful objects for gaining access to the file system. These are *drive list boxes,* which let you browse the valid drives on a system; *directory list boxes,* which let you navigate the folders on a particular drive; and *file list boxes,* which let you select a specific file in a folder. In the following exercise, you use the three file system objects to build a program called Browser that locates and displays files containing artwork on your system.

> **NOTE** You also use an image object in this program. An image object can display three kinds of graphics formats: bit maps (.bmp files), Windows metafiles (.wmf files, which are electronic artwork files that you can size), and icons (.ico files).

The Browser Program

The Browser program uses the three file system objects, an image object, and several lines of program code to create an artwork browser program. When you've finished creating Browser, you can use it in your daily work to examine the artwork on any floppy disk, hard disk, network drive, or CD-ROM drive. The file system objects support all drive types.

Build the Browser program

1. On the File menu, click New Project.

   The Hello World program disappears, and a blank form appears on the screen. You have a chance to save any unsaved changes in Hello World before it closes.

DriveListBox control

2. Click the DriveListBox control in the toolbox.
3. Move the mouse pointer to the upper left corner of the form, and then draw a drive list box, as shown in the following illustration:

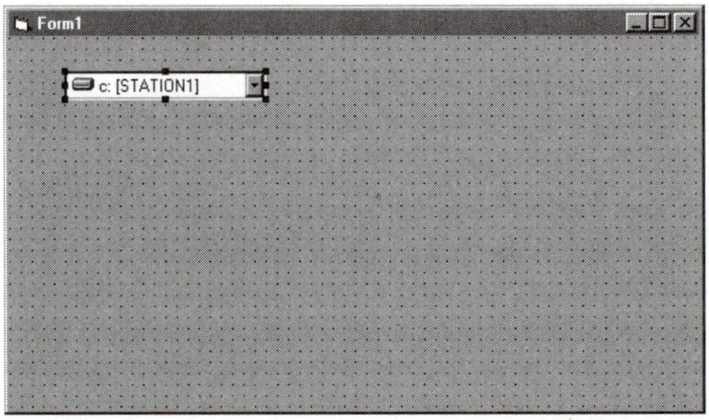

   Visual Basic includes the current drive and volume label in the object when you create it. This information is displayed to help the user identify the currently selected drive when he or she is using the program, and it also lets you see the information at design time so that you can size the object correctly. If you can't see all the drive and volume information, resize your drive list box accordingly.

DirListBox control

4. Click the DirListBox control in the toolbox, and then add a directory list box to the form, below the drive list box. Allow room for at least four or five folders to appear in the list box.

   A directory list box object provides access to the folders in the file system. When you place the object on a Visual Basic form, the folders appear as they will when the program runs. It's tempting to start clicking folders now, but since the list box isn't active, it won't do any good. Folders appear now only so that you can size the object appropriately.

FileListBox control

5. Click the FileListBox control in the toolbox, and then add a file list box to the form, below the directory list box. Allow room for at least four or five filenames to be displayed.

A file list box object lets a user select a specific file in the file system. When the user selects a file, Visual Basic puts the filename in the FileName property of the file list box object. In a similar manner, the Drive property of the drive list box object and the Path property of the directory list box object receive the drive and folder selections the user makes in the drive and directory list boxes. You'll use these three properties together in the Browser program to open the artwork file the user selects. This is a typical use of objects and properties in a program. The user changes a setting in an object while the program is running, the change is reflected in a property, and the property is processed in the program code.

> **NOTE** The Drive, Path, and FileName properties are available only at runtime. (They contain values that are assigned when the file system list boxes are used.) You cannot set them by using the Properties window.

Image control

6 Click the Image control in the toolbox, and then add a large image box to the form, to the right of the drive, directory, and file list boxes.

After you add the image object, your screen should look similar to the following:

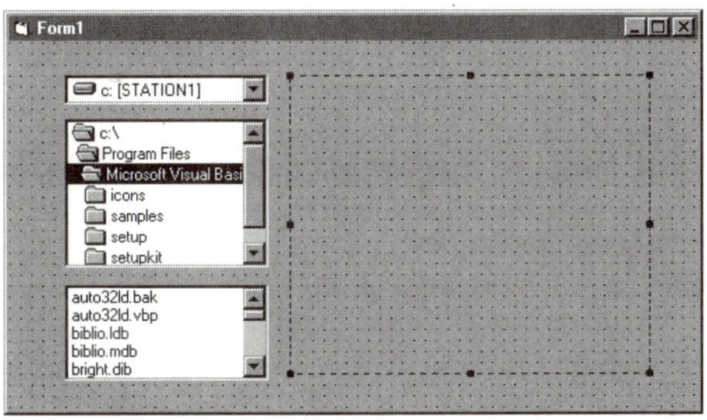

7 Now set the following properties by using the Properties window:

Object	Property	Setting
File1	Pattern	*.bmp;*.wmf;*.ico
Image1	Stretch	True
Image1	BorderStyle	1 - Fixed Single

The Pattern setting in the file list box is especially important in this case. It lists the valid graphics formats that Visual Basic can display in a program by using an image box. If the property were left blank, the file list box would list all file types in a folder, and if the user selected a graphics format that Visual Basic doesn't support (such as TIFF), the selection would result in a crash or a runtime error. If possible, it's best to eliminate such problems before they get started.

Now add a few lines of program code to the procedures associated with the file system objects. These procedures are called *event procedures* because they are run when an event, such as a mouse click, occurs in the object.

Double-click an object to display its default event procedure.

8 Double-click the drive list box object on the form, and then type the following program statement between the Private Sub and End Sub statements in the Drive1_Change event procedure:

```
Dir1.Path = Drive1.Drive
```

This statement updates the Path property in the directory list box when the user selects a drive in the drive list box. The statement hooks the two objects together so that the directory list box lists folders for the correct drive.

9 Close the Code window (click the Close button in the upper right corner), and then double-click the directory list box on the form and add the following program statement to the Dir1_Change event procedure:

```
File1.Path = Dir1.Path
```

This statement links the file list box to the directory list box so that the files in the list box match the selected folder.

10 Close the Code window, and then double-click the file list box on the form and add the following code to the File1_Click event procedure:

```
SelectedFile = File1.Path & "\" & File1.FileName
Image1.Picture = LoadPicture(SelectedFile)
```

You'll learn more about operators, variables, and functions in Lesson 4.

These two lines are the heart of the program. The first line uses the & operator to combine File1's Path property, the \ character, and File1's FileName property, and then stores the resulting pathname in the SelectedFile variable. A *variable* is a temporary storage space or holding tank for information in a program. In this case, the SelectedFile variable holds the complete name of the file that has been selected by the user (including drive and folder names). The second statement in the event procedure uses the SelectedFile variable when it loads the file into the image box (Image1) on the form with the LoadPicture function and the Picture property.

After you enter the code for the File1_Click event procedure, the Code window should look similar to the following illustration:

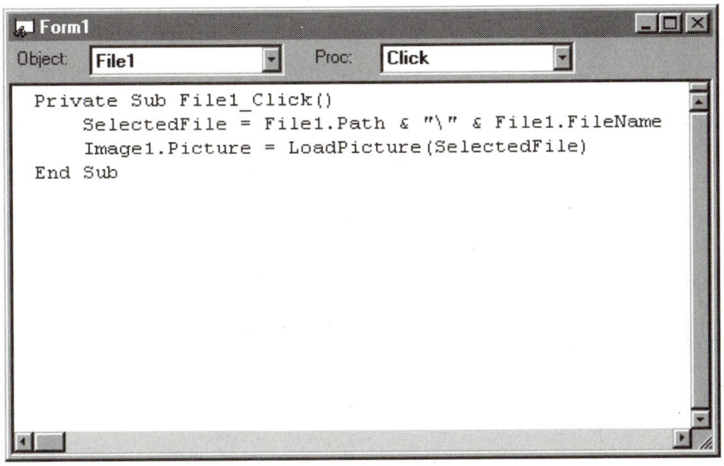

The complete Browser.vbp program is located on disk in the Lesson 2 folder.

Now you're ready to run the Browser program and save it to disk.

Run the Browser program

Start button

1. Click the Start button on the toolbar.

   The Browser program starts to run in the programming environment.

2. Open the folder \Vb\Practice\Lesson 2 by using the directory list box.

   The Windows metafiles in the selected folder appear in the file list box.

3. Scroll to the bottom of the box, and then click the filename Satedish.wmf.

   The selected file (a picture of a satellite dish) appears in the image box, as shown here:

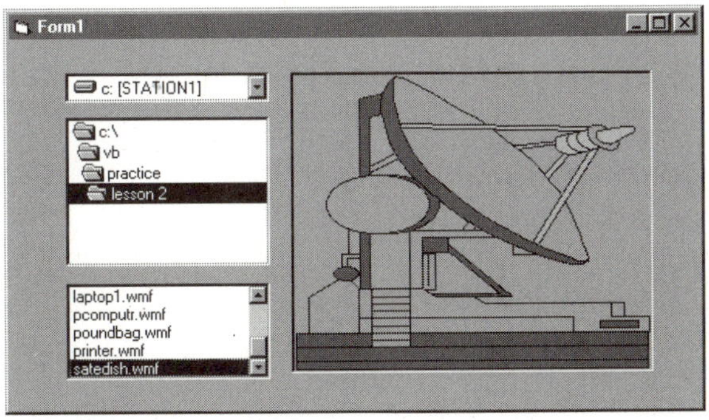

4. Scroll to the top of the file list box, and click the Calcultr.wmf filename.

   A picture of a calculator appears in the image box.

5 Use the drive, directory, and file list boxes to view other bit maps, Windows metafiles, and icons on your system.

You'll probably find several interesting bit maps in the \Windows folder.

When you've finished experimenting with Browser, stop the program and save it to disk.

6 Click the Close button on the form.

7 On the File menu, click Save Project As, and then save the form as **My Browser** and the project as **My Browser**.

What If My Program Crashes?

If you use the Browser program a lot, you might notice that it produces a runtime error, or *crashes,* in two specific situations. Since this program was created quickly for demonstration purposes, you didn't add the code necessary to protect the program against out-of-the-ordinary problems. As you begin to write more complex programs, however, you'll want to test your code carefully to make sure you can't break it under either normal or extreme operating conditions.

The first problem with Browser is that it crashes if the user selects a drive in the drive list box that doesn't contain a disk or is otherwise unready for work. (An example of an unready drive would be a drive containing a floppy disk that isn't formatted or an offline network drive.) To watch this happen, verify that drive A in your system doesn't have a disk in it, and then select A: in the Browser drive list box. The program immediately stops, and Visual Basic displays the message "Run-time error '68': Device unavailable." This statement means that Visual Basic couldn't find the floppy disk and quit running the program because it didn't know how to proceed. The Browser program relies on the user not making any mistakes with disks, which is probably not a safe assumption.

The second problem Browser has is with viewing artwork located in the root folder. Since files in the root folder have a pathname of only the backward slash (\), the program statement

```
SelectedFile = File1.Path & "\" & File1.FileName
```

causes trouble because it creates a pathname containing two backward slashes. (The statement would describe a file named Truck.wmf in the root folder as C:\\Truck.wmf.) When Visual Basic tries to load a file whose name contains two backward slashes side by side, it causes a runtime error and the program stops.

The way around these problems is to use program statements that avoid the error condition (you can do this with the pathname problem) or to create special routines called *error handlers* that will help your program recover if errors occur. Error handlers are beyond the scope of our current discussion, but for now you should note that although Visual Basic can handle most operating conditions, now and then users can create problems that make all but the sturdiest programs break. We'll discuss tracking down and fixing bugs in Lessons 5 and 7.

NOTE Visual Basic 4 Professional Edition and Visual Basic 4 Enterprise Edition include two custom controls (TreeView and ListView) that let programmers using Windows 95 display lists of folders and files the way they are presented by Windows Explorer. If you have Professional Edition, or Enterprise Edition, you can consult the Visual Basic online Help for more information about using the TreeView and ListView custom controls.

Objects for Gathering Input

Visual Basic provides several objects for gathering input in a program. Text boxes accept typed input, menus present commands that can be clicked, and dialog boxes offer a variety of elements that can be chosen individually or selected in a group. In this exercise, you'll learn to use four important objects that will help you gather input in several different situations. You'll learn about option button objects, check box objects, list box objects, and combo box objects. You will explore each of these objects as you use a Visual Basic program called Online Shopper, a simple tool that can be used to order computers and office equipment graphically. As you run the program, you'll get some hands-on experience with the input objects. In the next lesson, we'll discuss how these objects can be used along with menus in a full-fledged program.

The Online Shopper Program

The Online Shopper program simulates an electronic ordering environment in which you see what you're ordering as you make your selection. If you work in a business that does a lot of order entry, you may want to expand this program into a full-featured graphical order entry program someday. (They seem to be the thing of the future.) As you experiment with Online Shopper, spend some time observing how the option button, check box, list box, and combo box elements work in the program. They were created in a few short steps by using Visual Basic.

Run the Online Shopper program

1. On the Visual Basic File menu, click Open Project.

   The Open Project dialog box appears.

2. Open the Online Shopper.vbp file in the \Vb\Practice\Lesson 2 folder.
3. Click the View Form button in the Project window.

View Form button

The Online Shopper form appears, as shown in the following illustration:

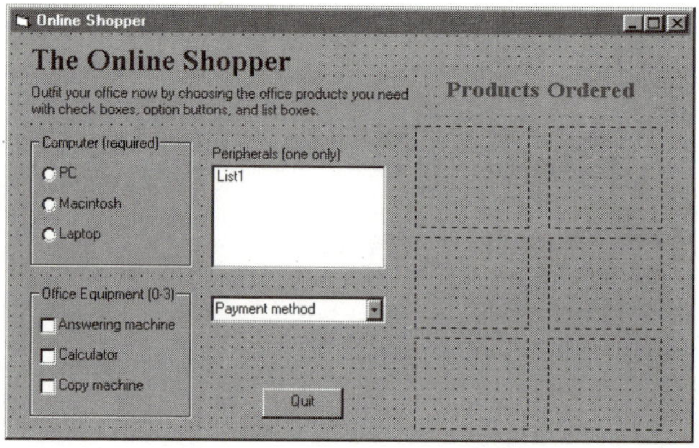

The Online Shopper form contains option button, check box, list box, combo box, image box, command button, and label objects. These work together to create a simple order entry program that demonstrates how the Visual Basic input objects work. When the Online Shopper program is run, it loads Windows metafiles from the \Vb\Practice\Lesson 2 folder on drive C and displays them in the six image boxes on the form.

NOTE If you installed the practice files in a location other than the default C:\Vb\Practice folder, the statements in the program that load the artwork from disk will contain an incorrect pathname. (Each statement begins with c:\vb\practice\lesson 2, as you'll see soon.) If this is the case, you can make the program work by renaming the practice files folder to \Vb\Practice or by changing the pathnames in the Code window by using the editing keys or by using the Replace command on the Edit menu.

Start button

Option buttons allow the user to select one item from a list.

4 Click the Start button on the toolbar.

The program runs in the programming environment.

5 Click the Laptop option button in the Computer box.

The image of a laptop computer appears in the Products Ordered area on the right side of the form. In the Computer box, a group of *option buttons* is used to gather input from the user. Option buttons force the user to choose one (and only one) item from a list of possibilities. The user can click the various option buttons repeatedly. After each click, the current choice is graphically depicted in the order area to the right.

6 Click the Answering Machine, Calculator, and Copy Machine check boxes in the Office Equipment box.

Check boxes let the user select any number of items.

Check boxes are used in a program when more than one option at a time can be selected from a list. Click the Calculator check box again, and notice that the picture of the calculator disappears from the order area. Since each user interface element is live and responds to click events as they occur, order choices are reflected immediately.

7 Click Satellite Dish in the Peripherals list box.

List boxes let the user select one item from a variable-length list of choices.

A picture of a satellite dish is added to the order area. A *list box* is used to get a single response from a list of choices. List boxes can contain many items to choose from (scroll bars appear if the list is longer than the list box), and unlike option buttons, a default selection is not required. In a Visual Basic program, items can be added to, removed from, or sorted in a list box while the program is running.

8 Now choose U.S. Dollars (sorry, no credit) from the payment list in the Payment Method combo box.

Combo boxes take up less space than list boxes.

A *combo box,* or drop-down list box, is similar to a regular list box, but it takes up less space. Visual Basic automatically handles the opening, closing, and scrolling of the list box. All you do as a programmer is write code to add items to the list box before the program starts and to process the user's selection. You'll see examples of each task in the Online Shopper code.

After making your order selections, your screen should look something like this:

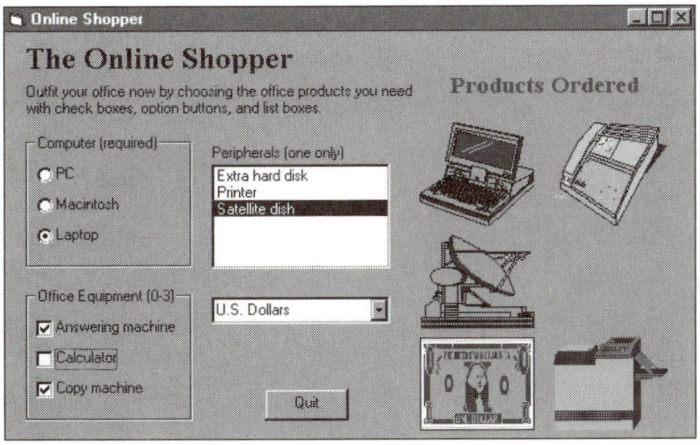

9 Practice making a few more changes to the order list in the program (try different computers, peripherals, and payment methods), and then click the Quit button in the program to exit.

The program closes when you click Quit, and the programming environment appears.

Looking at the Online Shopper Program Code

Lessons 4, 5, and 6 discuss program code in detail.

Although you haven't had much formal experience with program code yet, it's worth taking a quick look at a few event procedures in Online Shopper to see how the program processes input from the user interface elements. In these procedures, you'll see the If...Then and Select Case statements at work. You'll learn about these and other decision structures in Lesson 5. For now, concentrate on the Value property, which changes when a check box is selected, and the ListIndex property, which changes when a list box is selected.

Examine the check box code and list box code

1. Be sure the program has stopped running, and then double-click the Answering Machine check box in the Office Equipment box to display the Check1_Click event procedure in the Code window.

   You'll see the following program code:

In program code, an underscore (_) at the end of a line indicates that the program statement continues on the next line.

```
Private Sub Check1_Click()
    If Check1.Value = 1 Then
        Image2.Picture = _
          LoadPicture("c:\vb\practice\lesson 2\answmach.wmf")
        Image2.Visible = True
    Else
        Image2.Visible = False
    End If
End Sub
```

The Check1_Click event procedure contains the program code that is run when a user clicks the Answering Machine check box in the program. The important keyword here is Check1.Value, which should be read as "the Value property of the first check box object." Check1 is the name of the first check box created on a form; subsequent check boxes are named Check2, Check3, and so on. The Value property is the property that changes when a user clicks the check box on the form. When an "x" or a check mark appears in the check box, the Value property is set to 1; when the check box is blank, the Value property is set to 0 (zero).

The Value property can be set by using the Properties window when you are designing your check box (so that the check box can contain a default setting), or the property can be changed by the user when the program is running (when a check box is clicked). In the code above, the Value property is evaluated by an If...Then...Else decision structure. If the property evaluates to 1, the program loads the picture of an answering machine into the second image box on the form and makes the picture visible. Otherwise (if the Value property is 0), the answering machine picture is hidden from view. If this seems odd, don't worry. You'll learn about decision structures in detail in Lesson 5.

2 Close the Code window, and double-click the Peripherals list box on the form.

The List1_Click event procedure appears in the Code window. The following statements appear:

```
Private Sub List1_Click()
    Select Case List1.ListIndex
    Case 0
        Image3.Picture = _
          LoadPicture("c:\vb\practice\lesson 2\harddisk.wmf")
    Case 1
        Image3.Picture = _
          LoadPicture("c:\vb\practice\lesson 2\printer.wmf")
    Case 2
        Image3.Picture = _
          LoadPicture("c:\vb\practice\lesson 2\satedish.wmf")
    End Select
    Image3.Visible = True
End Sub
```

When the user clicks an item in a list box, Visual Basic returns the name of the item to the program in the List1.Text property.

Here you see code that executes when the user clicks an item in the Peripherals list box in the program. In this case, the important keyword is List1.ListIndex, which is read "the ListIndex property of the first list box object." After the user makes a choice in the list box, the ListIndex property returns a number that corresponds to the location of the item in the list box. (The first item is numbered 0, the second item is numbered 1, and so on.) The actual text of the choice (the name of the list box item) is also returned in the List1.Text property, and Visual Basic programmers often use this value in their programs. In the code above, List1.ListIndex is evaluated by the Select Case decision structure, and a different Windows metafile is loaded depending on the value of the ListIndex property. If the value is 0, a picture of a hard disk is loaded; if the value is 1, a picture of a printer is loaded; if the value is 2, a picture of a satellite dish (my dream peripheral) is loaded. You'll learn more about how the Select Case decision structure works in Lesson 5.

3 Close the Code window, and double-click the form (not any of the objects) to display the code associated with the form itself.

Statements in the Form_Load event procedure run when the program starts.

The Form_Load event procedure appears in the Code window. This is the procedure that is executed each time the Online Shopper program starts, or *loads*. Programmers put program statements in this special procedure when they want them executed every time a program loads. Often, as in the Online Shopper program, the statements define an aspect of the user interface that couldn't be created by using toolbox controls or the Properties window. The Form_Load code is shown on the following page.

```
Image1.Picture = LoadPicture("c:\vb\practice\lesson 2\pcomputr.wmf")
List1.AddItem "Extra hard disk"
List1.AddItem "Printer"
List1.AddItem "Satellite dish"

Combo1.AddItem "U.S. Dollars"
Combo1.AddItem "Check"
Combo1.AddItem "English Pounds"
```

The first line loads the personal computer Windows metafile into the first image box. This is the default setting reflected in the Computer option button box. The next three lines add items to the Peripherals list box (List1) in the program. The words in quotes will appear in the list box when it appears on the form. Below the list box program statements, the items in the Payment Method combo box (Combo1) are specified. The important keyword in both these groups is AddItem, which is a special function, or *method,* for the list box and combo box objects. Methods are special statements that perform an action or a service for a particular object, such as adding items to a list box. Methods differ from properties, which contain a value, and event procedures, which execute when a user manipulates an object. Methods can also be shared among objects, so when you learn how to use one method, you'll often be able to apply it to several circumstances. We'll discuss several important methods as you work through this book.

You're finished using the Online Shopper program. Take a few minutes to examine any other parts of the program you're interested in, and then move on to the next exercise.

A Word About Terminology

So far in this book I've used several different terms to describe items in a Visual Basic program. Although I haven't defined each of them formally, it's worth listing several of them now to clear up any confusion. Can you tell the difference yet?

Control A control is a tool you use to create objects on a Visual Basic form. You select controls from the toolbox and use them to draw objects on a form by using the mouse. You use most controls to create user interface elements, such as command buttons, image boxes, and list boxes.

Object An object is the name of a user interface element you create on a Visual Basic form by using a toolbox control. You can move, resize, and customize objects by using property settings. Objects also have what is known as *inherent functionality* —they know how to operate and can respond to certain situations on their own. (A list box "knows" how to scroll, for example.) You can program Visual Basic objects by using event procedures that are customized for different situations in a program. In Visual Basic the form itself is also an object.

A Word About Terminology, *continued*

Property A property is a value or characteristic held by a Visual Basic object, such as Caption or ForeColor. Properties can be set at design time by using the Properties window or at runtime by using statements in the program code. In code, the format for setting a property is

```
Object.Property = Value
```

where *Object* is the name of the object you're customizing, *Property* is the characteristic you want to change, and *Value* is the new property setting. For example,

```
Command1.Caption = "Hello"
```

could be used in the program code to set the Caption property of the Command1 object to "Hello".

Event procedure An event procedure is a block of code executed when an object is manipulated in a program. For example, when the first command button in a program is clicked, the Command1_Click event procedure is executed. Event procedures typically evaluate and set properties and use other program statements to perform the work of the program.

Program statement A program statement is a keyword in the code that does the work of the program. Visual Basic program statements create storage space for data, open files, perform calculations, and do several other important tasks.

Variable A variable is a special container used to hold data temporarily in a program. The programmer creates variables to store the results of a calculation, create filenames, process input, and so on. Numbers, names, and property values can be stored in variables.

Method A method is a special statement that performs an action or a service for a particular object in a program. In program code, the notation for using a method is

```
Object.Method Value
```

where *Object* is the name of the object you want to change, *Method* is the command you want to use to change the object, and *Value* is an optional argument to be used by the method. For example, the statement

```
List1.AddItem "Check"
```

uses the AddItem method to put the word *Check* in the List1 list box.

Using an OLE Object to Launch Applications

An OLE object lets you start applications for Windows from inside a Visual Basic application.

One of the most exciting features of Visual Basic is its ability to work closely with other applications for Windows. Using an OLE object, you can launch applications from your program while it is running and process several types of information. You can also use an OLE object to run individual components of other applications (such as the spelling checker in Microsoft Word) by using a special technology called *OLE Automation*. We'll discuss OLE objects and OLE Automation in detail in Lesson 10 of this book. In the next exercise, you'll learn how an OLE object works and how it can be used (without program code) to create an application named Bid Estimator that launches Word, Microsoft Excel, and Paint documents so that the user can enter estimate and bid information and site drawings for a construction project.

To run the Bid Estimator program, you'll need a copy of Word, Excel, and Paint on your hard disk. (Paint comes with Windows 95.) When you first create an OLE object, it displays an Insert Object dialog box that lists the available application objects you can use in your program. If you don't have Word, Excel, or Paint on your hard disk, the Insert Object dialog box won't list them, but feel free to choose another object instead. The purpose of this exercise is to practice using applications you'd like to start from a Visual Basic program. The completed utility will look like this when you run it:

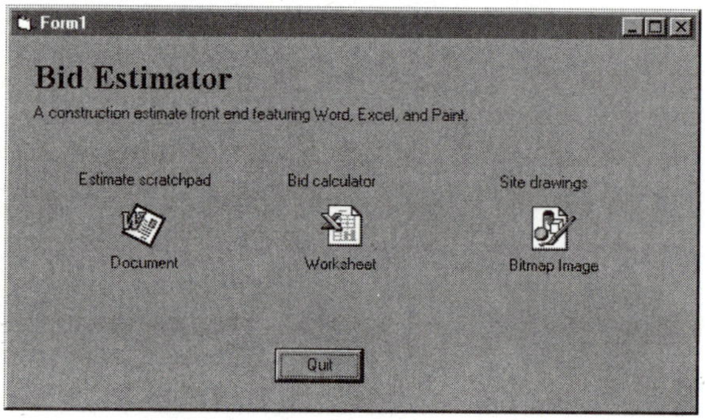

Create the Bid Estimator program

1. On the File menu, click New Project.

   The Online Shopper program closes, and a new form appears in the programming environment.

2. In the upper left corner of the form, create a label that has the caption "Bid Estimator". Below the label, create a second label that has the caption "A construction estimate front end featuring Word, Excel, and Paint."

   Leave some extra space in the first label—you'll increase the point size of the caption when you set properties later.

3. Below the second label, spaced equally across the form (see the illustration above), create three additional labels that have the captions "Estimate scratchpad", "Bid calculator", and "Site drawings".

These labels will be used to identify the OLE objects used to launch the Word, Excel, and Paint applications, respectively. Now add the OLE objects to the form.

OLE control

4 Click the OLE control in the toolbox.

5 Below the Estimate Scratchpad label, create a rectangle about the size of a matchbox by using the OLE control.

When you release the mouse button, Visual Basic displays the Insert Object dialog box, which contains a list of all the application objects you can use in your program. The exact list will vary from system to system.

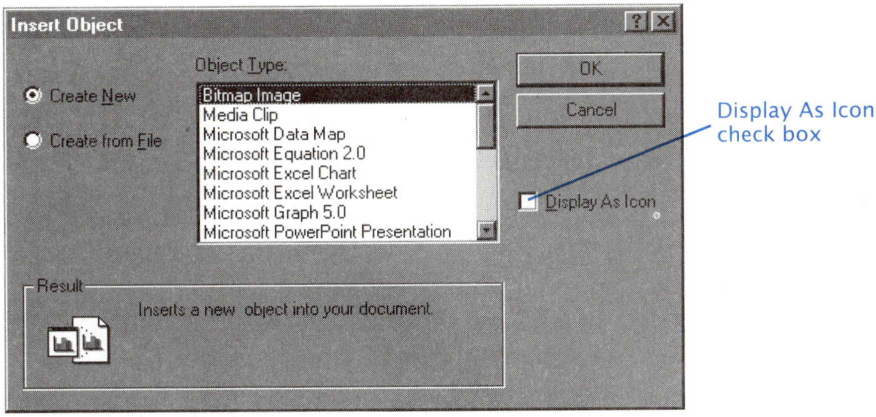

6 Scroll down the list of objects, and click the Microsoft Word Document object if you have Word for Windows 95 on your computer.

If you don't have Word for Windows 95, select an earlier version of Word, another Windows-based word processor, or a similar application in the dialog box.

7 Click the Display As Icon check box in the Insert Object dialog box so that the application will appear as an icon in your Visual Basic program.

If you don't click this check box, the application object (typically a document) will be displayed in a window in your application. You'll use this feature to considerable advantage later in this book. For now, however, just click Display As Icon.

8 Click OK to close the Insert Object dialog box and to open Word.

Word opens and displays a blank word processing document in a window. This document will become a *template* in the Bid Estimator program. It should contain any information a contractor would find useful when using the program, such as information about the construction company, names, addresses, prices, materials, and so on.

9 For now just type **Estimate Notes --**. Then use the Date And Time command on the Insert menu to add today's date to the template.

The text appears in the Word document as it will when you run the program.

10 On the Word File menu, click Exit.

If you are asked whether you want to update the source document, click Yes. You will receive this prompt when you close certain application objects.

When you're finished with the first OLE object, your form should look like the following. Resize your OLE object or label if any text is hidden from view.

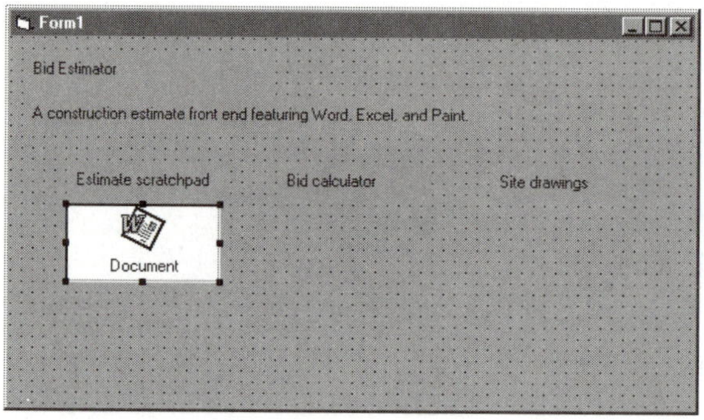

NOTE The three-dimensional appearance of the OLE object is controlled by the Appearance property, which has 3D and Flat settings. In step 13, you will set the Appearance property of each OLE object to Flat and the BackColor property of each OLE object to light gray to make the objects match the form.

11 Repeat steps 4 through 10 to add a Microsoft Excel Worksheet object (or its equivalent) to the form below the Bid Calculator label and a Bitmap Image object to the form below the Site Drawings label.

Be sure to click the Display As Icon check box in the Insert Object dialog box both times, and add some template information (such as notes or instructions) to the Excel worksheet and the Paint canvas if you're comfortable using those programs. In the Excel worksheet, it is easy to imagine a well-organized contractor including several rows and columns of bidding information, including costs of lumber, paint, and labor. The beauty of using other Windows-based applications in your program is that you have access to all these applications' features automatically—you don't have to reinvent the wheel!

12 Place a command button at the bottom of the form. After you've added the button, double-click the object and type the statement **End** in the Command1_Click event procedure.

The End program statement will terminate the program when the user is finished using it.

13 Set the following properties for the objects on the form, by using the Properties window:

Object	Property	Setting
Command1	Caption	"Quit"
Label1	Font	Times New Roman, Bold, 18-point
OLE1	BorderStyle	0 - None
	Appearance	0 - Flat
	BackColor	Light gray
OLE2	BorderStyle	0 - None
	Appearance	0 - Flat
	BackColor	Light gray
OLE3	BorderStyle	0 - None
	Appearance	0 - Flat
	BackColor	Light gray

14 On the File menu, click Save Project As, and save the form to disk with the name **My Bid Estimator**. Save the project to disk with the name **My Bid Estimator**.

When you've finished, your My Bid Estimator form should look similar to the following:

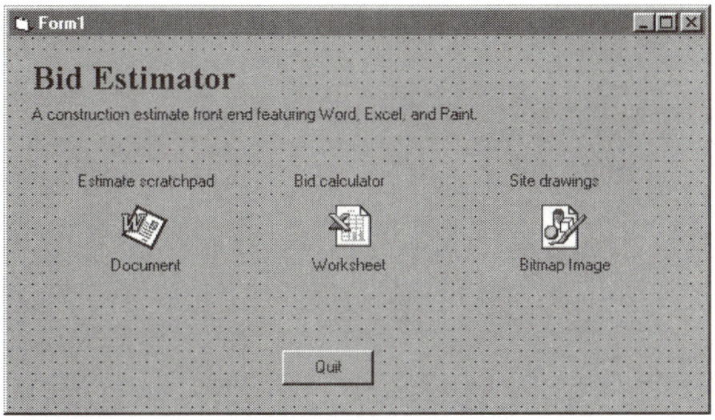

Now try running the program to see how the OLE objects operate at runtime.

The complete Bid Estimator program is located on disk in the Lesson 2 folder.

Run the My Bid Estimator program

1 Click the Start button on the toolbar.

The program runs in the programming environment. The OLE 1 object (the Document icon) is surrounded by a dotted line, indicating that it has the attention, or *focus,* of the program.

NOTE The focus is important for keyboard operations. When the user presses ENTER, the object that has the focus is selected, or activated, in the program. The user can switch the focus to another object in the program by pressing the TAB key or by clicking the object. You can change the order in which objects receive the focus in the program by changing each object's TabIndex property.

2 Double-click the Document icon in the program.

The word processor starts, and the Word template document appears in a window.

3 Type a few lines of text (pretend you're an important contractor), and then, on the File menu, click Exit to return to the My Bid Estimator program.

4 Double-click the Worksheet icon in the program.

The spreadsheet starts, and the Excel template appears in a window.

5 Enter a few rows and columns of information in the spreadsheet (feel free to use Excel functions and formatting features if you like), and then, on the File menu, click Exit to return to the My Bid Estimator program.

6 Double-click the Bitmap Image icon.

The Paint accessory starts and appears in a window. Paint is a simple illustration program containing drawing tools and color palettes for creating rudimentary artwork.

7 Create a simple construction site sketch with the Paint accessory (or pretend you did), and then, on the File menu, click Exit & Return To.

8 Click the Quit button to end the program.

Congratulations! You've built your first program that uses Microsoft Office application objects. You can use this technique to include in a program any application object installed on your system. Now try working with another type of file in the Windows environment—a preexisting database containing customer names and addresses.

Using a Data Object to View a Microsoft Access Database

If you work in a corporate setting or share information with other computer users regularly, you might use databases to track important information about clients, employees, or ongoing projects. A *database* is an organized collection of information stored electronically in a file. Database applications, such as Access, dBASE, and Paradox, are special programs that create and process information stored in databases. They provide the tools to design the database, manipulate the information in it, and search for specific items.

To enhance your work with databases, Visual Basic provides three objects that let you display and modify the information in database files. The primary object, data, gives you access to the fields and records of a database file directly on your form. Practice using a data object now to display information in an Access database named Shops.mdb.

> **NOTE** The Access file used in this exercise is on disk in the Lesson 2 folder, so you can try this exercise even if you don't have Access installed. You can also substitute one of your own database files for the Access file if you like.

Fields and Records

Two important terms used to describe information in databases are *fields* and *records*. Fields are the categories of information stored in a database. Typical fields in a customer database might include customer names, addresses, phone numbers, and comments. All the information about a particular customer or business is called a record. In a personnel database, each card containing information about a particular employee is a record. When databases are created, information is entered in tables of fields and records. Often the records correspond to rows in the table, and the fields correspond to columns.

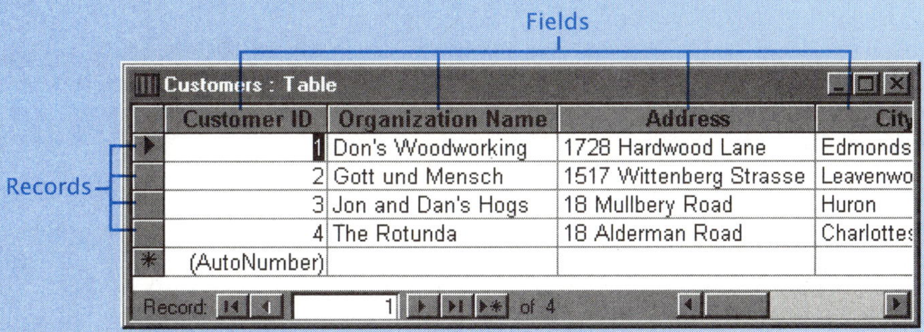

Create a data object

1 On the File menu, click New Project.

The My Bid Estimator program closes, and a new form appears in the programming environment. Save any changes to the My Bid Estimator program if you are prompted to.

2 Click the Data control in the toolbox.

Data control

3 Move the mouse pointer to the center of the form, near the bottom, and draw a rectangular box by using the control.

A data object named Data1 appears on the form, as shown in the following illustration:

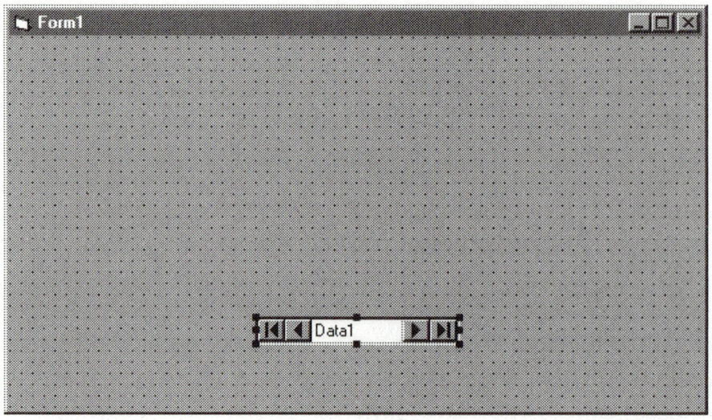

The object contains arrows that let you scroll through the records of your database when the program runs. The object also contains a caption (currently Data1) that you can use to describe the database you'll access by using the object. Typically the caption is set to the name of the database. The arrows near the outside edges of the object are used to move to the beginning or the end of the database.

There are many sophisticated operations you can perform with a database in Visual Basic. In this exercise, you display the Name field of the Shops.mdb database. (You'll actually be able to scroll through the database and view each name in the file.) To display the Name field on the form, an additional object is needed to hold the data. Since the data you want to display is text, you'll add a text box object to the form. (You'll also place a label next to the text box to identify the database field.) Finally, you'll establish a connection between the data object and the text box object, or *bind* them together, by using several property settings.

Create text box and label objects

TextBox control

Label control

1. Click the TextBox control in the toolbox.
2. Create a text box on the form, above the data object.

   The text box should be about the same size as the data object. The box should be wide enough to display shop names up to 20 characters long.
3. Click the Label control in the toolbox.
4. Create a label to the left of the text box on the form.

When you've finished creating the objects, your screen should look like this:

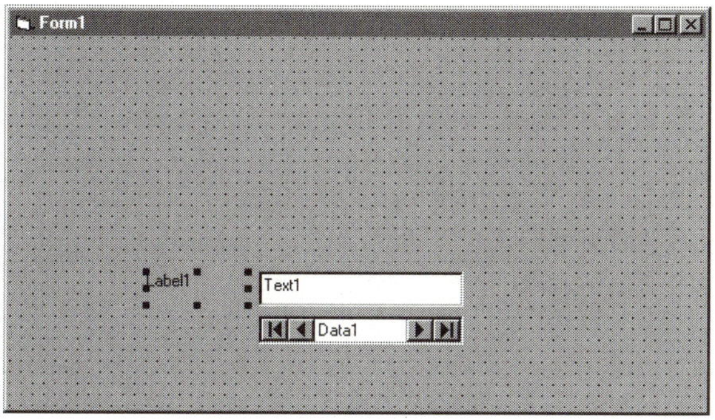

Now set the properties for the objects.

Set object properties

1 Click the data object, and then click the Properties button on the toolbar.

2 In the Properties window, verify that the Connect property is set to Access (the default).

Connect is the property that records the database format you'll be using. The formats Visual Basic can read include Access, dBASE, FoxPro, and Paradox.

3 In the Properties window, set the DatabaseName property to C:\Vb\Practice\Lesson 2\Shops.mdb by selecting the file in the DatabaseName dialog box.

Shops.mdb is the sample Access database you'll open in this exercise. It contains names, addresses, phone numbers, and other information used to track a group of fictitious shops.

4 In the Properties window, click the RecordSource property, and then click the drop-down list box button. When a list of database tables appears, click Customers in the list box.

The RecordSource property lets you specify the table (the collection of data) you want to open in the database.

5 In the Properties window, set the Caption property of the data object to "Shops.mdb".

The caption in the control changes to Shops.mdb to identify the database to the user. Now change the DataSource property of the text box to link the text box to the data object.

6 Click the text box object, and then click the Properties button on the toolbar.

7 In the Properties window, click the DataSource property, click the drop-down list box button, and then click Data1 (the first data object) in the list.

8 In the Properties window, click the DataField property, click the drop-down list box button, and then click OrganizationName (the field you want to display) in the list.

9 Click the Label object, click the Properties button on the toolbar, and then change the Caption property to "Name".

This will identify the database field in the text box when the program runs. Adding labels to your form to explain what things are is always a good idea, especially when you're working with database fields.

10 Save your form as **My Data Object** and your project as **My Data Object**.

That's it! Now run your program.

The complete Data Object.vbp program is located on disk in the Lesson 2 folder.

Run the My Data Object program

1 Click the Start button on the toolbar.

The program runs in the program environment, as shown in the following illustration:

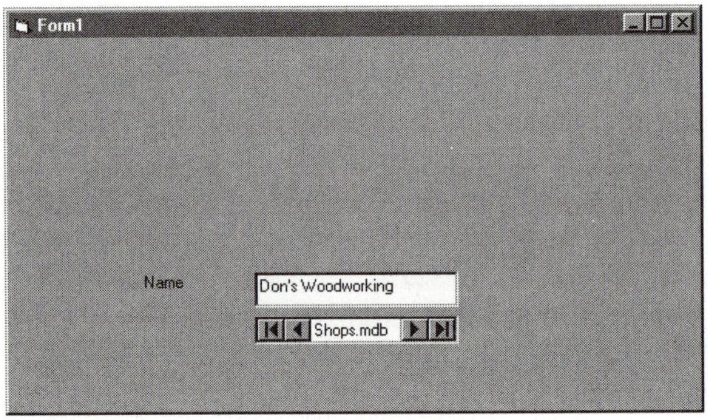

Visual Basic loads the Shops.mdb database and places the first OrganizationName field in the text box. Examine other field entries now by clicking buttons in the data object.

2 Click the inner right button in the data object.

The second name in the database appears in the text window.

3 Click the outer right button in the data object.

Visual Basic displays the last name in the database.

4 Click the outer left button in the data object.

Visual Basic displays the first name in the database again.

5 Click the Close button on the form to stop the program.

Modifying a Database

A data object also lets you modify the information in databases. To change a name in the Shops.mdb database, run the My Data Object program and scroll to the name you want to change. Then click in the Name text box, and edit the name as you see fit. When you change to a different record, the edit you made is copied to the original database immediately. Give it a try now.

Change a name in the database

1 Click Start on the toolbar to run the My Data Object program.

  The first name in the database appears in the text box.

2 Highlight the first name by using the mouse, press DEL, and then type **Pete's Shuttles**.

3 Click the inside right arrow in the data object to move to the next record.

  The first name in the database is changed to Pete's Shuttles.

4 Click the inside left arrow in the data object to move back to the first record.

  The first name now appears as Pete's Shuttles.

5 Click the Close button on the form to stop the program.

As you can see, a data object gives you quick access to preexisting databases. You can display any field in the database and process the information as you see fit. You'll learn more about data objects and how to manage files in Lesson 9.

One Step Further: Installing Custom Controls

You can extend the functionality of Visual Basic by installing the custom controls that come with Visual Basic or custom controls from third-party tool vendors. You install custom controls in the toolbox for a project by using the Custom Controls command on the Tools menu. New custom controls, which take advantage of 32-bit OLE technology, have the filename extension .ocx and can be used to add new features to Windows 95 and Microsoft Windows NT programs. Old custom controls, which were designed for 16-bit versions of Visual Basic and Windows 3.1, have the filename extension .vbx. You should always use the new .ocx controls if you have a choice. In many cases, Visual Basic will replace old controls with their new counterparts automatically when you install the new controls.

Install the Grid and the Outline custom controls

Visual Basic 4 includes extra custom controls you can use in your projects. For example, if you're writing a program to display data in a table, you can install the Grid custom control, which you can use to create a grid of cells on a form. (A grid object looks a lot like an Excel worksheet.) This custom control is located in the file Grid32.ocx. Another useful custom control, for displaying data hierarchically, is the Outline custom control, located in the file Msoutl32.ocx. Follow these steps to install the custom controls:

1 On the File menu, click New Project.

Save any changes to the My Data Object program if you are prompted to.

2 On the Tools menu, click the Custom Controls command.

The Custom Controls dialog box appears, as shown in the following illustration:

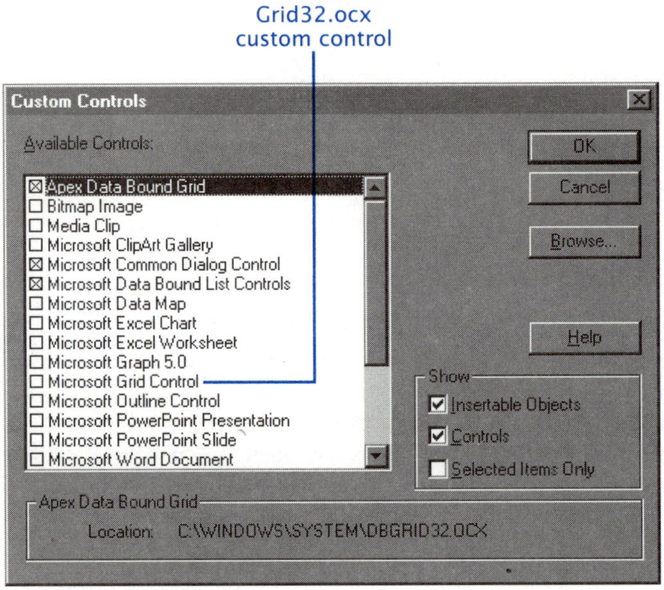

The Custom Controls dialog box presents an alphabetical list of the custom controls and insertable objects in your system that can be added to your project's toolbox. An *insertable object* is a program component supplied by another application for Windows, such as a Word document or an Excel worksheet. To give you flexibility in how you create your programs, every project is given its own unique toolbox containing the default Visual Basic controls and any custom controls or insertable objects you select. Accordingly, any controls or objects you add to this project now will appear in only this project's toolbox. In the following steps you'll add the Grid custom control (Grid32.ocx) and the Outline custom control (Msoutl32.ocx) to your toolbox.

3 Click the check box next to the control named Microsoft Grid Control.

The custom control is selected, and the location of the .ocx file appears at the bottom of the dialog box.

4 Scroll down the list, and click the check box next to the control named Microsoft Outline Control.

5 Click OK to add the selected custom controls to this project's toolbox.

The toolbox displays two new controls, as shown in the following illustration:

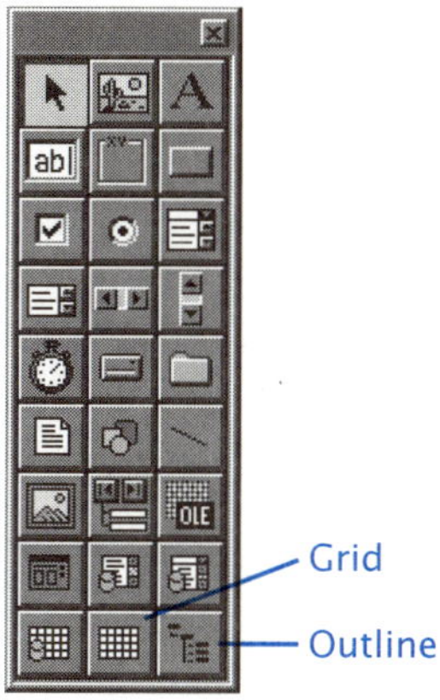

The Grid and Outline custom controls work exactly like the rest of the Visual Basic controls in the toolbox. In fact, if you didn't know they were custom controls, it would be difficult to tell them from the other controls. You select the custom controls by clicking them and you use them to create objects on a form the same way you use the other controls. The custom controls also have adjustable property settings and can be used in program code like the rest of the controls you've used in this lesson.

Windows 95 Custom Controls

If you're writing programs that will run under Windows 95, Visual Basic 4 Professional Edition and Visual Basic 4 Enterprise Edition include a special library of custom controls for user interface design. (These Windows 95 custom controls appear in the default toolbox.) For information about how the Windows 95 custom controls can be used in a program, run the Help file Custom Control Help, which is located in the Visual Basic 4.0 folder. The table on the following page gives a brief description of the Windows 95 custom controls.

Windows 95 Custom Controls, *continued*

Custom control	Purpose
ImageList	Maintains a list of bit maps in memory for use in toolbars, animation, and multilingual applications.
ListView	Displays lists of files and icons in the same way Windows Explorer displays them.
TreeView	Displays information in a hierarchy (for example, folders and subfolders) in the same way Windows Explorer displays it.
Tabstrip	Creates dialog boxes that have Windows 95–style tabs.
Toolbar	Adds standard toolbars to programs.
Slider	Adds a sliding gauge to a program that allows a user to quickly change his or her position in a file or media presentation.
Progress	Displays for the user how long it will take to complete the user's request.
StatusBar	Presents peripheral information to the user in a standard format.

If you want to continue to the next lesson

- Keep Visual Basic running, and turn to Lesson 3.

  If you are asked whether you want to save the changes to the current project later, click No To All.

If you want to quit Visual Basic for now

- On the File menu, click Exit.

  If you see a Save dialog box, click No To All. You don't need to save this project and its list of custom controls.

Lesson Summary

To	Do this	Button
Create a text box	Click the TextBox control, and draw the box.	
Create a command button	Click the CommandButton control, and draw the button.	
Change a property at runtime	Change the value of the property by using program code. For example: `Text1.Text = "Hello!"`	

To	Do this	Button
Create a drive list box	Click the DriveListBox control, and draw the box.	
Create a directory list box	Click the DirListBox control, and draw the box.	
Create a file list box	Click the FileListBox control, and draw the box.	
Prevent a program crash	Write an event procedure by using program code (see Lesson 7).	

Load a picture at runtime	Call the LoadPicture function, and assign the result to the Picture property of an image object or a picture box object. The syntax for this statement would be
	`Object.Picture = LoadPicture(SelectedFile)`
	where *Object* is the name of the object and *SelectedFile* is a variable that holds the filename of a graphic. For example:
	`SelectedFile = "c:\truck.bmp"`
	`Image1.Picture = LoadPicture(SelectedFile)`	

Create an option button	Use the OptionButton control. To create multiple option buttons, place more than one option button object inside a box you create by using the Frame control.	
Create a check box	Click the CheckBox control, and draw a check box.	
Create a list box	Click the ListBox control, and draw a list box.	
Create a drop-down list box	Click the ComboBox control, and draw a drop-down list box.	
Add items to a list box	Include statements with the AddItem method in the Form_Load procedure of your program. For example: `List1.AddItem "Printer"`	

To	Do this	Button
Launch applications for Windows in your program	Use the OLE control to draw a box for the application on your form, and select the desired application object in the Insert Object dialog box.	
Display existing databases within your program	Use the Data control to create an object to navigate the database, and then bind the data object to an object that can display the database records (typically a text box object).	
Modify records in a database	Display the database in the program. Edit the record in the text box object at runtime, and then click a navigation arrow to save the change to disk.	
Install custom controls	On the Tools menu, click the Custom Controls command. Select the custom controls or insertable objects you want to add to your project's toolbox, and then click the OK button.	

For online information about	Do this
Visual Basic controls	On the Visual Basic Help menu, click Search For Help On, and then type the control name and click Display.
The standard Windows 95 custom controls in Visual Basic Professional Edition and Visual Basic Enterprise Edition	In the Visual Basic 4.0 program folder, click the Custom Control Help icon, and then click the control you're interested in.

For more information on	In the Visual Basic *Programmer's Guide,* see
TextBox and CommandButton controls	Chapter 3, "Creating and Using Controls"
Controls that present choices to the user	Chapter 3, "Creating and Using Controls"
File system controls	Chapter 18, "Using the File-System Controls"
The OLE control	Chapter 8, "Using the OLE Container Control"
Data controls	Chapter 22, "Accessing Databases with the Data Control"

Preview of Next Lesson

In the next lesson, "Working with Menus and Dialog Boxes," you'll learn how to add menus to your programs and how to process input from the user by using dialog boxes. You'll also learn how to use the CommonDialog control to create a standard user interface for input and how to detect and correct errors in your programs.

Lesson

3

Working with Menus and Dialog Boxes

Estimated time
45 min.

In this lesson you will learn to:

- Add menus to your programs by using the Menu Editor.
- Process menu choices by using program code.
- Use common dialog objects to display standard dialog boxes.

In Lesson 2, you used several Microsoft Visual Basic objects to gather input from the user while he or she was using a program. In this lesson, you'll learn to present choices to the user by using professional-looking menus and dialog boxes. A *menu* is located on the menu bar and contains a list of related commands. When you click a menu title, a list of the menu commands appears in a list box. Most menu commands are executed immediately after they are clicked; for example, when the user clicks the Copy command on the Edit menu, information is copied to the Clipboard immediately. If a menu command is followed by an ellipsis (...), however, Visual Basic displays a dialog box requesting more information before the command is carried out. In this lesson, you'll learn to use the Menu Editor and the CommonDialog control to add menus and standard dialog boxes to your programs.

Adding Menus by Using the Menu Editor

The Menu Editor is a graphical tool that manages menus in your programs. It lets you add new menus, modify and reorder existing menus, and delete old menus. It also lets you add special effects to your menus, such as access keys, check marks, and keyboard shortcuts. After you have added menus to your form, you can use event procedures to process the menu commands. In the following exercise, you'll use the Menu Editor to create a Clock menu containing commands that display the current date and time.

Create a menu

1 Start Visual Basic.

If the programming environment is already running, on the File menu, click New Project to start a new project.

Menu Editor button

2 Click the Menu Editor button on the toolbar.

The Menu Editor appears, as shown in the following illustration:

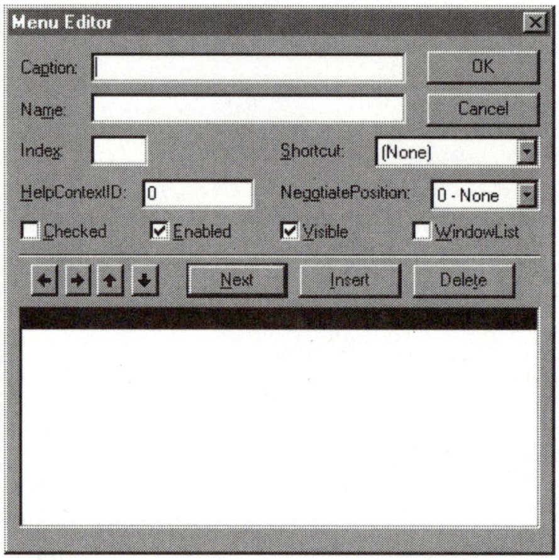

The Menu Editor helps you create and modify menus.

The Menu Editor displays menu-building commands and options in a dialog box. You specify the caption for a menu (the name of the menu on the screen) in the Caption text box. You specify the name for a menu (the name it will have in the program code) in the Name text box. These are the two most important settings for a menu. Additional settings, such as Index, HelpContextID, Shortcut, and Checked, are optional. You'll learn about the Shortcut setting at the end of this lesson. When you click the Next button in the Menu Editor dialog box, the Menu Editor clears the dialog box for the next menu item. The menu list box at the bottom of the dialog box displays menu items as you create them and shows the overall structure of the menu. Use the Menu Editor now to create a Clock menu.

3 Type **Clock** in the Caption text box, and then press TAB.

The word *Clock* is entered as the caption of your first menu, and the cursor moves to the Name text box. As you type the menu caption, the caption also appears in the menu list box below.

4 Type **mnuClock** in the Name text box.

By convention, mnu is used to identify a menu.

The word *mnuClock* is entered as the name of your menu in the program. By convention, the prefix *mnu* is used to identify a menu item in the program code. Prefixing user interface elements with a three-character label will help you differentiate event procedures as your programs get larger, and it will help you identify interface elements in the Code window.

NOTE The One Step Further section in Lesson 8 lists the naming conventions for all Visual Basic objects.

5 Click the Next button to add the Clock menu title to your program.

The Clock menu is added to the menu bar, and the Menu Editor clears the dialog box for your next menu item. The menu title still appears in the menu list box at the bottom of the dialog box. As you build your menu, each item will be added to the menu list box so that you can see the structure of the menu.

6 Type **Date** in the Caption text box, press TAB, and then type **mnuDateItem**.

The Date command appears in the menu list box. Since you wanted to make Date a command rather than a menu title, you used another naming convention—you added the word *Item* to the end of the name in the Name text box. This will help you differentiate menu commands from menu titles in the Code window.

7 With the Date item highlighted in the menu list box, click the right arrow button in the Menu Editor.

The Date command moves one indent (four spaces) to the right in the menu list box, indicating that the item is a menu command. The position of an item in the list box determines whether it is a menu title (flush left), a menu command (one indent), a submenu title (two indents), or a submenu command (three indents). You click the right arrow button in the Menu Editor dialog box to move items to the right, and you click the left arrow button to move items to the left. Now add a menu command named Time to the Clock menu.

8 Click the Next button, type **Time**, press TAB, and then type **mnuTimeItem**.

The Time command appears in the menu list box, as shown here:

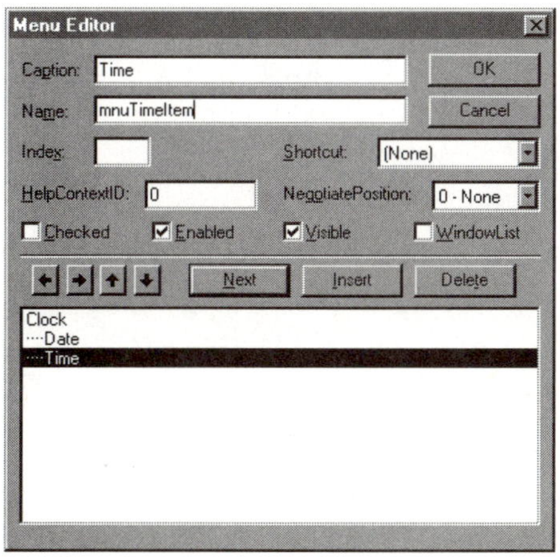

Notice that the Menu Editor assumed that the next item would be a menu command and indented Time one level. You've finished adding commands to the Clock menu, so you can close the Menu Editor.

9 Click OK to close the Menu Editor.

The Menu Editor closes, and your form appears in the programming environment with a menu bar and a Clock menu. Now open the Clock menu to see its contents.

10 Click the Clock menu.

The Date and Time commands appear, as shown here:

Clicking a menu command in the programming environment displays the event procedure that is executed when the menu command is chosen. You'll create event procedures for Date and Time a little later. First you'll add keyboard support to the menus.

11 Click the form (or press ESC twice) to close the Clock menu.

Adding Access Keys to Menu Commands

You define an access key by placing an ampersand (&) before the letter.

Visual Basic makes it easy to provide access key support for menus and menu commands. The access key for a command is the keyboard key the user can press to execute the command. When the user opens a menu at runtime, the access key for a command is indicated by an underlined letter in the command name. To add an access key to a menu item, all you need to do is start the Menu Editor and prefix the access key letter in the menu item caption with an ampersand (&). From that time forward, your program will support the access key. Try adding access keys to the Clock menu now.

Add access keys

Menu Editor button

1 Click the Menu Editor button on the toolbar.

The Menu Editor appears, and the menu list box displays the menu items that are in your program. The caption and name for the Clock menu appear in the dialog box.

2 Click in front of the word *Clock* in the Caption text box.

The cursor blinks before the letter "C" in *Clock.*

3 Type & to define the letter "C" as the access key for the Clock menu.

An ampersand (&) appears in the text box.

4 Click the Date command in the menu list.

The caption and name for the Date command appear in the dialog box.

5 Put an ampersand before the letter "D" in the Caption text box.

The letter "D" is now defined as the access key for the Date command.

6 Click the Time command in the menu list.

The caption and name for the Time command appear in the dialog box.

7 Put an ampersand before the letter "T" in the Caption text box.

The letter "T" is now defined as the access key for the Time command.

Menu Conventions

By convention, each menu title and menu command in an application for Microsoft Windows has an initial capital letter. File and Edit are often the first two menu names on the menu bar, and Help is the last. Other common menu names are View, Format, and Window. No matter what menus and commands you use in your applications, take care to be clear and consistent with them. Menus and commands should be easy to use and should have as much in common with those in other applications as possible. As you create menu items, use the following guidelines:

- Use short, specific captions consisting of one or two words at most.
- Assign each menu item in a program a unique access key. Use the first letter of the item if possible.
- If a command is used as an on/off toggle, place a check mark next to the item when it is active. You can add a check mark by clicking the Checked check box in the Menu Editor or by setting the menu item's Checked property to True.
- Place an ellipsis (...) after a menu command that requires the user to enter more information before the command can be executed.
- Use menu naming conventions such as the *mnu* prefix and the *Item* suffix when assigning menu names.

8. Click OK in the dialog box to close the Menu Editor.

   Now open the Clock menu to see how the access keys appear in the program.

9. Click the Clock menu.

   The menu title and menu commands are displayed with underlined access keys. When you run the program, you will be able to select the Clock menu items by pressing ALT plus the keyboard keys that correspond to the underlined letters or by clicking the commands by using the mouse.

10. Click the form to close the Clock menu.

Now practice using the Menu Editor to switch the order of the Date and Time commands on the Clock menu. Changing the order of menu items is an important skill to have; at times you'll think better of a decision you made when you first defined your menus.

Change the order of menu items

1. Click the Menu Editor button on the toolbar.

   The Menu Editor appears.

2. Click the Time command in the menu list.

   The caption and name for the Time command appear in the dialog box.

3. Click the up arrow button in the dialog box.

   The Time menu item is moved above the Date menu item.

4. Click the OK button.

   The Menu Editor closes, and the order of the Date and Time commands is switched in the Clock menu. You can also use the down arrow button in the Menu Editor to switch menu items; it moves commands down in the list.

You've finished creating the user interface for the Clock menu. Now use the menu event procedures to process the user's menu selections in the program.

NOTE You can also insert new menu items and delete unwanted menu items by using the Menu Editor. To insert a new menu item, click the item in the menu list that you want to place the new item in front of or above, and then click the Insert button. The Menu Editor will insert a blank item in the list, and you can define it by using the Caption and Name text boxes. To delete an unwanted menu item, click the unwanted item in the menu list, and then click the Delete button.

Processing Menu Choices

A menu command is processed by an event procedure associated with the command.

After menu items are placed on the menu bar, they become objects in the program. To make the menu objects do meaningful work, you need to write event procedures for them. Menu event procedures typically contain program statements that display or process information on the form and modify one or more menu properties. If more information is needed from the user to process the selected command, an event procedure will often display a dialog box by using a common dialog object or one of the input objects. In the following exercise, you'll add a label object to your form to display the output of the Time and Date commands on the Clock menu.

Add a label object to the form

Label control

1. Click the Label control in the toolbox.
2. Create a small label in the top middle of the form.

   The label appears on the form. It is named Label1 in the program code. Your screen should look like the following:

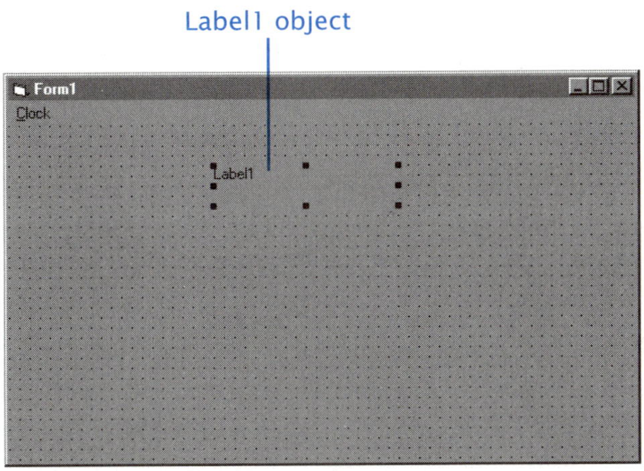

Set Label1 properties by using the Properties window.

3. Set the following properties for the label:

Object	Property	Setting
Label1	Alignment	2 - Center
	Border Style	1 - Fixed Single
	Caption	(none)
	Font	MS Sans Serif, Bold, 14-point

Now you'll add program statements to the Time and Date event procedures to process the menu commands.

NOTE In the following exercises, you'll enter program code to process menu choices. Type in the program statements exactly as they are printed. You won't learn how program statements work yet—only how they are used to support a functional user interface. You'll learn how program statements work in Lessons 4 through 6.

Edit the menu event procedures

1. Click the Clock menu on the menu bar.

   The Time and Date commands appear.

2. Click the Time command on the menu.

   The mnuTimeItem_Click event procedure appears in the Code window. You assigned the name mnuTimeItem to the Time command in the Menu Editor. When the user clicks the Time command in the program, the mnuTimeItem_Click event procedure is executed.

3. Press SPACEBAR four times, and then type

   ```
   Label1.Caption = Time
   ```

   This program statement displays the current time (from the system clock) in the caption of the Label1 object, replacing the previous Label1 caption. You can use the Time fuction at any time in your programs to display the time accurately down to the second.

NOTE Visual Basic's Time function returns the current system time. You can set the system time by using Control Panel's Date/Time option; you can change the system time format by using Control Panel's Regional Settings option.

4. Press the DOWN ARROW key.

   Visual Basic interprets the line and adjusts capitalization and spacing, if necessary. (Visual Basic checks each line for syntax errors as you enter it. You can enter a line by pressing ENTER, UP ARROW, or DOWN ARROW.)

5. Click the Close button on the Code window.
6. Click the Clock menu on the menu bar, and then click the Date command on the menu.

   The mnuDateItem_Click event procedure appears in the Code window. This event procedure is executed when the user clicks the Date command on the Clock menu.

7. Press SPACEBAR four times, and then type

   ```
   Label1.Caption = Date
   ```

This program statement displays the current date (from the system clock) in the caption of the Label1 object, replacing the previous Label1 caption. The Date function is also available for general use in your programs. Assign Date to an object caption whenever you want to display the current date on a form.

> **NOTE** Visual Basic's Date function returns the current system date. You can set the system date by using Control Panel's Date/Time option; you can change the system date format by using Control Panel's Regional Settings option.

8 Press the DOWN ARROW key to enter the line.

Your screen should look like the following:

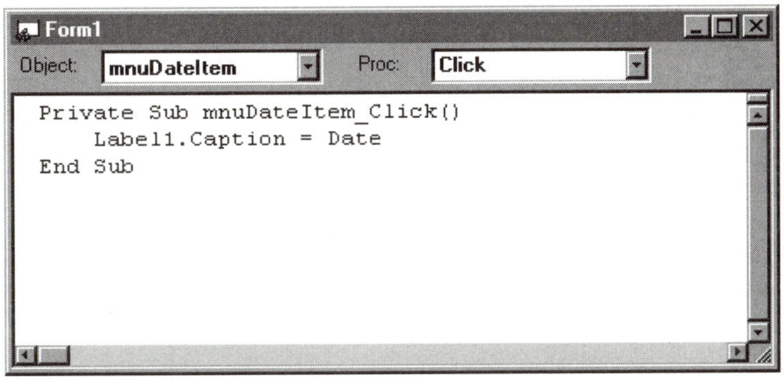

9 Close the Code window.

You've finished entering the menu demonstration program. Now you'll save the form and project to disk under the name My Menu.

Save the My Menu program

Save Project button

1 Click the Save Project button on the toolbar.

The Save Project button is the toolbar alternative to the Save Project command on the File menu. First enter the name of your project form.

2 Select the \Vb\Practice\Lesson 3 folder, and then type **My Menu** and press ENTER.

The form is saved to disk with the name My Menu.frm, and the Save Project dialog box appears. Enter the name of your project.

3 Type **My Menu** and press ENTER.

The project is saved to disk with the name My Menu.vbp.

Now your program is ready to run.

Run the My Menu program

Start button

The complete Menu.vbp program is located on disk in the \Vb\Practice\Lesson 3 folder.

1. Click the Start button on the toolbar.

   The My Menu program runs in the programming environment.

2. Click the Clock menu on the menu bar.

   The contents of the Clock menu appear.

3. Click the Time command.

   The current system time appears in the label box, as shown in the following illustration. Your time will probably be different.

Now try displaying the current date by using the access keys on the menu.

4. Press the ALT key.

   The Clock menu on the menu bar is highlighted.

5. Press C to display the Clock menu.

   The contents of the Clock menu appear.

6. Press D to display the current date.

   The current date appears in the label box.

   Congratulations! You have a working program that makes use of menus and access keys. In the next exercise, you'll learn how to use menus to display standard dialog boxes.

7. Click the End button to stop the program.

End button

System Clock Functions

You can use 10 functions to retrieve chronological values from the system clock. You can use these values to create custom calendars, clocks, and alarms in your programs. The following table lists the complete set of system clock functions. You'll use a few of these functions in the Part 2 Review & Practice. For more information, check the Visual Basic online Help.

Function	Description
Time	Returns the current time from the system clock.
Date	Returns the current date from the system clock.
Now	Returns an encoded value representing the current date and time. This function is most useful as an argument for other system clock functions.
Hour (*time*)	Returns the hour portion of the specified time (0 through 23).
Minute (*time*)	Returns the minute portion of the specified time (0 through 59).
Second (*time*)	Returns the second portion of the specified time (0 through 59).
Day (*date*)	Returns a whole number representing the day of the month (1 through 31).
Month (*date*)	Returns a whole number representing the month (1 through 12).
Year (*date*)	Returns the year portion of the specified date.
Weekday (*date*)	Returns a whole number representing the day of the week (1 is Sunday, 2 is Monday, and so on).

Using Common Dialog Objects

A common dialog object allows you to display five standard dialog boxes in your programs. Each common dialog box can be displayed from a single common dialog object. You display a particular common dialog box by using its corresponding common dialog object method. (As mentioned earlier, a method is a command that performs an action or a service for an object.) You control the contents of a common dialog box by setting its associated properties. When the user fills out a common dialog box in a program, the results are returned through one or more properties in the common dialog object, which can then be used in the program to perform meaningful work. The five common dialog boxes provided by the common dialog object are listed with the methods you use to specify them in the table on the following page.

Dialog Box	Purpose	Method
Open	Get the drive, folder name, and filename for an existing file	ShowOpen
Save As	Get the drive, folder name, and filename for a new file	ShowSave
Print	Let the user set printing options	ShowPrinter
Font	Let the user choose a new font type and style	ShowFont
Color	Let the user select a color from a palette	ShowColor

In the following exercises, you'll add a new menu to the My Menu program and practice using the Open and Color common dialog boxes. To retain a copy of the original My Menu program, you'll save the My Menu form and project with the name My Dialog before you start.

Save both the project and the form under a new name when you're renaming a project.

Save the My Menu files as My Dialog

1. If My Menu.vbp is not already open, load it from disk by clicking Open Project on the File menu.

   If you didn't create My Menu, open Menu.vbp from the \Vb\Practice\Lesson 3 folder. Its contents should match those of My Menu.
2. On the File menu, click the Save Project As command.

   The Save Project As dialog box appears.
3. Specify the \Vb\Practice\Lesson 3 folder, type **My Dialog.vbp**, and then press ENTER.

   A copy of the My Menu project file is saved to disk under the name My Dialog.vbp. Now save the form under the new name too.

WARNING If you don't save the form under a new name (as listed in steps 4 and 5), the My Menu and My Dialog programs will share the same form.

---

4. On the File menu, click the Save File As command.

   The Save File As dialog box appears.
5. Specify the \Vb\Practice\Lesson 3 folder, type **My Dialog.frm**, and then press ENTER.

   A copy of the My Menu form is saved to disk under the name My Dialog.frm.

Adding a Common Dialog Object

A common dialog object is not visible to the user at runtime.

Now use the CommonDialog control to add a common dialog object to the form. The common dialog object appears in only one size and is not visible to the user at runtime. (Since the object won't be visible, it can be placed anywhere on the form.) Placing the object on the form allows you to use any of the five common dialog boxes in your program.

Add a common dialog object

CommonDialog control

1. Click the CommonDialog control in the toolbox.
2. Draw a common dialog object in the lower left corner of the form.

   When you finish drawing the object, it resizes itself. The common dialog object is now ready for use in your program.

Now you'll create a picture box object by using the PictureBox control. You'll use the picture box to display artwork the user selects in your program by using the Open common dialog box.

Add a picture box object

PictureBox control

1. Click the PictureBox control in the toolbox.
2. Add a picture box object to the form, below the label.

   When you've finished, your screen should look like the following:

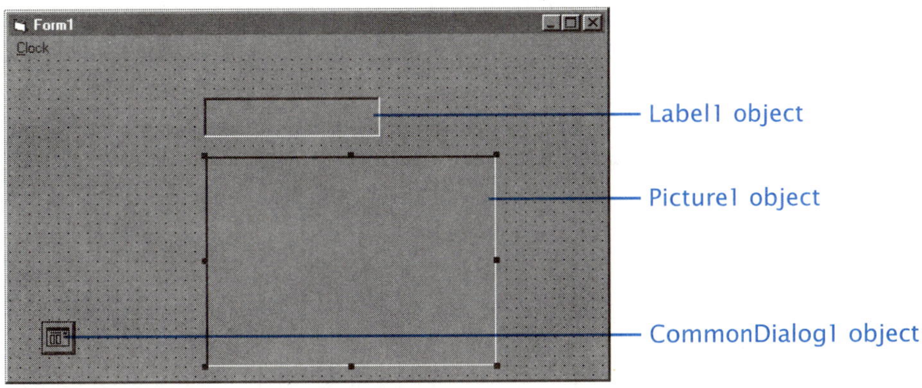

Now you'll use the Menu Editor to add a File menu to the My Dialog program.

Add a File menu

Menu Editor button

1. Click the Menu Editor button on the toolbar.

   The Menu Editor appears, and the current menu structure of the My Dialog program appears in the dialog box. Now add to the program a File menu that has Open, Close, and Exit commands.

2 Click the Insert button four times.

Four blank lines appear at the top of the menu item list. This creates space for the File menu commands you'll enter.

3 Click the Caption text box, type **&File**, press TAB, type **mnuFile**, and then click the Next button.

The File menu is added to the program. The letter "F" is specified as the access key.

4 Type **&Open...**, press TAB, type **mnuOpenItem**, click the right arrow button, and then click Next.

The menu item Open—a command that will open Windows metafiles—is added to the menu list and indented one level. Since the command will display a dialog box, you added an ellipsis (...) to the command caption.

5 Type **&Close**, press TAB, type **mnuCloseItem**, click the right arrow button, and then click Next.

The menu item Close (a command that will close the open file) is added to the menu list.

6 Type **E&xit**, press TAB, type **mnuExitItem**, and then click the right arrow button.

The menu item Exit—a command that will close the My Dialog application—is added to the menu list. It's traditional to use "x" as the access key for the Exit command. Your screen should look like the following:

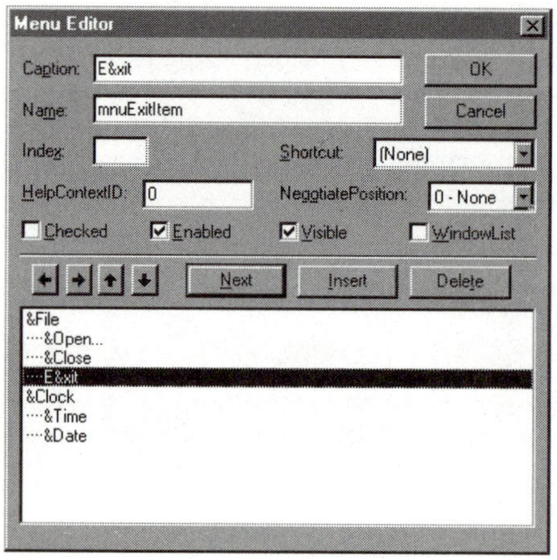

7 Click OK to close the Menu Editor and to add the items to the menu bar.

The File menu appears to the left of the Clock menu on the menu bar.

Disabling a Menu Command

In a typical application for Windows, not all menu commands are available at the same time. In a typical Edit menu, for example, the Paste command is available only when there is data on the Clipboard. You can disable a menu item by clearing the Enabled check box for that menu item in the Menu Editor. When a command is disabled, it appears in dimmed type on the menu bar.

In the following exercise, you'll disable the Close command. (Close is a command that can be used only after a file has been opened in the program.) Later in the lesson, you'll include a statement in the Open command event procedure that enables the Close command at the proper time.

Disable the Close command

1. Click the Menu Editor button on the toolbar.

   The Menu Editor appears.
2. Click the Close command in the menu list.

   The caption and name of the command appear in the dialog box.
3. Click the Enabled check box in the Menu Editor to remove the check mark.

   The check mark is removed from the check box, and the setting is disabled.
4. Click OK to close the Menu Editor.

   The Menu Editor closes.
5. Click the File menu on the form's menu bar.

   The commands in the File menu appear, as follows:

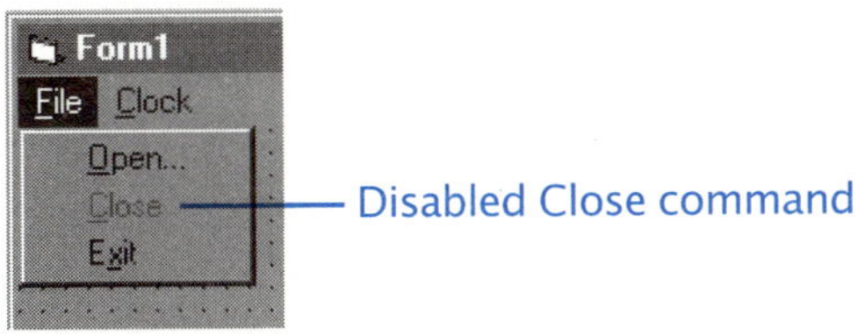

   The Close command appears in dimmed type.

Now you'll add a TextColor command to the Clock menu to demonstrate the Color common dialog box. The Color common dialog box returns a color setting to the program through the CommonDialog1.Color property. You'll use that property to change the color of the text in the label caption.

Add the TextColor command to the Clock menu

1. Click the Menu Editor button on the toolbar.
2. Click Date, the last menu item in the menu list.

   You'll place the TextColor command at the bottom of the Clock menu.
3. Click the Next button.

   A blank line appears at the bottom of the menu list.

4 Type **TextCo&lor...**, press TAB, and type **mnuTextColorItem**.

The command TextColor is added to the Clock menu. The command contains a trailing ellipsis to indicate that it will display a dialog box when the user selects it. The access key chosen for this command was "L" because "T" was already used in the menu, for Time. Your access keys won't behave correctly if you have duplicates at the same level within a particular menu or duplicates at the menu bar level.

5 Click OK to close the Menu Editor.

Event Procedures That Manage Common Dialog Boxes

To display a common dialog box in a program, you need to call the common dialog object by using the appropriate object method in an event procedure. If necessary, you also set one or more common dialog box properties before the call by using program code. After the user makes his or her picks in the common dialog box, you process the choices by using program code in the event procedure.

In the following exercise, you'll type in the program code for the mnuOpenItem_Click event procedure, the routine that executes when the Open command is clicked. First you'll set the Filter property in the CommonDialog1 object to define the file type in the Open common dialog box. (You'll specify Windows metafiles.) Then you'll use the ShowOpen method to display the Open common dialog box. After the user has selected a file and closed the common dialog box, you'll display the file in the picture box by setting the Picture property of the Picture1 object to the filename the user selected. Finally, you'll enable the Close command so that the user can unload the picture if he or she wants.

Edit the Open command event procedure

1 Click the File menu on the form's menu bar.

The commands on the File menu appear.

2 Click the Open command.

The mnuOpenItem_Click event procedure appears in the Code window.

3 Type the following program statements in the event procedure, between the Private Sub and End Sub statements. Indent each line four spaces to set the lines off as the text of the event procedure. Be sure to type each line exactly as it is printed, and press the DOWN ARROW key after the last line.

```
CommonDialog1.Filter = "Metafiles (*.WMF)|*.WMF"
CommonDialog1.ShowOpen
Picture1.Picture = LoadPicture(CommonDialog1.FileName)
mnuCloseItem.Enabled = True
```

Your screen should look like the following:

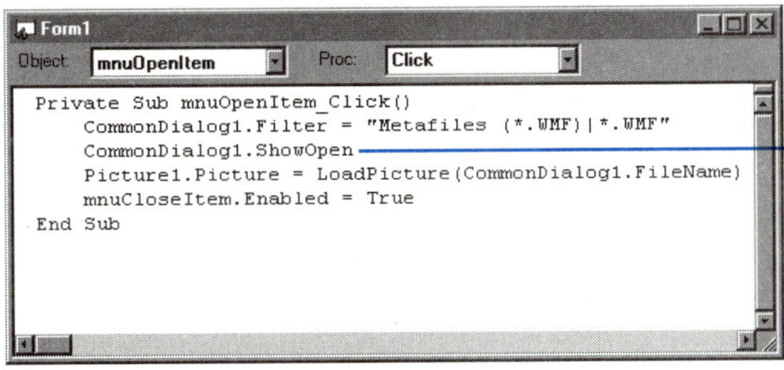

This statement displays the Open common dialog box

The Filter property defines the file types that will be listed in the Open dialog box.

The first three lines in the event procedure refer to three different properties of the CommonDialog1 object. The first line uses the Filter property to define a list of valid files. (In this case, the list has only one item: *.WMF.) This is important for the Open dialog box because a picture box, as you learned in Lesson 2, can display only three file types: bit maps (.bmp files), Windows metafiles (.wmf files), and icons (.ico files). (Attempting to display a .txt file in a picture box would cause a runtime error, for example.) To add additional items to the Filter list, you can type a semicolon between items. For example,

```
CommonDialog1.Filter = "Bitmaps (*.BMP)|*.BMP;Metafiles (*.WMF)|*.WMF"
```

would allow both bit maps and Windows metafiles to be chosen in the Open dialog box.

The second line displays the Open common dialog box in the program. Each common dialog box is displayed by using a different object method; the method for displaying the Open common dialog box is ShowOpen. (See the table earlier in this lesson for the methods that display other common dialog boxes.) This is the critical statement for the event procedure. Since the command's name is Open, the procedure needs to display an Open common dialog box and process the results.

The third line in the event procedure uses the filename selected by the user in the dialog box. When the user selects a drive, folder, and filename and then clicks OK, the complete pathname is passed to the program through the CommonDialog1.FileName property. The LoadPicture function, a special routine that loads electronic artwork, is then used to copy the specified Windows metafile into the Picture1 picture box.

The final line in the procedure enables the Close command on the File menu. Now that a file has been opened in the program, the Close command should be available so that users can close the file.

Now type in the program code for the mnuTextColorItem_Click event procedure, the routine that runs when the TextColor command on the Clock menu is clicked.

Edit the TextColor command event procedure

1. Close the Code window, and then click the TextColor command on the Clock menu.

   The event procedure for the TextColor command appears in the Code window.

2 Type the following program statements (indented four spaces) in the event procedure, between the Private Sub and End Sub statements.

```
CommonDialog1.Flags = &H1&
CommonDialog1.ShowColor
Label1.ForeColor = CommonDialog1.Color
```

Your screen should look like the following:

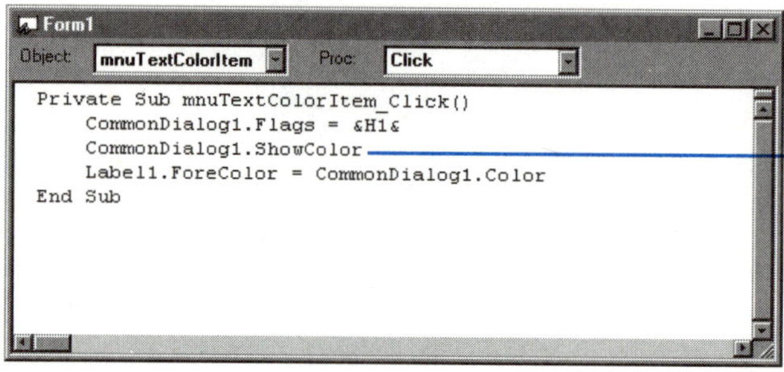

This statement displays the Color common dialog box

Controlling Color Choices by Using Flags

The Flags property defines the type of Color common dialog box that will be displayed.

The mnuTextColorItem_Click event procedure makes heavy use of the common dialog object's properties and methods. The first line sets a property named Flags to &H1&, a hexadecimal value that directs the Color common dialog box to present a list of standard color choices to the user, with custom colors as an option and a default color choice highlighted. The following table shows the four possible values for the Flags property.

Flag	Meaning
&H1&	Display a standard Color common dialog box (with custom colors as an option) and specify the current color as the default.
&H2&	Display a standard and custom Color common dialog box.
&H4&	Display a standard Color common dialog box with the Define Custom Colors button disabled.
&H8&	Display a Help button in the Color common dialog box.

You can use any combination of these values to prepare your Color common dialog box before you open it. To combine two or more values, use the Or operator. For example,

```
CommonDialog1.Flags = &H1& Or &H8&
```

displays the same Color common dialog box as before, but with an added Help button.

The second line in the event procedure uses the ShowColor method to open the Color common dialog box, and the third line assigns the selected color to the ForeColor property of the Label1 object. You might remember Label1 from the My Menu program earlier in this lesson—it's the label box you used to display the current time and date on the form. You'll use the color returned from the Color common dialog box to set the color of the foreground text in the label.

NOTE The Color common dialog box can be used to set the color of any user interface element that supports color. Other possibilities include the form background color, the colors of shapes on the form, and the foreground and background colors of objects.

Now you'll type in the program code for the mnuCloseItem_Click event procedure, the routine that closes the file displayed in the picture box when the Close command on the File menu is clicked.

Edit the Close command event procedure

1. Click the Object drop-down list box in the Code window, and then click the mnuCloseItem object in the list box.

   The event procedure for the File Close command appears in the Code window.

NOTE You need to use the Object list box to view the code of a menu item that is disabled.

2. Type the following program statements (indented four spaces) in the event procedure, between the Private Sub and End Sub statements.

Use the LoadPicture function with empty quotes to clear a picture box or an image box.

```
Picture1.Picture = LoadPicture("")
mnuCloseItem.Enabled = False
```

   The first line closes the open Windows metafile by loading a blank picture into the Picture1 object. (This is the technique used to clear a picture box or an image box object.) The second line dims the Close command on the File menu because there is no longer an open file.

Now you'll type in the program code for the mnuExitItem_Click event procedure, the routine that stops the program when the Exit command on the File menu is clicked. This is the last event procedure in the program.

Edit the Exit command event procedure

1. Click the mnuExitItem object in the Object drop-down list box.

   The event procedure for the File Exit command appears in the Code window.

2. Type the following program statement (indented four spaces) in the event procedure, between the Private Sub and End Sub statements.

```
End
```

   This statement stops the program when the user is finished. (It might look familiar by now.)

3 Close the Code window.

Save Project button

4 Click the Save Project button on the toolbar to save the completed project to disk.

Visual Basic saves your changes in the My Dialog form and project files.

Now you'll run the My Dialog program and experiment with the menus and dialog boxes you've created.

Run the My Dialog program

Start button

The complete Dialog.vbp program is located on disk in the Lesson 3 folder.

1 Click the Start button on the toolbar.

The program runs in the programming environment, and the File and Clock menus appear on the menu bar.

2 On the form's File menu, click Open.

The Open common dialog box appears, as shown in the following illustration:

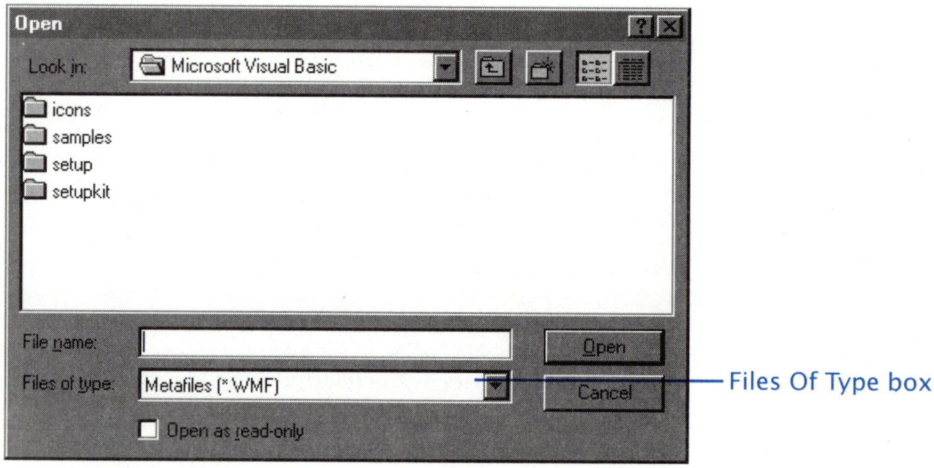

Notice the Metafiles (∗.WMF) entry in the Files Of Type box. You defined this entry with the statement

```
CommonDialog1.Filter = "Metafiles (*.WMF)|*.WMF"
```

in the mnuOpenItem_Click event procedure. The first part of the text in quotes—Metafiles (∗.WMF)—specifies which items are listed in the Files Of Type box. The second part—∗.WMF—specifies the default filename extension of the files that are to be listed in the dialog box. The dialog box also contains list boxes that you can use to locate a Windows metafile on your hard disk.

3 Specify the \Vb\Practice\Lesson 2 folder on your hard disk.

The sample Windows metafiles in the Lesson 2 folder appear in the file list box.

4 Double-click the file Pcomputr.wmf.

A picture of a computer appears in the picture box.

Now practice using the Clock menu.

5 On the Clock menu, click the Time command.

The current time appears in the label box.

6 On the Clock menu, click the TextColor command.

The Color common dialog box appears, as shown here:

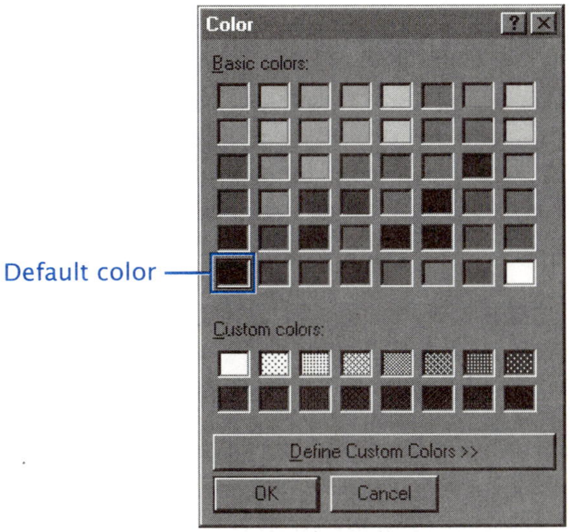

The Color common dialog box contains elements that let you change the color of the clock text in your program. The current color setting, black, is selected.

7 Click the dark red box, and then click the OK button.

The Color common dialog box closes, and the color of the text in the clock label changes to dark red.

8 On the Clock menu, click the Date command.

The current date is displayed in dark red type. Now that the text color has been set in the label, it will remain dark red until the color is changed again or the program closes.

9 Click the File menu.

Notice that the Close command is now enabled. (You enabled it in the mnuOpenItem_Click event procedure by using the statement mnuCloseItem.Enabled = True.)

10 Press C to close the computer Windows metafile.

The file closes, and the Windows metafile is removed from the picture box.

11 Click the File menu.

The Close command is now dimmed because there is no picture in the picture box.

12 Click the Exit command.

The My Dialog program closes, and the Visual Basic programming environment appears.

That's it! You've learned several important commands and techniques for creating menus and dialog boxes in your programs. After you learn more about program code, you'll be able to put these skills to work in your own programs.

Adding Nonstandard Dialog Boxes to Programs

What if you need to add a dialog box to your program that isn't one of the five common dialog box types? No problem—but you'll need to do a little extra design work. As you'll learn in future lessons, a Visual Basic program can use more than one form to receive and display information. To create nonstandard dialog boxes, you'll need to add new forms to your program, add input and output objects, and process the dialog box clicks in your program code. (These techniques will be introduced in Lesson 7.) In the next lesson, you'll learn how to use two handy dialog boxes that are specifically designed for receiving text input (InputBox) and displaying text output (MsgBox). These dialog boxes will help bridge the gap between the common dialog boxes and those that you need to create on your own.

One Step Further: Assigning Shortcut Keys to Menus

The Menu Editor also lets you assign shortcut keys to your menus. Shortcut keys are key combinations that a user can press to activate a command without using the menu bar. For example, on a typical Edit menu in an application for Windows (such as Visual Basic), you can copy selected text to the Clipboard by pressing CTRL+C. Try assigning shortcut keys to the Clock menu in the My Dialog program now.

Assign shortcut keys to the Clock menu

Menu Editor button

1 Click the Menu Editor button on the toolbar.

The Menu Editor appears.

2 Click the Time command in the menu list box.

The caption and name of the Time command appear in the dialog box. You assign a shortcut key by selecting the desired key combination in the Shortcut drop-down list box. Assign Ctrl+T as the shortcut key for the Time command.

3 Click the Shortcut drop-down list box, scroll down in the list box, and then click Ctrl+T.

You can't assign a shortcut key to a menu title.

Ctrl+T is assigned as the shortcut key for the Time menu item, and the key combination appears in the menu list box.

4 Click the Next button.

The caption and name of the Date command appear in the dialog box. Assign Ctrl+D as the shortcut key for this command.

5 Click the Shortcut drop-down list box, and then click Ctrl+D.

Your screen should look like the following:

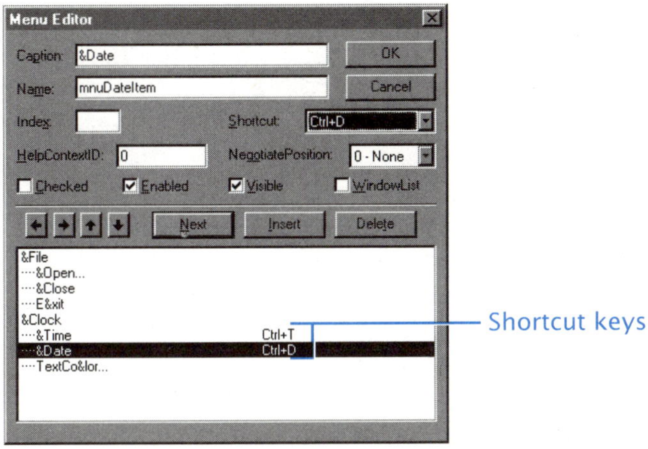

6 Click OK to close the Menu Editor.

Now run the program and try the shortcut keys.

Start button

7 Click Start on the toolbar.

8 Press CTRL+T to choose the Time command.

The current time appears in the program.

9 Press CTRL+D to choose the Date command.

The current date appears in the program.

10 Click the Clock menu.

The shortcut keys are listed beside the Time and Date commands. Visual Basic adds these key combinations when you define the shortcuts by using the Menu Editor.

11 On the File menu, click the Exit command.

The program stops, and the programming environment appears.

12 Click the Save Project button to save your shortcut keys to disk.

Save Project button

If you want to continue to the next lesson

➤ Keep Visual Basic running, and turn to the Part 1 Review & Practice section or to Lesson 4.

If you want to quit Visual Basic for now

➤ From the File menu, click Exit.

If you see a Save dialog box, click Yes.

Lesson Summary

To	Do this	Button
Create a menu item	Click the Menu Editor button, and define the menu item's caption, name, and position.	
Add an access key to a menu item	Start the Menu Editor, click the menu item you want, and then click in the Caption text box. Type an ampersand (&) before the letter you want to use as an access key.	
Assign a shortcut key to a menu item	Start the Menu Editor, and click the menu item you want. Specify the shortcut key in the Shortcut drop-down list box.	
Change the order of menu items	Start the Menu Editor. Click the menu item you want to move, and click the up arrow button or the down arrow button to move the item.	
Use a standard dialog box in your program	Add a common dialog object to your form, and then use one of the five common dialog methods in your program code to display the dialog box.	
Disable a menu command	Remove the check mark from the Enabled check box associated with the menu command in the Menu Editor.	
Enable a menu command by using program code	Use the program statement `mnuCloseItem.Enabled = True.` but substitute your command name for *mnuCloseItem*.	
Clear a picture box	Use the program statement `Picture1.Picture = LoadPicture("")`	

For online information about	On the Visual Basic Help menu, click Search For Help On, and then
The Menu Editor	Type **Menu Editor**
The CommonDialog control	Type **CommonDialog**
Common dialog types and methods	Type **ShowOpen**, **ShowSave**, **ShowPrinter**, **ShowFont**, or **ShowColor**

For more information on	In the Visual Basic *Programmer's Guide*, see
Creating and controlling menus	Chapter 10, "Menus"
Creating standard and custom dialog boxes	Chapter 11, "Dialogs"

Preview of the Next Lesson

The next section in this book is the first of your Review & Practice exercises. You can work through this Review & Practice section to review what you learned in Part 1. Following that, Part 2 (Lessons 4 through 6) covers the programming fundamentals you can use to get the most out of program code. In Lesson 4, "Visual Basic Variables and Operators," you'll learn how to create variables in your programs. You'll also learn how to work with operators and mathematical functions.

Part

1

Review & Practice

You will review and practice how to:

- Start Visual Basic.
- Add objects by using controls.
- Set object properties.
- Add menu commands to the menu bar.
- Write program code.
- Run and test a program.
- Create an executable file.

Estimated time
30 min.

Before you move on to Part 2, which focuses on Microsoft Visual Basic programming fundamentals, you can practice the skills you learned in Part 1 by solving the programming problem in this Review & Practice section. You will start Visual Basic, create the user interface for a program named Bit Map Browser, write code for the program, run and test the program, and create an executable file.

Scenario

Experienced computer users often have dozens or even hundreds of bit-mapped files on their hard disks. Bit-mapped files contain graphics images created by using painting programs such as Paint. The images are organized as a collection of pixels in the file. Bit maps are used for wallpaper on the Microsoft Windows desktop, for icons and toolbar buttons, and for electronic artwork in desktop publishing programs. Windows 95 contains several bit maps you can use in your programming projects, and if you have Visual Basic Professional Edition, you'll find several dozen toolbar bit maps in the \Program Files\Microsoft Visual Basic\Bitmaps folder.

In this Review & Practice, your programming problem is to create a Visual Basic utility that allows a user to browse the bit-mapped files on his or her computer. The program should contain a File menu that lets the user open and close bit maps and exit from the program. It should also contain a label that describes the purpose of the program and a picture box that displays the bit map.

If you like, you can try solving the problem before looking at the following practice steps. This will give you some "real world" experience at using Visual Basic to create a utility on your own, without any help. Or you can solve the problem by following these steps carefully and reviewing the related sections in Part 1 when the need arises. The solution to the problem is in the \Vb\Practice\Review folder, in the file named Problem 1.vbp.

Step 1: Start Visual Basic

Starting Visual Basic is the first step in any programming project. Begin your project now by starting Visual Basic.

1. Click the Start button, point to Programs, and then point to the Visual Basic 4.0 folder.
2. Click the Visual Basic 4.0 program icon.

For more information on	See
Starting Visual Basic	Lesson 1
Using the Visual Basic programming environment	Lesson 1
Preparing to write a program	"Getting Ready"

Step 2: Add Objects by Using Controls, and Set Properties

To start building the Bit Map Browser program, you need to create a user interface on the form. This involves adding descriptive text by using a label object, adding a container for the bit maps by using a picture box object, and preparing an Open dialog box for the user. You can use the three file system objects or one common dialog object to create an Open dialog box. In this solution, you'll use one common dialog object.

1. Use the Label control to create a label in the top center of the form.
2. Use the PictureBox control to create a large picture box in the center of the form.
3. Add a common dialog object to the lower left corner of the form.
4. Set the following properties for the Label1 object:

Object	Property	Setting
Label1	Caption	"A program that displays bit maps."
	Font	Times New Roman, Bold, 12-point
	ForeColor	Dark blue

5 Save the form to disk under the name **My Practice 1.frm**, and save the project to disk under the name **My Practice 1.vbp**. Specify the \Vb\Practice\Review folder.

For more information on	See
Using controls	Lessons 1 and 2
Setting properties	Lessons 1 and 2
Common dialog objects	Lesson 3

Step 3: Add Menu Commands to the Menu Bar

The second part of creating the Bit Map Browser user interface involves adding menu commands to the menu bar. Menus provide access to the commands and dialog boxes of a program, and they usually provide a mechanism for quitting the program. In your program, you'll need a File menu that has Open, Close, and Exit commands.

1. Click the Menu Editor button on the toolbar.
2. Create a menu title that has the caption "File", the name "mnuFile", and the access key "F". (Hint: You can create an access key by placing the ampersand character [&] in front of the letter you want to use as the access key.)
3. Create a command that has the caption "Open...", the name "mnuOpenItem", and the access key "O".
4. Create a command that has the caption "Close", the name "mnuCloseItem", and the access key "C".
5. Create a command that has the caption "Exit", the name "mnuExitItem", and the access key "x".
6. Close the Menu Editor.
7. Use the Properties window to set the Enabled property of the mnuCloseItem object to False. (This will disable the Close menu item when the program starts.)

For more information on	See
Creating menus and menu commands	Lesson 3
Adding access keys to menus	Lesson 3
Setting menu properties	Lesson 3

Step 4: Write the Program Code

The final step in building a program is writing the program code associated with the objects in the user interface. To complete Bit Map Browser, you need to write code for the event procedures associated with the program's menu commands (Open, Close, and Exit).

1. Click the File menu on the form, and then click the Open command.

2 Type the following program statements in the mnuOpenItem_Click event procedure:

```
CommonDialog1.Filter = "Bitmaps (*.BMP)|*.BMP"
CommonDialog1.ShowOpen
Picture1.Picture = LoadPicture(CommonDialog1.FileName)
mnuCloseItem.Enabled = True
```

3 In the Object drop-down list box in the Code window, click mnuCloseItem.

4 Type the following statements in the mnuCloseItem_Click event procedure:

```
Picture1.Picture = LoadPicture("")
mnuCloseItem.Enabled = False
```

5 Close the Code window, click the File menu, and then click the Exit command.

6 Type **End** in the mnuExitItem_Click event procedure, and then close the Code window.

For more information on	See
Using the Code window	Lesson 1
Writing program statements	Lessons 1 through 3
Loading pictures by using menu commands	Lesson 3

Step 5: Run and Test the Program

After the program is complete, you need to run it in the programming environment and test each feature to make sure the program is working correctly. Always be on the lookout for bugs!

1 Click the Start button on the toolbar.

2 On the File menu, click the Open command, and then open a bit-mapped file in the Windows folder. (You might need to scroll to the right to view the bit maps since there are so many subfolders in the Windows folder.) Verify that the bit map appears correctly.

3 On the File menu, click the Close command to close the file.

4 Open several more bit-mapped files on your hard disk. (If you have Visual Basic Professional Edition, you can find a number of interesting bit maps in the \Program Files\Microsoft Visual Basic\Bitmaps\Assorted folder.)

5 Test each of the access keys on the File menu.

6 When you've finished, on the File menu, click the Exit command.

7 If a part of the program isn't working correctly, retrace your programming steps to track down the problem, and then fix it. The program code and the property settings are the easiest places to make mistakes.

8 When you've finished testing, save the project to disk.

For more information on	See
Running a program	Lesson 1
Testing a browser program	Lesson 2

Step 6: Create an Executable File

As an optional step at the end of the programming process, you can create an executable (.exe) program file that can run without the Visual Basic programming environment.

1. On the File menu, click the Make EXE File command.
2. Specify the folder and the filename you want for the program file.
3. Click OK to create the file.

For more information on	See
Creating an executable file	Lesson 1

Part

2

Programming Fundamentals

Lesson

4

Visual Basic Variables and Operators

Estimated time
50 min.

In this lesson you will learn how to:

- Use variables to store data in your programs.
- Get input by using the InputBox function.
- Display messages by using the MsgBox function.
- Use mathematical operators and functions in formulas.

In Part 1, you learned how to create the user interface of a Microsoft Visual Basic program and how to build and run a program in the Visual Basic programming environment. In the next three lessons, you'll learn more about Visual Basic program code—the statements and keywords that form the core of a Visual Basic program. In this lesson, you'll learn how to use variables to store data temporarily in your program and how to use mathematical operators to perform tasks such as addition and multiplication. You'll also learn how to use mathematical functions to perform calculations involving numbers, and you'll use the InputBox and MsgBox functions to gather and present information by using dialog boxes. After you complete Part 2, you'll be ready for more advanced topics.

The Anatomy of a Visual Basic Program Statement

As you learned in Lesson 1, a line of code in a Visual Basic program is called a program statement. A *program statement* is any combination of Visual Basic keywords, properties, functions, operators, and symbols that collectively create a valid instruction recognized

A program statement is a valid instruction for the Visual Basic compiler.

by the Visual Basic compiler. A complete program statement can be a simple keyword such as

```
Beep
```

which sounds a note from your computer's speaker, or it can be a combination of elements, such as the following statement, which assigns the current system time to the Caption property of a label:

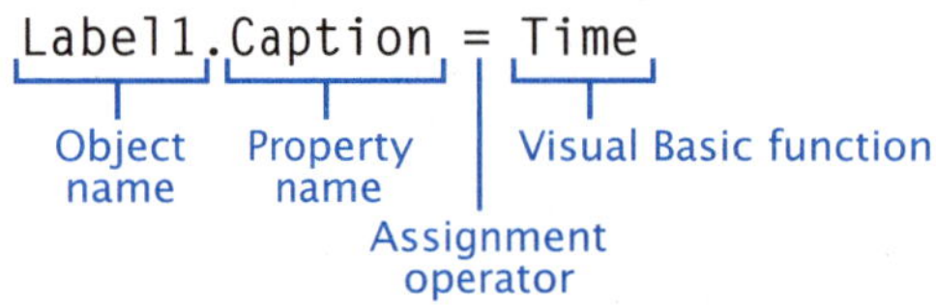

The rules of construction that must be used when you build a programming statement are called statement *syntax*. Visual Basic shares many of its syntax rules with earlier versions of the Basic programming language and with other language compilers. The trick to writing good program statements is learning the syntax of the most useful language elements and then using those elements correctly to process the data in your program. Fortunately, Visual Basic does a lot of the toughest work for you, so the time you spend writing program code will be relatively short, and the results can be used again in future programs.

In the following lessons, you'll learn the most important Visual Basic keywords and program statements. You'll find that they will complement nicely the programming skills you've already learned and will help you to write powerful programs in the future. Variables and data types, the first topics, are critical features of nearly every program.

Using Variables to Store Information

A *variable* is a temporary storage location for data in your program. You can use one or many variables in your code, and they can contain words, numbers, dates, or properties. Variables are useful because they let you assign a short, easy to remember name to a piece of data you plan to work with. Variables can hold information entered by the user at runtime, the result of a specific calculation, or a piece of data you want to display on your form. In short, variables are simple tools you can use to track almost any type of information.

Using variables in a Visual Basic program is a little like getting a table at a fancy restaurant. You can start using one at any time in your program code, but the management is happiest if you make reservations for it in advance. I'll cover the process of making reservations for, or *declaring,* a variable in the next two sections.

Making Reservations for Variables: The Dim Statement

Dim reserves space for a variable.

To explicitly declare a variable, before you use the variable (typically at the beginning of an event procedure), you type the variable name after the Dim statement. This action reserves room in memory for the variable when the program runs, and it lets Visual Basic know what type of data it should expect to see later. For example, the following statement creates space for a variable named LastName in a program:

```
Dim LastName
```

After the variable name, you can specify the variable type if you like. (You'll learn about several fundamental data types later in this lesson.) Visual Basic lets you identify the type in advance so that you can control how much memory your program uses. For example, if the variable will be holding a small number without any decimal places (an integer), you can declare the variable as an integer and save some memory space. By default, however, Visual Basic reserves space for a variable type called a *variant*, which is a variable that can hold data of any size or format. The general-purpose variant variable is extremely flexible, and it may be the only variable you use in your programs.

You store data in a variable by using the assignment operator (=).

After you declare a variable, you are free to assign information to it in your code. For example, the following program statement assigns the name "Jefferson" to the LastName variable.

```
LastName = "Jefferson"
```

After this assignment, the LastName variable can be used in place of the name "Jefferson" in your code. For example, the assignment statement

```
Label1.Caption = LastName
```

would display *Jefferson* in the first label (Label1) on your form.

Declaring Variables Without Dim

You can also declare a variable without the Dim statement; this process is called *implicit declaration*. To declare a variable in this way, you simply use the variable on its own, skipping the Dim statement altogether:

```
LastName = "Charles V"
```

Implicit declaration has a speed advantage because you don't spend time typing the Dim statement, but "the management" often discourages it because the implicit declaration doesn't force you to organize and list your variables in advance and because it prevents Visual Basic from displaying an error message if you mistype the variable name later. (See the following note.) In this book, I'll declare variables by using both techniques.

NOTE If you decide to always declare your variables by using the Dim statement, you might want to put the statement Option Explicit at the beginning of the Form_Load event procedure of your program. For example:

```
Private Sub Form_Load()
    Option Explicit
    .
    .
    .
End Sub
```

When you use Option Explicit, Visual Basic generates an error message whenever it finds a variable that has not been explicitly declared in the code. (The likely reason for this would be a spelling error in the variable name.) If you're worried about spelling errors, this statement can help you track them down.

Using Variables in a Program

Variables can maintain the same value throughout a program or they can change values several times, depending on your needs. The following exercise demonstrates how a variable named LastName can contain both text and a number, and how the variable can be assigned to object properties.

Change the value of a variable

1. Start Visual Basic.
2. On the File menu, click the Open Project command.

   The Open Project dialog box appears.
3. Open the sample project Variable Test in the \Vb\Practice\Lesson 4 folder.

   The Variable Test project opens in the programming environment. Variable Test is a skeleton program—it contains a form with labels and buttons for displaying output, but it contains little program code. You'll add the code in this exercise.

4. Click the View Form button in the Project window.

   The Variable Test form appears on the screen, as follows:

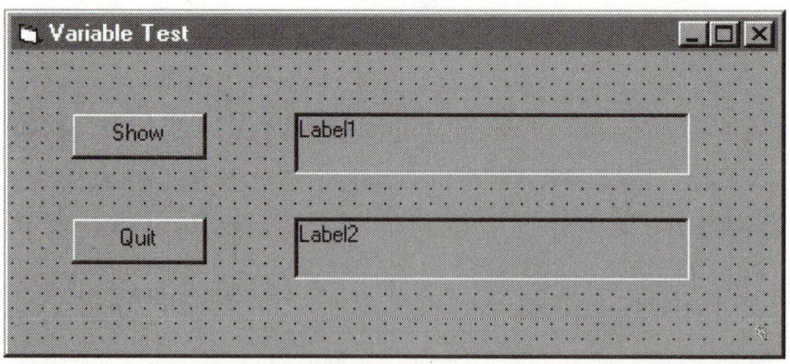

The form contains two labels and two command buttons. You'll use variables to display information in each of the labels.

5 Double-click the Show command button.

The Command1_Click event procedure appears in the Code window.

6 Type the following program statements to declare and use the LastName variable:

```
Dim LastName

LastName = "Smart"
Label1.Caption = LastName

LastName = 99
Label2.Caption = LastName
```

Variables can transfer information to a property.

The program statements are arranged in three groups. The first statement declares the LastName variable by using the Dim statement. Since no type was specified, the variable is declared as a variant type—a variable that can hold text or numbers. The second and third lines assign the name "Smart" to the LastName variable and then display this name in the first label on the form. This demonstrates one of the most common uses of variables in a program—transferring information to a property.

The fourth line assigns the number 99 to the LastName variable. This operation removes the text string from the variable and replaces it with a number. The number wasn't placed in quotation marks. Text strings require quotation marks, but numbers don't. (If you had placed quotation marks around the number, the number would be treated as a text string and couldn't be used in mathematical formulas.)

Your screen should look like the following:

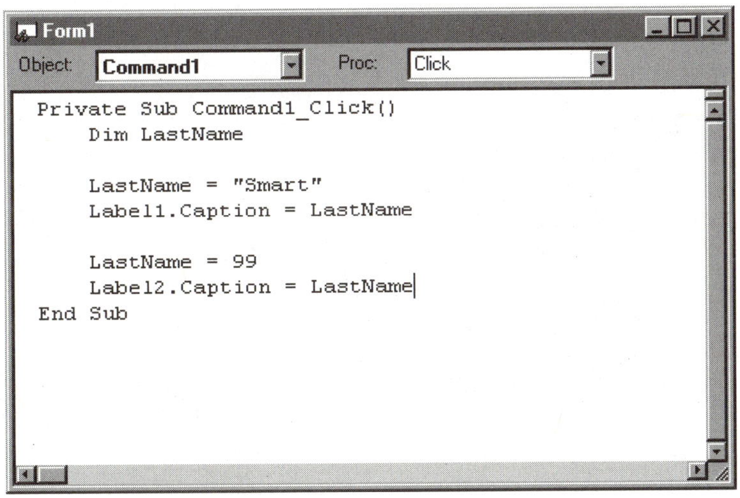

Start button

7 Click the Start button on the toolbar to run the program.

The program runs in the programming environment.

8 Click the Show button.

The program declares the variable, assigns data to it twice, and copies it to the two labels on the form. The program produces the following output:

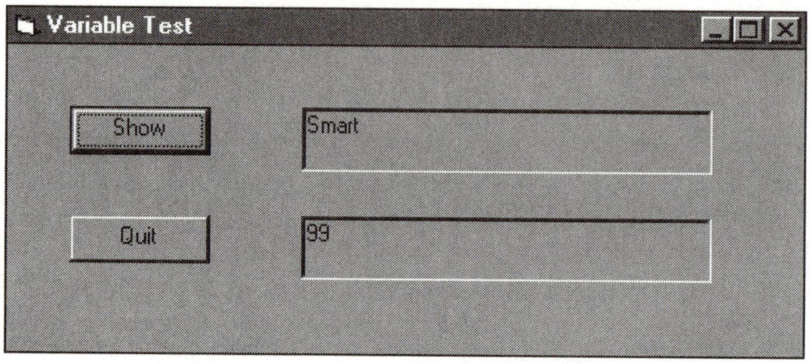

9 Click the Quit button to stop the program.

The program stops, and the programming environment returns.

10 Save your form changes to disk under the name **My Variable Test.frm** by using the Save File As command. Save your project changes to disk under the name **My Variable Form.vbp** by using the Save Project As command.

Variable Naming Conventions

Naming variables can be a little tricky because you need to use names that are short but intuitive and easy to remember. To avoid confusion, use the following conventions when naming variables:

- Begin each variable name with a letter. This is a Visual Basic requirement. Variable names must be fewer than 256 characters long and cannot contain periods.
- Choose descriptive names, combining one or more words into a variable name when it makes sense to do so. For example, the variable name SalesTaxRate is much clearer than Tax or Rate.
- Use a combination of uppercase and lowercase characters and numbers if you wish. An accepted convention is to capitalize the first letter of each word in a variable; for example, DateOfBirth.
- Don't use Visual Basic keywords, objects, or properties as variable names.

Using a Variable to Store Input

You can get input from the user effectively by using the InputBox function and a variable.

One excellent use for a variable is to hold information input from the user. You can often use an object (such as a file list box or a text box) to retrieve this information, but at times you'll want to deal directly with the user and save the input in a variable rather than in a property. One way to do this is to use the InputBox function to display a dialog box on the screen and then to store the text the user types in a variable. You'll try this technique in the next example.

Get input by using InputBox

1. On the File menu, click the Open Project command.

   The Open Project dialog box appears.
2. Open the project Input Box in the \Vb\Practice\Lesson 4 folder.

   The Input Box project opens in the programming environment. Input Box is a skeleton program—it contains a form with buttons and a label for displaying output, but it contains little program code.
3. Click the View Form button in the Project window.

   The Input Box form appears on the screen. The form contains one label and two command buttons. You'll use the InputBox function to get input from the user, and then you'll display the input in the label on the form.
4. Double-click the Input Box command button.

   The Command1_Click event procedure appears in the Code window.
5. Type the following program statements to declare two variables and call the InputBox function:

   ```
   Dim Prompt, FullName
   Prompt = "Please enter your name."

   FullName = InputBox$(Prompt)
   Label1.Caption = FullName
   ```

   This time you're declaring two variables by using the Dim statement: Prompt and FullName. The second line in the event procedure assigns a group of characters, or a *text string,* to the Prompt variable. This message will be used as a text argument for the InputBox function. (An *argument* is a value or expression passed to a sub procedure or a function.) The next line calls the InputBox function and assigns the result of the call (the text string the user enters) to the FullName variable. InputBox is a special Visual Basic function that displays a dialog box on the screen and prompts the user for input. In addition to a prompt string, the InputBox function supports other arguments you may want to use occasionally. Consult the Visual Basic online Help for details.

After InputBox has returned a text string to the program, the fourth statement in the procedure places the user's name in the Caption property of the Label1 object, which displays it on the form.

Start button

6 Click the Start button on the toolbar to run the program.

The program runs in the programming environment.

7 Click the Input Box button.

Visual Basic executes the Command1_Click event procedure, and the Input Box dialog box appears on your screen:

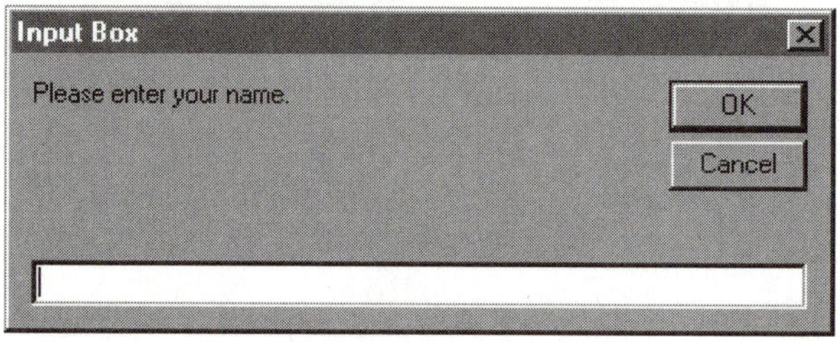

8 Type your full name, and click OK.

The InputBox function returns your name to the program and places it in the FullName variable. The program then uses the variable to display your name on the form:

You can use the InputBox function in your programs anytime you want to prompt the user for information. You can use it in combination with the other input controls to regulate the flow of data into and out of a program. In the next exercise, you'll learn how to use a similar function to display text in a dialog box.

9 Click the Quit button to stop the program.

The program stops, and the programming environment returns.

10 Save your form and project changes to disk under the name **My Input Box**.

What Is a Function?

InputBox is a special Visual Basic keyword known as a *function*. A function is a statement that performs meaningful work (such as prompting the user for information or calculating an equation) and then returns a result to the program. The value returned by a function can be assigned to a variable, as it was in the My Input Box program, or it can be assigned to a property or another statement or function. Visual Basic functions often use one or more arguments to define their activities. For example, the InputBox function you just executed used the Prompt variable to display dialog box instructions for the user. When a function uses one or more arguments, the arguments are separated by commas, and the whole group of arguments is enclosed in parentheses. The following statement shows a function call that has two arguments:

```
FullName = InputBox$ (Prompt, Title)
```

Variable name — Function name — Assignment operator — Arguments

Using a Variable for Output

The MsgBox function uses text strings to display output in a dialog box. It supports a number of optional arguments.

You can display the contents of a variable by assigning the variable to a property (such as the Caption property of a label object) or by passing the variable as an argument to a dialog box function. One useful dialog box function for displaying output is the MsgBox function. Like InputBox, it takes one or more arguments as input, and the results of the function call can be assigned to a variable. The syntax for the MsgBox function is:

```
ButtonClicked = MsgBox(Message, NumberOfButtons, Title)
```

where *Message* is the text to be displayed on the screen, *NumberOfButtons* is a button style number (1 through 5), and *Title* is the text displayed in the message box title bar. The variable *ButtonClicked* is assigned the result returned by the function, which indicates which button was clicked in the dialog box. If you're just displaying a message in MsgBox, the assignment operator (=), the *ButtonClicked* variable, and the *NumberOfButtons* argument are optional. You won't be using these in the following exercise; for more information about them (including the different buttons you can include in MsgBox), search for *MsgBox* in the Visual Basic online Help.

Now add a MsgBox function to the My Input Box program to display the name the user enters in the Input Box dialog box.

Display a message by using MsgBox

1. Double-click the Input Box button on the My Input Box form.

   The event procedure for the Command1_Click procedure appears in the Code window. (This is the code you entered in the last exercise.)

2 Use the mouse to select the following statement in the event procedure (the last line):

```
Label1.Caption = FullName
```

This is the statement that displays the contents of the FullName variable in the label.

3 Press DEL to delete the line.

The statement is removed from the Code window.

4 Type the following line into the event procedure as a replacement:

```
MsgBox(FullName), , "Input Results"
```

This new statement will call the MsgBox function, display the contents of the FullName variable in the dialog box, and place the words *Input Results* in the title bar. (The optional *NumberOfButtons* argument and the *ButtonClicked* variable have been omitted.) Your event procedure should look like the following:

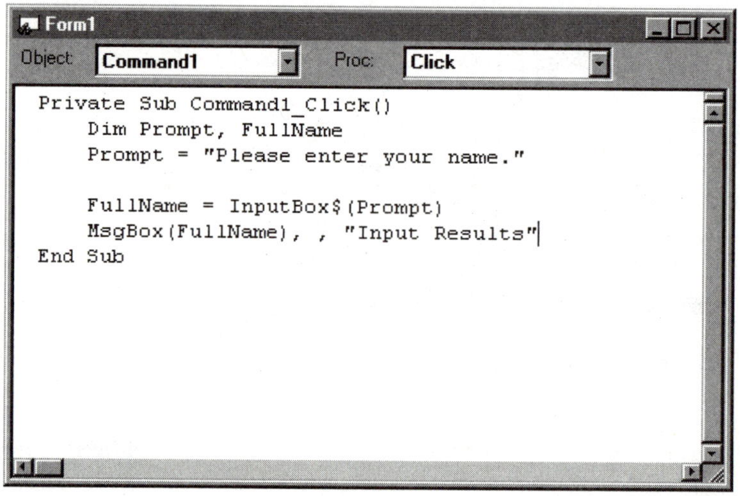

NOTE When no *ButtonClicked* variable is included, the parentheses go around only the first argument.

Start button

5 Click the Start button on the toolbar.

6 Click the Input Box button, type your name in the input box, and then click OK.

The input is stored in the program in the FullName variable and is then displayed in a message box. Your screen should look like the following:

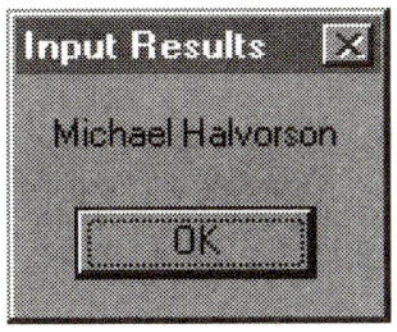

7 Click OK to close the message box, and then click Quit to close the program.

The program closes, and the programming environment returns.

8 Save the form and project as **My Output** to keep a copy of your program.

Working with Specific Data Types

If a variable will always contain a specific data type, you can increase program performance by declaring the variable as that type.

In most cases, the variant data type will be the only data type you need. Variant variables can store all of Visual Basic's fundamental (predefined) data types and switch formats automatically. Variants are also easy to use, and you don't have to give much thought to the eventual size of the variable when you declare it. If you want to create especially fast and concise code, however, you may want to use more specific data types when appropriate. For example, if a variable will always contain small integer values (numbers without a decimal point), you can save space in memory when you run your program by declaring the variable as an integer rather than as a variant. An integer variable will speed up arithmetic operations too, so you'll also gain a small speed advantage when you use it. The following chart lists the fundamental data types in Visual Basic. In the next exercise, you'll see how several of these data types work.

Variable storage size is measured in bytes—the amount of storage space required to store 8 bits (approximately 1 character).

Data type	Size	Range	Sample usage
Integer	2 bytes	–32,768 through 32,767	Dim Birds% Birds% = 37
Long integer	4 bytes	–2,147,483,648 through 2,147,483,647	Dim Loan& Loan& = 350,000
Single precision floating point	4 bytes	–3.042823E38 through 3.402823E38	Dim Price! Price! = 899.99
Double precision floating point	8 bytes	–1.79769313486232D308 through 1.79769313486232D308	Dim Pie# Pie# = 3.1415926535
Currency	8 bytes	–922337203685477.5808 through 922337203685477.5807	Dim Debt@ Debt@ = 7600300.50
String	1 byte per character	0 through 65,535 characters	Dim Dog$ Dog$ = "pointer"
Boolean	2 bytes	True or False	Dim Flag as Boolean Flag = True

Data type	Size	Range	Sample usage
Date	8 bytes	January 1, 100, through December 31, 9999	Dim Birthday as Date Birthday = #3-1-63#
Variant	16 bytes (with numbers); 22 bytes + 1 byte per character (with strings)	All data type ranges	Dim Total Total = 289.13

NOTE You can specify some fundamental data types by appending a type-declaration character to the variable's name. For example, you can declare a variable as type integer by adding a % character to the end of its name. So, in Visual Basic, the following two declaration statements are equivalent:

```
Dim I As Integer
Dim I%
```

For more information about fundamental data types, variable sizes, and supported ranges, see Chapter 6, "Variables, Constants, and Data Types," in the Visual Basic *Programmer's Guide.*

Use fundamental data types in code

The Data program demonstrates fundamental data types in program code.

1. On the File menu, click the Open Project command.

   The Open Project dialog box appears.

2. Open the Data project in the \Vb\Practice\Lesson 4 folder.

   The Data project opens in the programming environment. Data is a complete Visual Basic program that demonstrates how several fundamental data types work. You'll run the program to see what the data types look like, and then you'll look at how the variables are declared and used in the program code.

Start button

3. Click the Start button on the toolbar.

   The following application window appears:

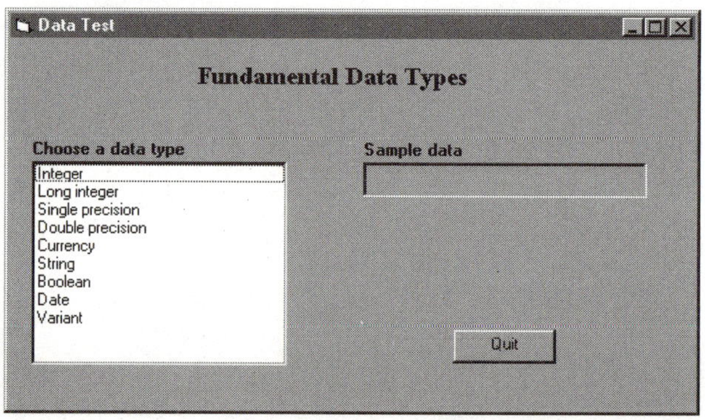

The Data program lets you experiment with nine data types, including integer, single precision floating point, and date. The program displays an example of each type when you click its name in the list box.

4 Click the Integer type in the list box.

The number 37 appears in the Sample Data box.

5 Click the Date type in the list box.

The date Tuesday, November 19, 1963, appears in the Sample Data box.

6 Click each data type in the list box to see how Visual Basic displays it in the Sample Data box.

7 Click the Quit button to stop the program.

Now examine how the fundamental data types are declared and used in the List1_Click event procedure.

8 Click the View Form button in the Project window.

9 Double-click the list box object on the form.

The List1_Click event procedure appears in the Code window:

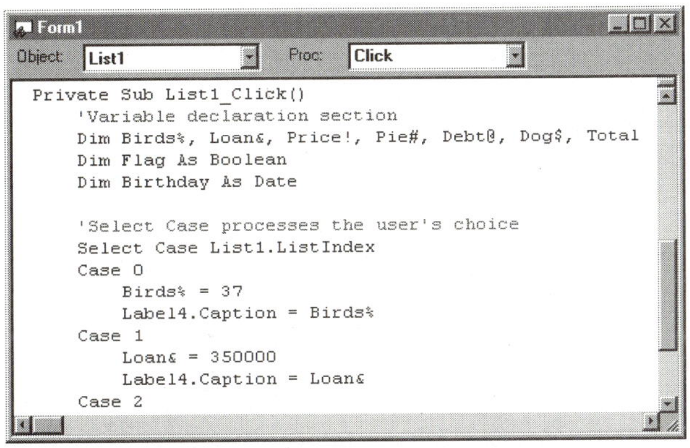

The first few lines of the procedure declare variables with specific data types in the procedure. These variables will be *local* to the procedure: they'll have no meaning in other event procedures in the program. Several of the variables are declared using special data type characters, such as %, #, and @. These symbols identify each variable as a specific fundamental data type in the program and mark the variables for the Visual Basic compiler and for people reading your program code.

The next section of the event procedure is called a Select Case decision structure. We'll discuss how this group of program statements selects one choice from many in the next lesson. For now, notice how each section of the Select Case block assigns a sample value to one of the fundamental data type variables and then assigns the variable to the caption of the Label4 object on the form. You can use both of these techniques to manipulate fundamental data types in your own programs. The Date data type is especially useful if you plan to work with date and time values regularly. The date is assigned to the variable Birthday with # characters surrounding the date, and the date is formatted with the Format function.

NOTE Variables can also be *global* in nature, or available in all form procedures and modules of a program. (*Modules* are special files that contain declarations and procedures not associated with a particular form.) For a variable to have this range, or *scope*, it needs to be declared at the module level. For information about creating a global variable, search for *Public* in the Visual Basic online Help.

User-Defined Data Types

Visual Basic also lets you create your own data types. This feature is most useful when you're dealing with a group of data items that naturally fit together but fall into different data categories. You create a user-defined type by using the Type statement, and you declare variables associated with the new type by using the Dim statement. (The Type statement must be located in the Declarations section of a standard module; to learn more about standard modules, search for *module* in the Visual Basic online Help.) For example, the following declaration creates a user-defined data type named Employee that can store the name, date of birth, and hire date associated with a worker:

```
Type Employee
    Name As String
    DateOfBirth As Date
    HireDate As Date
End Type
```

After you create a new data type, it can be used in the program code. The following statements make use of the new Employee type. The first statement creates a variable named ProductManager, of the Employee type, and the second statement assigns the name "Erick Cody" to the Name component of the variable:

```
Dim ProductManager As Employee
ProductManager.Name = "Erick Cody"
```

This looks a little like setting a property, doesn't it? Visual Basic uses the same notation for the relationship between objects and properties as it uses for the relationship between user-defined data types and component variables. You can learn more about creating and using user-defined data types in Chapter 6 of the Visual Basic *Programmer's Guide*.

10 Scroll through the Code window, and examine each of the variable assignments closely.

If you wish, you can change the data in a few of the variable assignment statements and run the program again to see what the data looks like.

11 When you've finished, close the Code window.

If you made any changes you want to save to disk, click the Save Project button on the toolbar.

Constants: Variables That Don't Change

If a variable in your program contains a value that never changes (such as π, a fixed mathematical entity), you might consider storing the value as a constant instead of as a variable. A *constant* is a meaningful name that takes the place of a number or text string that doesn't change. Constants are useful because they increase the readability of program code, they can save memory, and they make global changes easier to accomplish later. Constants operate a lot like variables, but you can't modify their values at runtime. They are declared with the Const keyword, as shown in the following example:

```
Const Pi = 3.14159265
```

The statement above creates a constant called Pi that can be used in place of the value of π in the program code. To create a constant available to all procedures in a program, you should create the constant in a standard module, with the Public keyword in front of it. For example:

```
Public Const Pi = 3.14159265
```

NOTE For more information about standard modules, search for *module* in the Visual Basic online Help. For more information about the Public keyword, search for *Public* in the Visual Basic online Help.

The following exercise demonstrates how you can use a constant in an event procedure.

Use a constant in an event procedure

1 On the File menu, click the Open Project command.

The Open Project dialog box appears.

2 Open the Constant project in the \Vb\Practice\Lesson 4 folder.

3 Click the View Form button in the Project window.

The Constant program form appears on the screen. Constant is a skeleton program. The user interface is finished, but you need to type in the program code.

4 Double-click the Show Constant button on the form.

The Command1_Click event procedure appears in the Code window.

5 Type the following statements in the event procedure:

```
Const Pi = 3.14159265
Label1.Caption = Pi
```

Start button

6 Click the Start button to run the program.

7 Click the Show Constant button in the program.

The Pi constant appears in the label box, as shown here:

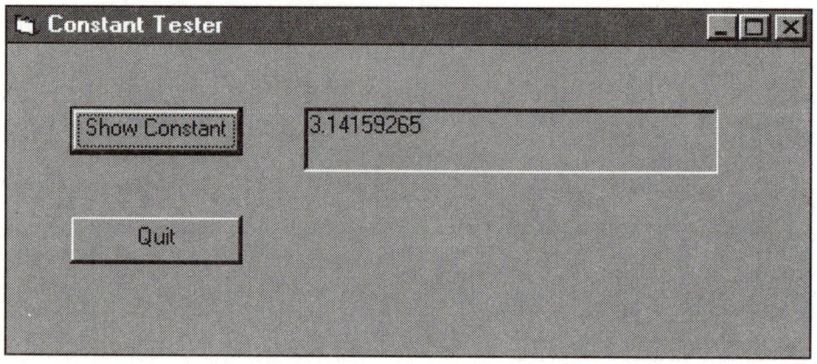

8 Click the Quit button to stop the program.

If you would like to keep a copy of the modified Constant program, save the form and project to disk under the name **My Constant**.

Constants are very useful in program code, especially in involved mathematical formulas, such as Area = $2\pi r^2$. The next section describes how you can use operators and variables to write similar formulas.

Working with Visual Basic Operators

Visual Basic operators hold together a formula.

A *formula* is a statement that combines numbers, variables, operators, and keywords, or some of these elements, to create a new value. Visual Basic contains several language elements designed for use in formulas. In this section, you'll practice working with mathematical operators, the symbols used to tie together the parts of a formula. With a few exceptions, the mathematical symbols you'll use are the ones you use in everyday life, and their operations are fairly intuitive. You'll see each demonstrated in the following exercises.

Visual Basic provides the following operators:

Operator	Mathematical operation
+	Addition
–	Subtraction
*	Multiplication
/	Division
\	Integer (whole number) division

Operator	Mathematical operation
Mod	Remainder division
^	Exponentiation (raising to a power)
&	String concatenation (combination)

Basic Math: The +, –, *, and / Operators

The operators for addition, subtraction, multiplication, and division are straightforward and can be used in any formula where numbers or numeric variables are used. The following exercise demonstrates how you can use them in a program.

Work with basic operators

1. On the File menu, click the Open Project command.
2. Open the Basic Operators project in the \Vb\Practice\Lesson 4 folder.
3. Click the View Form button in the Project window.

   The form for the Basic Operators program appears on the screen. Basic Operators demonstrates how the addition, subtraction, multiplication, and division operators work with numbers you type in from the keyboard. It also demonstrates how you can use text box, option button, and command button objects to process user input in a program.

A text box object is a useful tool for getting keyboard input from the user.

4. Click the Start button on the toolbar.

   The Basic Operators program runs in the programming environment. The program displays two text boxes in which you enter numeric values, a group of operator option buttons, a result box, and two command buttons.
5. Type **100** in the Variable 1 text box, and then press TAB.

   The cursor moves to the second text box.
6. Type **17** in the Variable 2 text box.

   You can now apply any of the mathematical operators to the values in the text boxes.
7. Click the Addition option button, and then click the Calculate command button.

   The operator is applied to the two values, and the number 117 appears in the Result box, as shown in the following illustration:

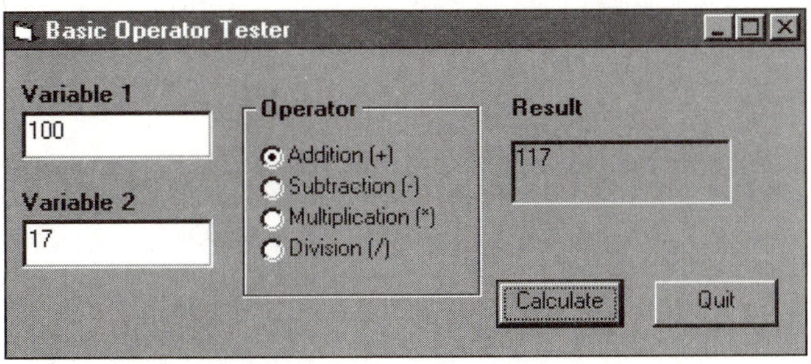

8 Practice using the subtraction, multiplication, and division operators with the two numbers in the variable boxes. (Click Calculate to calculate each formula.)

The results appear in the Result box. Feel free to experiment with different numbers in the variable text boxes. (Try a few numbers with decimal points if you like.)

9 When you've finished calculating, click the Quit button.

The program stops, and the programming environment returns.

Now take a look at the program code to see how the results were calculated. Basic Operators uses a few of the standard input controls you experimented with in Lesson 2 and an event procedure that uses variables and operators to calculate simple mathematical formulas. The procedure also uses the Val function to convert the string input received from the text boxes to numbers.

Examine the Basic Operators program code

1 Click the View Form button in the Project window. The form for the Basic Operators program appears on the screen.

2 Double-click the Calculate button on the form.

The Command1_Click event procedure appears in the Code window, as shown here:

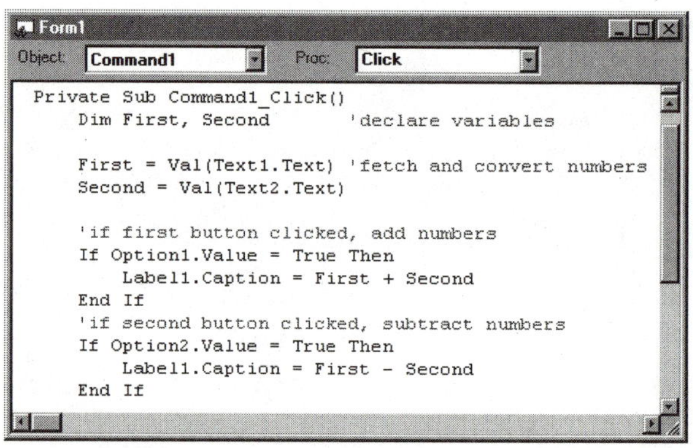

The first statement in the procedure declares two general-purpose variables of the variant type. The variants will be used to hold the values typed in the two text boxes, and they will be flexible enough to handle any numeric data type you want to use. The next two statements load the data from the text boxes into the variables and convert the text strings to numbers by using the Val function:

```
First = Val(Text1.Text) 'fetch and convert numbers
Second = Val(Text2.Text)
```

The Val function converts text values to numeric values.

The Val function is a special routine that converts a text argument to a numeric value. This conversion is necessary for the addition operation to work correctly in this program. The default data type returned by a text box object is text. This isn't a problem for three of the operators. The –, *, and / operators work only with numbers, so when the user selects one of these three operators in the program, Visual Basic automatically converts the values returned to the First and Second variables to numbers. The + operator works with both text strings and numbers. Because the default data type returned by the text box object is text, Visual Basic would automatically treat First's and Second's values as text when the + operator is used. Visual Basic would combine, or *concatenate,* the two values rather than add them mathematically. (In other words, "100" + "17" would equal "10017.") You'll learn more about string concatenation in the next exercise. For now, make a mental note that even though the variant data type can hold any fundamental data type, you need to watch closely how it is used in a program. It might default to something you don't expect.

IMPORTANT It is always important to test each calculation in a program to verify that the whole program is working correctly. Testing one part of the program is not enough.

---

3 Scroll down the Code window, and examine the four formulas that use basic mathematical operators.

The first formula in the procedure uses the addition operator (+) in an If...Then decision structure:

```
'if first button clicked, add numbers
If Option1.Value = True Then
    Label1.Caption = First + Second
End If
```

If the Value property of the first option button is set to True (if the button has been clicked), then the two variables are added together with the + operator and the result is assigned to the label. The three remaining formulas have a similar logic, each using an If...Then decision structure and the Caption property of the Label1 object. Decision structures such as If...Then are extremely useful in determining which option a user selects in your program when several options are available. You'll learn more about If...Then in the next lesson.

4 Close the Code window.

You're done using the Basic Operators program.

Using Advanced Operators: \, Mod, ^, and &

In addition to the four basic mathematical operators, Visual Basic includes four advanced operators, which perform integer division (\), remainder division (Mod), exponentiation (^), and string concatenation (&). These operators are useful in special-purpose mathematical formulas and text processing applications. The following utility (a slight modification of the Basic Operators program) shows how you can use each of these operators in a program.

Work with advanced operators

1. On the File menu, click the Open Project command.
2. Open the Advanced Operators project in the \Vb\Practice\Lesson 4 folder.
3. Click the View Form button in the Project window.

   The form for the Advanced Operators program appears on the screen. The Advanced Operators program is identical to the Basic Operators program, with the exception of the operators shown on the option buttons and the operators used in the program.
4. Click the Start button on the toolbar.

   The program displays two text boxes in which you enter numeric values, a group of operator option buttons, a result box, and two command buttons.
5. Type **9** in the Variable 1 text box, and then press TAB.
6. Type **2** in the Variable 2 text box.

   You can now apply any of the advanced operators to the values in the text boxes.
7. Click the Integer Division option button, and then click the Calculate button.

   The operator is applied to the two values, and the number 4 appears in the Result box, as shown here:

   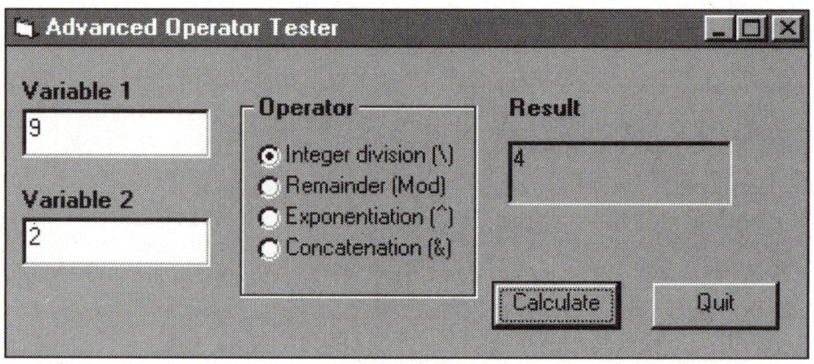

   Integer division produces only the whole number result of the division operation. Although 9 divided by 2 equals 4.5, the integer division operation returns only the first part (the number 4). You might find this result useful if you're working with quantities that can't easily be divided into fractional components, such as the number of adults that can fit in a car.
8. Click the Remainder option button, and then click the Calculate button.

   The number 1 appears in the Result box. Remainder division (modulus arithmetic) returns the remainder (the part left over that won't evenly divide) after two numbers are divided. Since 9 divided by 2 equals 4 with a remainder of 1 (2 × 4 + 1 = 9), the result produced by the Mod operator is 1. In addition to adding a 1960s sound to your programs, the Mod operator can help you track "leftovers" in your calculations, such as the amount of change left over after a financial transaction.

9 Click the Exponentiation option button, and then click the Calculate button.

The number 81 appears in the Result box. The exponentiation operator (^) raises a number to a power of itself. Since 9^2 equals 81, the result produced by the ^ operator is 81. In a Visual Basic formula, 9^2 is written 9 ^ 2.

10 Click the Concatenation option button, and then click the Calculate button.

The string "92" appears in the Result box. The string concatenation operator (&) combines two strings in a formula. The result ("92" in this case) is not a number; it is a combination of the "9" character and the "2" character. String concatenation can be performed only on text variables, strings delimited by quotation marks, and variant variables. Since the variables used in this program are variants, they were automatically converted to text for the operation. To see how this works with letters, type a few words in each variable box and click the Calculate button again.

11 Click the Quit button to stop the program.

The program stops, and the programming environment returns.

Now take a look at the Command1_Click event procedure to see how the operators were used.

12 Double-click the Calculate button on the form.

The event procedure appears in the Code window, as shown in the following illustration:

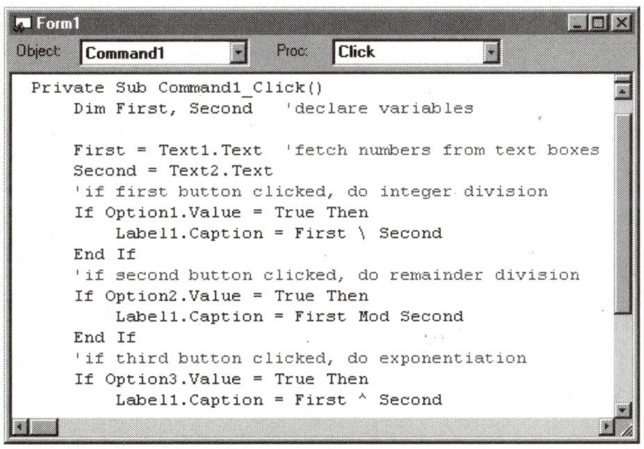

This Command1_Click procedure looks similar to the Command1_Click procedure in the Basic Operators program. The code declares two variant variables, assigns data to the variables from the text boxes, and computes the selected formula with If...Then decision structures. There is one important difference, however: this event procedure doesn't use the Val function to convert the data to a numeric type when it reads it from the text box objects. The conversion isn't necessary for the advanced operators because, unlike the + operator, each of the advanced operators works with only one type of data: \, Mod, and ^ work only with numbers; & works only with text. Because there's no type ambiguity, the variant variables can adequately convert the strings returned by the text boxes to numbers for the operations that require numbers.

13 Close the Code window.

You're finished working with the Advanced Operators program.

Operator Precedence

In the last two exercises, you experimented with seven mathematical operators and one string operator. Visual Basic lets you mix as many mathematical operators as you like in a formula, as long as each numeric variable and expression is separated from another by one operator. For example, this is an acceptable Visual Basic formula:

```
Total = 10 + 15 * 2 / 4 ^ 2
```

The formula processes several values and assigns the result to a variable named Total. But how is such an expression evaluated by Visual Basic? In other words, which mathematical operators does Visual Basic use first when solving the formula? You might not have noticed, but the order of evaluation matters a great deal in this example.

Visual Basic Mathematical Functions

Now and then you'll want to do a little extra number crunching in your programs. You may need to convert a value to a different type, calculate a complex mathematical expression, or introduce randomness to your programs. The following Visual Basic functions can help you work with numbers in your formulas. As with any function, the mathematical functions need to be used in a program statement, and they will return a value to the program. In the following table, the argument *n* represents the number, variable, or expression you want the function to evaluate.

Function	Purpose
Abs(*n*)	Returns the absolute value of *n*.
Atn(*n*)	Returns the arctangent, in radians, of *n*.
Cos(*n*)	Returns the cosine of the angle *n*. The angle *n* is expressed in radians.
Exp(*n*)	Returns the constant *e* raised to the power *n*.
Rnd(*n*)	Generates a random number between 0 and 1.
Sgn(*n*)	Returns –1 if *n* is less than zero, 0 if *n* is zero, and +1 if *n* is greater than zero.
Sin(*n*)	Returns the sine of the angle *n*. The angle *n* is expressed in radians.
Sqr(*n*)	Returns the square root of *n*.
Str(*n*)	Converts a numeric value to a string.
Tan(*n*)	Returns the tangent of the angle *n*. The angle *n* is expressed in radians.
Val(*n*)	Converts a string value to a number.

The operator order of evaluation is always important to keep in mind when you are building mathematical formulas.

Visual Basic solves this dilemma by establishing a specific *order of precedence* for mathematical operations. This list of rules tells Visual Basic which operators to use first when evaluating an expression that contains more than one operator. The following table shows the order, with the operators listed first to last, in which they will be evaluated. (Operators on the same level in this table are evaluated from left to right as they appear in an expression.)

Operator(s)	Order of precedence
( )	The values between parentheses are always evaluated first.
^	Exponentiation (raising a number to a power) is second.
-	Negation (creating a negative number) is third.
* /	Multiplication and division are fourth.
\	Integer division is fifth.
Mod	Remainder division is sixth.
+ –	Addition and subtraction are last.

Given the order of precedence in the above table, the expression

```
Total = 10 + 15 * 2 / 4 ^ 2
```

would be evaluated by Visual Basic in the following steps. (Boldface type is used to show the order of evaluation and the result):

```
Total = 10 + 15 * 2 / 4 ^ 2
Total = 10 + 15 * 2 / 16
Total = 10 + 30 / 16
Total = 10 + 1.875
Total = 11.875
```

One Step Further: Using Parentheses in a Formula

Parentheses clarify and influence the order of evaluation.

You can use one or more pairs of parentheses in a formula to clarify the order of precedence. For example, Visual Basic would calculate the formula

```
Number = (8 - 5 * 3) ^ 2
```

by determining the value between the parentheses (–7) before doing the exponentiation—even though exponentiation has a higher order of precedence than subtraction and multiplication do. You can further refine the calculation by placing nested parentheses in the formula. For example,

```
Number = ((8 - 5) * 3) ^ 2
```

directs Visual Basic to calculate the difference in the inner set of parentheses first, and then the outer parentheses, and then the exponent. The result produced by the two formulas is different: the first formula evaluates to 49 and the second to 81. Parentheses can change the result of a mathematical operation, in addition to making it easier to read.

If you want to continue to the next lesson

- Keep Visual Basic running, and turn to Lesson 5.

If you want to quit Visual Basic for now

- On the File menu, click Exit.

  If you see a Save dialog box, click Yes.

Lesson Summary

To	Do this

Declare a variable	Type **Dim** followed by the variable name in the program code. (You can also specify a data type; the variant type is the default.) For example:
	`Dim Temp%                'Integer type`
	`Dim Storage              'Variant type`

Change the value of a variable	Assign a new value with the assignment operator (=). For example: `Country = "Japan"`
Get input with a dialog box	Use the InputBox function, and assign the result to a variable. For example: `UserName = InputBox("What is your name?")`

Display output in a dialog box	Use the MsgBox function. (The string to be displayed in the dialog box can be stored in a variable.) For example:
	`Forecast = "Rain, mainly on the plain."`
	`MsgBox(Forecast),, "Spain Weather Report"`

Declare a variable of a specific data type	Type **Dim** followed by the variable name and a type declaration character.
	or
	Type **Dim** followed by the variable name, the keyword **As**, and one of the eight fundamental data types. For example:
	`Dim MyBirthday As Date  'Date type`
	`Dim Price! 'single precision floating point`

To	Do this
Create a constant	Type the **Const** keyword followed by the constant name, the assignment operator (=), and the fixed value. For example: `Const JackBennysAge = 39`
Create a formula	Link together numeric variables or values with one of the seven mathematical operators, and then assign the result to a variable or property. For example: `Result = 1 ^ 2 * 3 \ 4  'this equals 0`
Combine text strings	Use the string concatenation operator (&). For example: `Msg = "Hello" & "," & "world!"`
Convert text characters to number characters	Use the Val function. For example: `Pi = Val("3.1415926535897932")`
Use a mathematical function	Add the function and any necessary arguments to a formula. For example: `Hypotenuse = Sqr(x ^ 2 + y ^ 2)`

Control the evaluation order in a formula	Use parentheses in the formula. For example:
	`Result = 1 + 2 ^ 3 \ 4          'this equals 3`
	`Result = (1 + 2) ^ ( 3 \ 4)    'this equals 1`

For online information about	On the Visual Basic Help menu, click Search For Help On, and then
Declaring variables	Type **variable**
Fundamental data types	Type the symbol for the data type you want to examine
User-defined data types	Type **Type**
Using the InputBox function	Type **InputBox**
Using the MsgBox function	Type **MsgBox**
Operators and precedence	Type the operator you want to examine
Mathematical functions	Type the function name you want to examine

For more information on	In the Visual Basic *Programmer's Guide*, see
Declaring variables and constants	Chapter 6, "Variables, Constants, and Data Types"
Using InputBox and MsgBox functions	Chapter 11, "Dialogs"
Converting data types	Chapter 6, "Variables, Constants, and Data Types"
Creating user-defined data types	Chapter 6, "Variables, Constants, and Data Types"

Preview of the Next Lesson

In the next lesson, "Using Decision Structures," you'll learn how to control program flow in your event procedures. You'll learn how to use the If...Then and Select Case statements and how to execute different blocks of code depending on different conditions in your program. You'll also learn how to track down logic errors and syntax errors in a program and make corrections.

Lesson

5

Using Decision Structures

In this lesson you will learn how to:

Estimated time **45 min.**

- Write conditional expressions.
- Use an If...Then statement to branch to a set of program statements based on a condition.
- Use a Select Case statement to select one choice from many options in program code.
- Find and correct errors in your program code.

In the last few lessons, you used several Microsoft Visual Basic tools to process input from the user. You used menus, objects, and dialog boxes to display choices for the user, and you processed input by using properties and variables. In this lesson, you'll learn how to branch conditionally to a specific program code section based on input you receive from the user. You'll learn how to evaluate one or more properties or variables by using conditional expressions and then execute one or more program statements based on the results. You'll also learn how to detect and fix programming mistakes in your code by using the Debug window.

Event-Driven Programming

Visual Basic programs are event driven.

The programs you have written so far in this book have displayed menus, objects, and dialog boxes on the screen, and these programs have encouraged users to manipulate the screen elements in whatever order they saw fit. The programs put the user in charge, waited patiently for a response, and then processed the input predictably. In programming circles, this methodology is known as *event-driven programming*. You build a program by creating a group of "intelligent" objects that know how to respond when the user interacts with them, and then you process the input by using event procedures associated with the objects. The following diagram shows how an event-driven program works in Visual Basic:

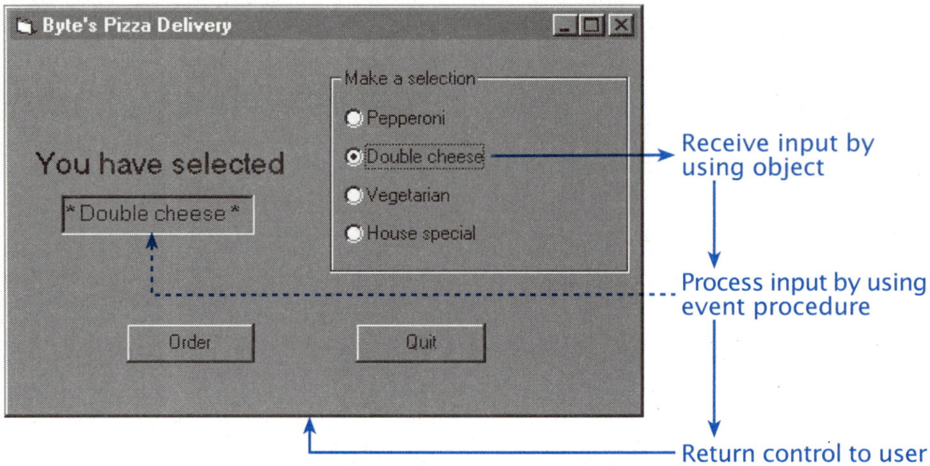

Program input can also come from the computer system itself. For example, your program might be notified when a piece of electronic mail arrives or when a certain period of time has elapsed on the system clock. These events are triggered by the computer, not by the user. Regardless of how an event is triggered, Visual Basic reacts by calling the event procedure associated with the object that recognized the event. Although so far you've dealt primarily with the Click and Change events, Visual Basic objects can respond to several types of events.

The event-driven nature of Visual Basic means that most of the computing done in your programs will be accomplished by event procedures. These event-specific blocks of code process input, calculate new values, display output, and handle other tasks. In the previous lesson, you learned how to use variables, operators, and mathematical formulas to perform calculations in your event procedures. In this lesson, you'll learn how to use *decision structures* to compare variables, properties, and values and how to execute one or more statements based on the results. In the next lesson, you'll learn how to use *loops* to execute a group of statements over and over until a condition is met. Together, these powerful flow-control structures will help you build your procedures so that they can respond to almost any situation.

Events Supported by Visual Basic Objects

Each object in Visual Basic has a predefined set of events it can respond to. These events are listed for each object in the Proc (Procedure) drop-down list box in the Code window. You can write an event procedure for any of these events, and if an event occurs in the program, Visual Basic will execute the event procedure that is associated with it. For example, a list box object supports the Click, DblClick, DragDrop, DragOver, GotFocus, KeyDown, KeyPress, KeyUp, LostFocus, MouseDown, MouseMove, and MouseUp events. Although you probably won't need to program for more than one or two of these events in your application, it's nice to know that you have so many choices when you create elements in your interface. The following illustration shows a partial listing of the events for a list box object in the Code window:

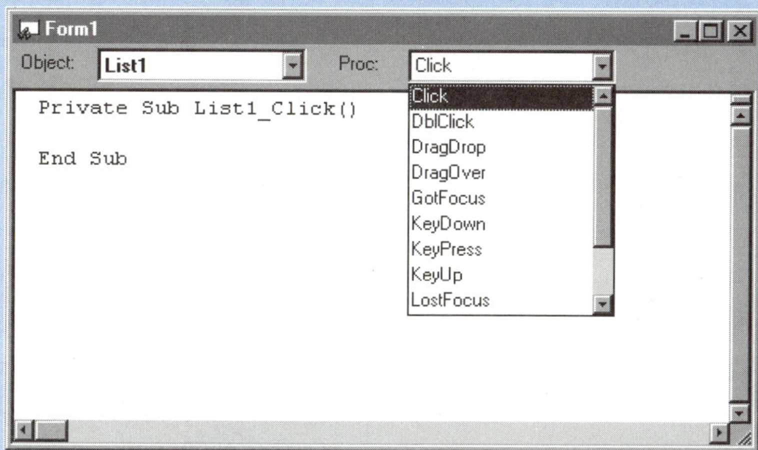

Using Conditional Expressions

Conditional expressions ask True-or-False questions.

One of the most useful tools for processing information in an event procedure is a conditional expression. A *conditional expression* is a part of a complete program statement that asks a True-or-False question about a property, a variable, or another piece of data in the program code. For example, the conditional expression

```
Price < 100
```

evaluates to True if the Price variable contains a value that is less than 100, and it evaluates to False if Price contains a value that is greater than or equal to 100. You can use the comparison operators listed on the next page in a conditional expression.

Comparison operator	Meaning
=	Equal to
< >	Not equal to
>	Greater than
<	Less than
> =	Greater than or equal to
< =	Less than or equal to

NOTE Expressions that can be evaluated as True or False are also known as Boolean expressions, and the True or False result can be assigned to a Boolean variable or property. You can assign Boolean values to certain object properties, variant variables, or Boolean variables that have been created by using the Dim statement and the As Boolean keywords.

The following table shows some conditional expressions and their results. In the next exercise, you'll work with the operators shown in the table.

Conditional expression	Result
10 < > 20	True (10 is not equal to 20)
Score < 20	True if Score is less than 20; otherwise, False
Score = Label1.Caption	True if the Caption property of the Label1 object contains the same value as the Score variable; otherwise, False
Text1.Text = "Bill"	True if the word *Bill* is in the first text box; otherwise, False

If...Then Decision Structures

If...Then decision structures let you add logic to your programs.

Conditional expressions can control the order in which statements are executed when they are used in a special block of statements known as a *decision structure.* An If...Then decision structure lets you evaluate a condition in the program and take a course of action based on the result. In its simplest form, an If...Then decision structure is written on a single line:

```
If condition Then statement
```

where *condition* is a conditional expression and *statement* is a valid Visual Basic program statement. For example,

```
If Score >= 20 Then Label1.Caption = "You win!"
```

is an If...Then decision structure that uses the conditional expression

```
Score >= 20
```

to determine whether the program should set the Caption property of the Label1 object to "You win!" If the Score variable contains a value that is greater than or equal to 20, Visual Basic sets the Caption property; otherwise, it skips the assignment statement and executes the next line in the event procedure. This sort of comparison always results in a True or False value. A conditional expression never results in maybe.

Testing Several Conditions in an If...Then Decision Structure

Visual Basic also supports an If...Then decision structure that allows you to include several conditional expressions. This block of statements can be several lines long and contains the important keywords ElseIf, Else, and End If.

ElseIf and Else clauses let you ask additional questions in an If...Then structure.

```
If condition1 Then
    statements executed if condition1 is True
ElseIf condition2 Then
    statements executed if condition2 is True
[Additional ElseIf clauses and statements can be placed here]
Else
    statements executed if none of the conditions is True
End If
```

In this structure, *condition1* is evaluated first. If this conditional expression is True, the block of statements below it is executed, one statement at a time. (You can include one or more program statements.) If the first condition is not True, the second conditional expression (*condition2*) is evaluated. If the second condition is True, the second block of statements is executed. (You can add additional ElseIf conditions and statements if you have more conditions to evaluate.) Finally, if none of the conditional expressions is True, the statements below the Else keyword are executed. The whole structure is closed at the bottom with the End If keywords.

The following code shows how a multiline If...Then structure could be used to determine the amount of tax due in a hypothetical progressive tax return. (The numbers are from the United States Internal Revenue Service 1994 tax rate schedule for single filing status.)

```
If AdjustedIncome <= 22750 Then         '15% tax bracket
    TaxDue = AdjustedIncome * 0.15
ElseIf AdjustedIncome <= 55100 Then     '28% tax bracket
    TaxDue = 3412 + ((AdjustedIncome - 22750) * 0.28)
```

```
ElseIf AdjustedIncome <= 115000 Then    '31% tax bracket
    TaxDue = 12470 + ((AdjustedIncome - 55100) * 0.31)
ElseIf AdjustedIncome <= 250000 Then    '36% tax bracket
    TaxDue = 31039 + ((AdjustedIncome - 115000) * 0.36)
Else                                    '39.6% tax bracket
    TaxDue = 79639 + ((AdjustedIncome - 250000) * 0.396)
End If
```

Multiline If...Then structures are perfect for calculating values that fall in different ranges, such as numbers in a tax return.

In this decision structure, the variable AdjustedIncome is tested at the first income level and subsequent income levels until one of the conditional expressions evaluates to True and an income tax is determined for the taxpayer. This simple decision structure is quite useful. It could be used to compute the tax owed by any taxpayer in a progressive tax system (such as the one in the United States), provided the tax rates are complete and up to date and the value in the AdjustedIncome variable is correct. If the tax rates change, it is a simple matter to update the conditional expressions.

IMPORTANT The order of the conditional expressions in your If...Then and ElseIf clauses is critical. If you reversed the order of the conditional expressions in the tax computation example (if you listed rates in the structure from highest to lowest), taxpayers in the 15 percent, 28 percent, and 31 percent tax brackets would be placed in the 36 percent tax bracket because they all would have an income that is less than or equal to 250,000. (Visual Basic stops at the first conditional expression that is True, even if others are also True.) Since all the conditional expressions in this example test the same variable, they need to be listed in ascending order to get the taxpayers to fall out at the right spots. Moral: When you use more than one conditional expression, watch their order carefully.

In the next exercise, you'll use an If...Then decision structure to validate users as they log in to a program. You might use similar program logic if you write a network application.

Validate users by using If...Then

1. Start Visual Basic.

   If Visual Basic is already running, click the New Project command on the File menu.

CommandButton control

2. Use the CommandButton control to create a command button in the upper left corner of the form.
3. Set the Caption property of the command button to "Log in".
4. Double-click the Log In button.

   The Command1_Click event procedure appears in the Code window.

By convention, statements below If...Then, ElseIf, and Else clauses are indented.

5 Type the following program statements in the procedure:

```
UserName = InputBox("Enter your first name.")
If UserName = "Laura" Then
    MsgBox("Welcome, Laura!  Ready to start your PC?")
    Form1.Picture = _
      LoadPicture("c:\vb\practice\lesson 5\pcomputr.wmf")
ElseIf UserName = "Marc" Then
    MsgBox("Welcome, Marc!  Ready to display your Rolodex?")
    Form1.Picture = _
      LoadPicture("c:\vb\practice\lesson 5\rolodex.wmf")
Else
    MsgBox("Sorry, I don't recognize you.")
    End   'quit the program
End If
```

The line continuation characters (_) used after the Form1.Picture properties break two long program statements into four lines so that they can be printed in this book. If you choose, you can type each of these long statements on one line; the Code window will scroll to the right.

NOTE Program lines can be 1023 characters long in the Visual Basic Code window, but it is usually easiest to work with lines fewer than 80 or so characters long. You can divide long program statements among multiple lines by using a line continuation character (_) at the end of each line in the statement except the last line. (You cannot use a line continuation character to break a string that is in quotation marks, however.)

When you've finished, your screen should look like the following:

The complete Login program is available on disk in the \Vb\Practice\Lesson 5 folder.

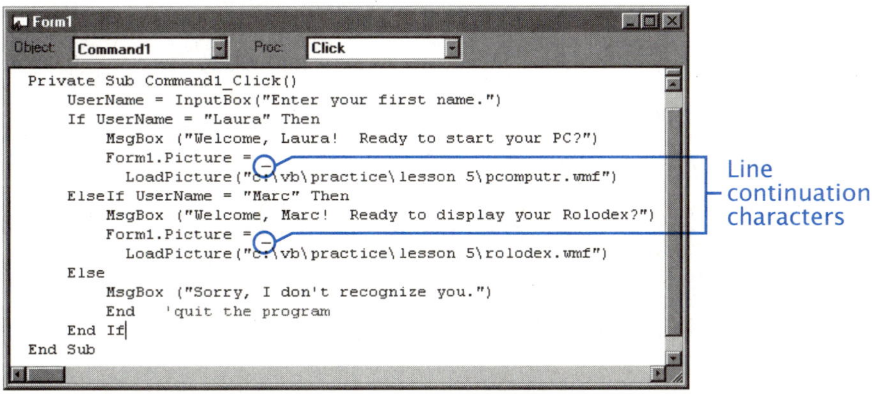

Start button

6 Click the Start button on the toolbar.

The program runs in the programming environment. A blank form appears on the screen, with a Log In button in the upper left corner.

7 Click the Log In button.

The InputBox function in the Command1_Click event procedure displays a dialog box that asks you to enter your first name.

8 Type **Laura** and press ENTER.

The If...Then decision structure compares the name you typed with the text "Laura" in the first conditional expression. If you typed *Laura*, the expression evaluates to True and the If...Then statement displays a welcome message by using the MsgBox function.

9 Click OK in the message box.

The message box closes, and a Windows metafile of a PC is loaded on the form, as shown in the following illustration:

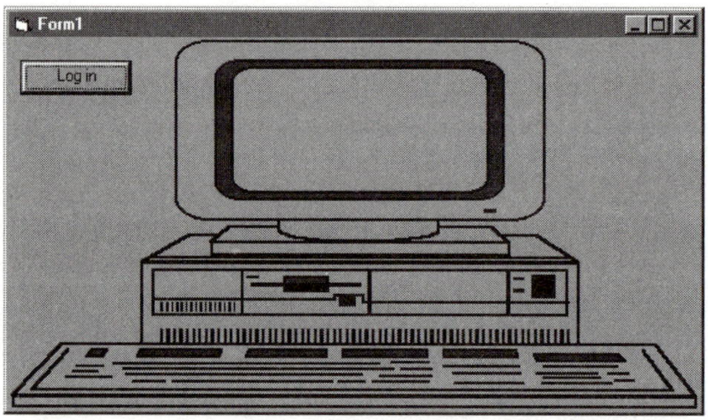

In this program, the Windows metafile is loaded directly on the form by using the Picture property. (Forms have Picture properties, just like image objects and picture box objects do.) When a graphic is loaded on a form, it appears in the background. Any control visible on the form appears on top of the graphic.

10 Click the Log In button, type **Marc**, and click OK.

This time the decision structure selects the ElseIf clause and admits Marc to the program. A welcome message is displayed on the screen again by the MsgBox function.

11 Click OK to display the Rolodex artwork.

The Rolodex Windows metafile is loaded on the form.

12 Click the Log In button, type **Frasier**, and click OK.

The Else clause in the decision structure is executed, and the following message appears in a MsgBox object:

13 Click OK to close the message box.

The message box closes, and the program closes. An unauthorized user has been prohibited from using the program.

14 Save the form as **My Login.frm** and the project as **My Login.vbp**.

Using Logical Operators in Conditional Expressions

Logical operators let you add tests to your expressions.

Visual Basic lets you test more than one conditional expression in your If...Then and ElseIf clauses if you want to include more than one selection criterion in your decision structure. The extra conditions are linked together by using one or more of the following logical operators:

Logical operator	Meaning
And	If both conditional expressions are True, then the result is True.
Or	If either conditional expression is True, then the result is True.
Not	If the conditional expression is False, then the result is True. If the conditional expression is True, then the result is False.
Xor	If one and only one of the conditional expressions is True, then the result is True. If both are True or both are False, then the result is False.

NOTE When your program evaluates a complex expression that mixes different operator types, it evaluates all mathematical operators first, all comparison operators second, and all logical operators third.

The table on the following page lists some examples of the logical operators at work. In the expressions, it is assumed that the variable Vehicle contains a value of "Bike" and the variable Price contains a value of 200.

Logical expression	Result
Vehicle = "Bike" And Price < 300	True (both expressions are True)
Vehicle = "Car" Or Price < 500	True (one condition is True)
Not Price < 100	True (condition is False)
Vehicle = "Bike" Xor Price < 300	False (both conditions are True)

In the following exercise, you modify the My Login program to prompt the user for a password during the validation process. An input box gets the password from the user, and you modify the If...Then and ElseIf clauses in the decision structure so that they use the And operator to verify the password.

Add password protection by using the And operator

1 Open the Command1_Click event procedure in the Code window.

2 Insert the following statement between the InputBox statement and the If...Then statement in the procedure (between the first and second lines):

```
Pass = InputBox("Enter your password.")
```

3 Modify the If...Then statement to the following:

```
If UserName = "Laura" And Pass = "May17" Then
```

The statement now includes the And logical operator, which verifies the user name and password before Laura is admitted to the program.

The complete Password application is available on disk in the Lesson 5 folder.

4 Modify the ElseIf statement to the following:

```
ElseIf UserName = "Marc" And Pass = "trek" Then
```

The And logical operator adds a check for the "trek" password in Marc's account.

5 Save the form as **My Password.frm** and the project as **My Password.vbp**.

Start button

6 Click the Start button on the toolbar.

The program runs in the programming environment.

7 Click the Log In button, type **Laura**, and then click OK.

The program prompts you for a password.

8 Type **May17** and click OK.

The And conditional expression evaluates to True, and Laura is welcomed to the program.

9 Click OK to close the message box.

End button

10 Click the End button on the toolbar to quit the program.

The program stops, and the programming environment returns.

> **NOTE** If you are writing a full-featured version of the My Password program, you should consider using a text box object to receive the password input in the program. Text box objects support the PasswordChar property, which lets you display a placeholder character, such as an asterisk (*), as the user types; and the MaxLength property, which lets you limit the number of characters entered.

Select Case Decision Structures

Select Case decision structures base branching decisions on one key variable.

Visual Basic also lets you control the execution of statements in your programs by using Select Case decision structures. You used Select Case structures earlier in this book when you wrote event procedures to process list box, combo box, and menu item choices. A Select Case structure is similar to an If...Then...ElseIf structure, but it is more efficient when the branching depends on one key variable, or *test case*. You can also use Select Case structures to make your program code more readable and efficient.

The syntax for a Select Case structure looks like this:

```
Select Case variable
Case value1
    program statements executed if value1 matches variable
Case value2
    program statements executed if value2 matches variable
Case value3
    program statements executed if value3 matches variable
.
.
.
End Select
```

A Select Case structure begins with the Select Case keywords and ends with the End Select keywords. You replace *variable* with the variable, property, or other expression that is to be the key value, or test case, for the structure. You replace *value1*, *value2*, and *value3* with numbers, strings, or other values related to the test case being considered. If one of the values matches the variable, the statements below its Case clause are executed and Visual Basic continues executing program code after the End Select statement. You can include any number of Case clauses in a Select Case structure, and you can include more than one value in a Case clause. If you list multiple values after a case, separate them with commas.

The example on the following page shows how a Select Case structure could be used to print an appropriate message about a person's age in a program. If the Age variable matches one of the Case values, an appropriate message is displayed by using a label.

```
Select Case Age
Case 16
    Label1.Caption = "You can drive now!"
Case 18
    Label1.Caption = "You can vote now!"
Case 21
    Label1.Caption = "You can drink wine with your meals."
Case 65
    Label1.Caption = "Time to retire and have fun!"
End Select
```

The organization of a Select Case structure can make it clearer than an equivalent If...Then structure.

A Select Case structure also supports a Case Else clause that you can use to display a message if none of the earlier cases matches. Here's how it works with the Age example:

```
Select Case Age
Case 16
    Label1.Caption = "You can drive now!"
Case 18
    Label1.Caption = "You can vote now!"
Case 21
    Label1.Caption = "You can drink wine with your meals."
Case 65
    Label1.Caption = "Time to retire and have fun!"
Case Else
    Label1.Caption = "You're a great age! Enjoy it!"
End Select
```

Using Comparison Operators with a Select Case Structure

A Select Case structure supports comparison operators just like an If...Then structure does.

Visual Basic lets you use comparison operators to include a range of test values in a Select Case structure. The Visual Basic comparison operators that can be used are =, < >, >, <, > =, and < =. To use the comparison operators, you need to include the Is keyword or the To keyword in the expression to identify the comparison you're making. The Is keyword instructs the compiler to compare the test variable to the expression listed after the Is keyword. The To keyword identifies a range of values. The following structure uses Is, To, and several comparison operators to test the Age variable and to display one of five messages:

```
Select Case Age
Case Is < 13
    Label1.Caption = "Enjoy your youth!"
Case 13 To 19
    Label1.Caption = "Enjoy your teens!"
Case 21
    Label1.Caption = "You can drink wine with your meals."
Case Is > 100
    Label1.Caption = "Looking good!"
```

```
Case Else
    Label1.Caption = "That's a nice age to be."
End Select
```

If the value of the Age variable is less than 13, the message "Enjoy your youth!" is displayed. For the ages 13 through 19, the message "Enjoy your teens!" is displayed, and so on.

A Select Case decision structure is usually much clearer than an If...Then structure and is more efficient when you're making three or more branching decisions based on one variable or property. However, when you're making two or fewer comparisons, or when you're working with several different values, you'll probably want to use an If...Then decision structure.

In the following exercise, you'll see how you can use a Select Case structure to process input from a list box. You'll use the List1.Text and List1.ListIndex properties to collect the input, and then you'll use a Select Case structure to display a greeting in one of four languages.

Label control

Use a Select Case structure to process a list box

1. On the File menu, click the New Project command.

   A blank form appears in the programming environment.

ListBox control

2. Click the Label control in the toolbox, and then create a large box in the top middle of the form to display a title for the program.
3. Click the ListBox control in the toolbox, and then create a list box on the left side of the form.

CommandButton control

4. Create a small label above the list box object, and then create two small labels on the right side of the screen, to display program output.
5. Click the CommandButton control in the toolbox, and then create a small command button in the bottom middle of the form.

Properties button

6. Click the Properties button on the toolbar, and then set the following object properties on the form:

Object	Property	Setting
Label1	Caption Font	"International Welcome Program" Times New Roman, Bold, 14-point
Label2	Caption	"Choose a country"
Label3	Caption	(Empty)
Label4	Caption BorderStyle ForeColor	(Empty) 1 - Fixed Single Dark red (&H00000080&)
Command1	Caption	"Quit"

When you've finished setting properties, your form should look similar to the following:

Now enter the program code to initialize the list box.

7 Double-click the form.

The Form_Load event procedure appears in the Code window.

8 Type the following program code to initialize the list box:

You load values in a list box by using the AddItem method.

```
List1.AddItem "England"
List1.AddItem "Germany"
List1.AddItem "Spain"
List1.AddItem "Italy"
```

These lines use the AddItem method of the list box object to add entries to the list box on your form.

9 Open the Object drop-down list box, and then click the List1 object in the list box.

The List1_Click event procedure appears in the Code window.

10 Type the following lines to process the list box selection made by the user:

The ListIndex property contains the number of the list item selected.

```
Label3.Caption = List1.Text
Select Case List1.ListIndex
Case 0
    Label4.Caption = "Hello, programmer"
Case 1
    Label4.Caption = "Hallo, Programmierer"
Case 2
    Label4.Caption = "Hola, programador"
Case 3
    Label4.Caption = "Ciao, programmatori"
End Select
```

The first line copies the name of the selected list box item to the caption of the third label on the form. The most important property used in the statement is List1.Text, which contains the exact text of the item selected in the list box. The remaining statements are part of the Select Case decision structure. The structure uses the property List1.ListIndex as a test case variable and compares it to several values. The ListIndex property always contains the number of the item selected in the list box; the item at the top is 0 (zero), the second item is 1, the next item is 2, and so on. Using ListIndex, the Select Case structure can quickly identify the user's choice and display the correct greeting on the form.

11 Open the Object drop-down list box, and then click the Command1 object in the list box.

The Command1_Click event procedure appears in the Code window.

12 Type **End** in the event procedure, and then close the Code window.

13 Save the form to disk under the name **My Case.frm**, and then save the project to disk under the name **My Case.vbp**.

Start button

The complete Case project is located on disk in the Lesson 5 folder.

14 Click the Start button to run the My Case program.

15 Click each of the country names in the Choose A Country list box.

The program displays a greeting for each of the countries listed. The following illustration shows the greeting for Italy:

16 Click the Quit button to stop the program.

The program stops, and the programming environment returns. You've finished working with Select Case structures in this lesson.

Finding and Correcting Errors

The process of finding and correcting errors in programs is called debugging.

The errors you have encountered in your programs so far have probably been simple typing mistakes or syntax errors. But what if you discover a nastier problem in your program—one you can't find and correct by a simple review of the objects, properties, and statements in your program? The Visual Basic programming environment contains several tools you can use to track down and fix errors, or *bugs,* in your programs. These tools won't stop you from making mistakes, but they'll often ease the pain when you encounter a mistake.

Consider the following If...Then decision structure, which evaluates two conditional expressions and then displays one of two messages based on the result:

```
If Age > 13 AND Age < 20 Then
    Text2.Text = "You're a teenager."
Else
    Text2.Text = "You're not a teenager."
End If
```

Can you spot the problem with this decision structure? A teenager is a person who is between 13 and 19 years old, inclusive, yet the structure fails to identify the person who is exactly 13. (For this age, the structure erroneously displays the message "You're not a teenager.") This type of mistake is not a syntax error (the statements follow the rules of Visual Basic); it is a mental mistake, or *logic error*. The correct decision structure contains a greater than or equal to operator (>=) in the first comparison after the If...Then statement:

```
If Age >= 13 AND Age < 20 Then
```

Believe it or not, this type of mistake is the most common problem in a Visual Basic program. Code that works most of the time—but not all of the time—is the hardest to track down and fix.

Three Types of Errors

Three types of errors can occur in a Visual Basic program: syntax errors, runtime errors, and logic errors.

- A *syntax error* (or *compiler error*) is a programming mistake that violates the rules of Visual Basic (such as a misspelled property or keyword). Visual Basic points out several types of syntax errors in your programs while you type program statements, and Visual Basic won't let you run a program until each syntax error is fixed.
- A *runtime error* is a mistake that causes a program to stop unexpectedly during execution. Runtime errors occur when an outside event or an undiscovered syntax error forces a program to stop while it is running. A misspelled filename in a LoadPicture function or an open floppy drive are conditions that can produce runtime errors.
- A *logic error* is a human error—a programming mistake that makes the program code produce the wrong results. Most debugging efforts are focused on tracking down logic errors introduced by the programmer.

Be sure to use the Visual Basic online Help resources when you encounter error messages produced by syntax errors or runtime errors. If a runtime error dialog box appears, click the Help button.

Using the Debug Window

The Debug window lets you see how your program is executed.

One way to identify a logic error is to execute your program code one line at a time and examine the content of one or more variables or properties as it changes. To do this, you can enter *break mode* while your program is running and then view your code in the Debug window. The Debug window is a special debugging window divided into two panes. The top pane is a Watch pane, in which you examine variables. The bottom pane, called the Immediate pane, allows you to type and execute debugging statements. The Debug window gives you a close-up look at your program while the Visual Basic compiler is executing it. It's kind of like pulling up a chair behind the pilot and copilot and watching them fly the airplane. But in this case, you can touch the controls.

In the following exercise, you'll use the Debug window to find and correct the logic error you discovered in the If...Then structure on the previous page. (The error is part of an actual program.) To find the problem, you'll use the Step Into button on the toolbar to execute program instructions one at a time and you'll use the Instant Watch button to watch the content of the Age variable change. Practice this technique carefully. You can use it to correct many types of bugs in your programs.

Debug the If Bug program

Open Project button

1 Click the Open Project button on the toolbar.

The Open Project dialog box appears.

2 Open the project If Bug in the \Vb\Practice\Lesson 5 folder.

3 Click the View Form button in the Project window.

The form for the If Bug program appears. This program prompts the user for his or her age. When the user clicks the Test button, the program lets the user know whether he or she is a teenager. The program still has the problem with 13-year-olds that you identified earlier in the lesson. Run the program now, and use the Debug window to find the problem.

Start button

4 Click the Start button on the toolbar.

The program runs in the programming environment.

5 Remove the 0 from the Age text box, type **14**, and then click the Test button.

The program displays the message "You're a teenager." So far the program displays the correct result.

6 Type **13** in the Age text box, and then click the Test button.

The program displays the message "You're not a teenager.", as shown in the following illustration:

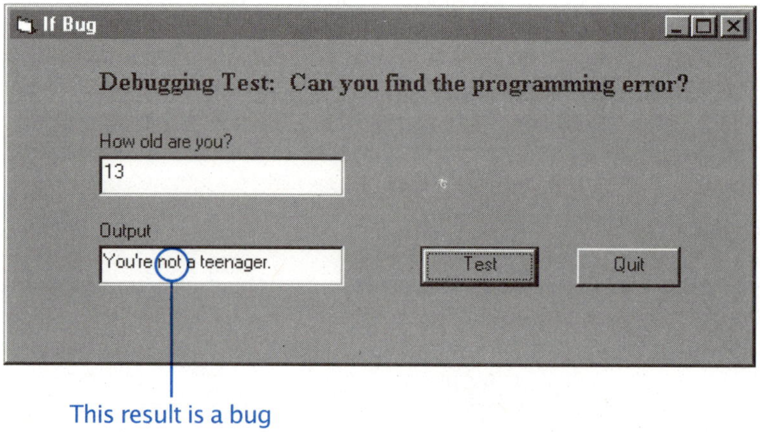

This answer is incorrect, and you need to look at the program code to fix the problem. Rather than quitting the program and searching the program code on your own, let Visual Basic help you out.

Break button

7 Click the Break button on the toolbar. (The Break button is just to the right of the Start button.)

The program pauses, and Visual Basic displays the *Debug window*, a special window you can use to test program statements and examine important variables and properties. Your screen should look like the following:

The Debug window is currently empty, but in step 12 you'll add the Age variable to it. Notice also that only the Immediate pane is currently visible. To view the Watch pane, double-click the split box at the top of the vertical scroll bar.

Step Into button

8 Click the Step Into button on the toolbar to execute the next program statement.

Visual Basic returns control to the form in the program and waits for input.

9 Click the If Bug form, verify that 13 is still in the text box, and then click the Test button.

Since Visual Basic is in break mode, something unusual happens. Visual Basic opens the Code window and displays the Command1_Click event procedure—the program code about to be executed by the compiler. This gives you the opportunity to see firsthand how the logic in your program is evaluated.

10 Click the Step Into button to execute the first statement in the procedure.

The Sub statement is executed, and the statement containing the Age variable is outlined. Age is the critical test variable in this program, so you'll place it in the Watch pane now to see how it changes as the program executes.

Instant Watch button

11 Select the Age variable by using the mouse, and then click the Instant Watch button on the toolbar. (The Instant Watch button contains a picture of a pair of eyeglasses.)

A dialog box appears on the screen showing the context, name, and value of the Age variable in the program. You'll also see this dialog box if you click the Instant Watch command on the Tools menu.

12 Click Add in the Instant Watch dialog box, and then click the Debug window. (The Debug window will be partially covered by the program form and the Code window.)

The Watch pane displays variables added by using the Instant Watch command.

The Age variable appears in the Watch pane of the Debug window. The variable currently has no value because Age hasn't been used yet in the event procedure. (Since the Age variable wasn't declared globally in the program, it is used as a local variable in the procedure and is reinitialized every time the procedure is called.) If you type a program statement in the Immediate pane and then press ENTER, the statement will be executed in the current event procedure. Your Debug window should look like the one shown on the following page.

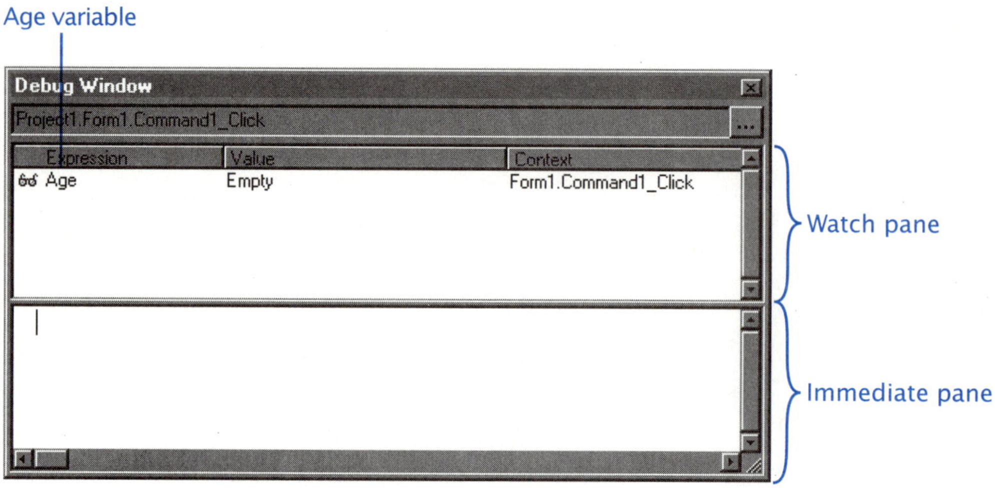

NOTE To remove a watch variable from the Watch pane, double-click the variable in the Watch pane, click the Delete button in the Edit Watch dialog box, and then click OK. You can also use the Edit Watch dialog box to edit the watch expression, adjust the watch context, and set the watch type.

13 Click the Code window again, and then click the Step Into button to execute the next instruction.

Visual Basic copies the number 13 from the text box to the Age variable, and the Age variable in the Debug window is updated. Visual Basic now highlights the first statement in the If...Then structure, the most important (and flawed) statement in the program. Since a 13-year-old is a teenager, Visual Basic should execute the Then clause after it evaluates this instruction.

14 Click the Step Into button.

When a decision structure branches incorrectly, look for the bug in the conditional expression and fix it if possible.

Visual Basic outlines the Else clause in the If...Then structure instead. The test fails on this value, and you need to find and fix the problem now if possible. (Visual Basic helped you find the problem, but you still have to recognize and fix it.) This time, you already know the answer. The first comparison needs the > = operator.

15 Click after the > operator in the If...Then statement, and then type =. Your screen should look like the following:

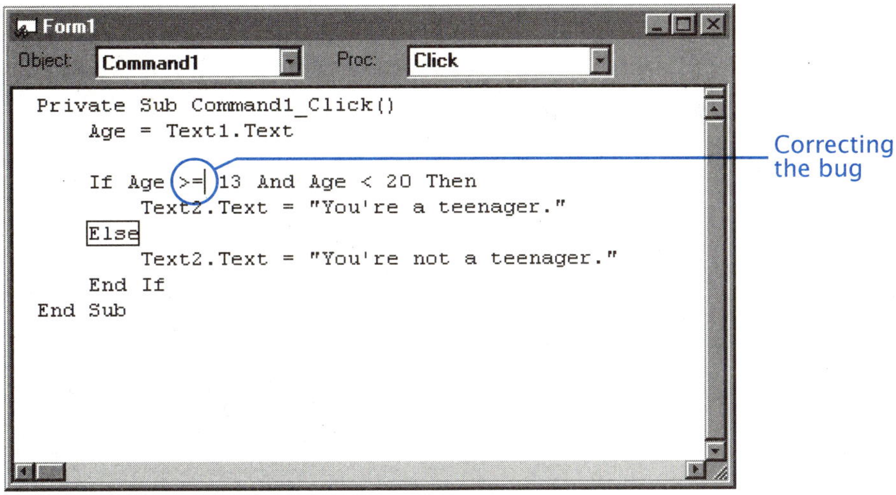

Visual Basic lets you fix errors while in break mode, but if the changes you make are in statements that have already been executed, your corrections won't take effect until the next time the statements are run. To test your correction in this decision structure, you need to click the Test button again.

16 Click the Step Into button three times.

Visual Basic finishes executing the decision structure.

17 Click the Start button (now labeled Continue) on the toolbar to resume full-speed execution of the program.

The If Bug form reappears.

18 Click the Test button to test your bug fix, verify the message "You're a teenager." in the Output box, and then click the Quit button to stop the program.

Congratulations! You've successfully used the Debug window to find and correct a logic error in a program. As you continue to work with Visual Basic, feel free to use the Debug window to analyze your code. You'll learn more about debugging in future lessons.

One Step Further: Using a Stop Statement to Enter Break Mode

You can enter break mode by using a Stop statement.

If you know the exact place in the program code where you want to enter break mode and start debugging, you can place a Stop statement in your code at that place to pause the program and display the Debug window. For example, as an alternative to clicking the Break button, you could have entered break mode in the previous exercise by inserting a Stop statement at the beginning of the Command1_Click event procedure, as shown on the following page.

```
Private Sub Command1_Click()
    Stop    'enter break mode
    Age = Text1.Text

    If Age > 13 And Age < 20 Then
        Text2.Text = "You're a teenager."
    Else
        Text2.Text = "You're not a teenager."
    End If
End Sub
```

When you run a program that includes a Stop statement, Visual Basic enters break mode as soon as it hits the Stop statement. While in break mode, you can use the Debug window, Step Into button, and Instant Watch button just as you would if you had entered break mode manually. When you've finished debugging, remove the Stop statement.

If you want to continue to the next lesson

- Keep Visual Basic running, and turn to Lesson 6.

If you want to quit Visual Basic for now

- On the File menu, click Exit.

If you see a Save dialog box, click Yes.

Lesson Summary

To	Do this	Button
Write a conditional expression	Use a comparison operator between two values.	
Use a decision structure	Use an If...Then or Select Case statement and supporting expressions and keywords.	
Make two comparisons in a conditional expression	Use a logical operator between comparisons (And, Or, Not, or Xor).	
Enter break mode for debugging	Click the Break button on the toolbar. *or* Place a Stop statement at the place you want to enter break mode.	
Execute one line of code in the Debug window	Click the Step Into button. *or* On the Run menu, click the Step Into command.	

To	Do this	Button
Examine a variable in the Debug window	Highlight the variable you want to examine, and then click the Instant Watch button or click the Instant Watch command on the Tools menu.	
Remove a watch expression	Double-click the expression in the Watch pane, click Delete in the Edit Watch dialog box, and then click OK.	
Test a program statement in the Debug window	Click the Immediate pane in the Debug window, type the program statement, and press ENTER.	

For online information about	On the Visual Basic Help menu, click Search For Help On, and then
Comparison operators	Type **comparison operators**
Logical operators	Type **logical**
If...Then decision structures	Type **If**
Select Case decision structures	Type **Select**
Using the Debug window	Type **Debug window**

For more information on	In the Visual Basic *Programmer's Guide*, see
If...Then decision structures	Chapter 5, "Programming Fundamentals"
Select Case decision structures	Chapter 5, "Programming Fundamentals"
Correcting errors and using the Debug window	Chapter 20, "Debugging"

Preview of the Next Lesson

In the next lesson, "Using Loops and Timers," you'll learn how to handle repetitive actions in your programs. You'll learn how to use the For...Next, Do, and While statements and how to use the Timer control.

Lesson

6

Using Loops and Timers

Estimated time
50 min.

In this lesson you will learn how to:

- Use a For...Next loop to execute statements a set number of times.
- Use the Print method to display output on a form.
- Use a Do loop to execute statements until a specific condition is met.
- Use a timer object to loop for a specific amount of time.

In Lesson 5, you learned how to use the If...Then and Select Case decision structures to choose which statements to execute in a program. In this lesson, you'll learn how to execute a block of statements over and over again by using a *loop*. You'll use a For...Next loop to execute statements a set number of times, and you'll use a Do loop to execute statements until a conditional expression in the loop evaluates to True. You'll also learn how to use the Print method to display text and numbers on a form and how to use a timer object to execute code at specific intervals in your program.

Writing For...Next Loops

A For...Next loop lets you execute a specific group of program statements a set number of times in an event procedure. This can be useful if you are performing several related calculations, working with elements on the screen, or processing several pieces of user input. A For...Next loop is really just a shorthand way of writing out a long list of program statements. Since each group of statements in the list would do essentially the same thing, Visual Basic lets you define one group of statements and request that it be executed as many times as you want.

The syntax for a For...Next loop looks like this:

In a For...Next loop, start *and* end *determine how long the loop runs.*

```
For variable = start To end
    statements to be repeated
Next variable
```

In this syntax statement, For, To, and Next are required keywords and = is a required operator. You replace *variable* with the name of a numeric variable that keeps track of the current loop count, and you replace *start* and *end* with numeric values representing the starting and stopping points for the loop. The line or lines between the For and Next statements are the instructions that are repeated each time the loop is executed.

For example, the following For...Next loop sounds four beeps in rapid succession from the computer's speaker:

```
For i = 1 To 4
    Beep
Next i
```

This loop is the functional equivalent of writing the Beep statement four times in a procedure. It looks the same to the compiler as

```
Beep
Beep
Beep
Beep
```

The variable used in the loop is i, a single letter that, by convention, stands for the first integer counter in a For...Next loop. Each time the loop is executed, the counter variable is incremented by one. (The first time through the loop, the variable contains a value of 1, the value of *start;* the last time through, it contains a value of 4, the value of *end.*) As you'll see in the following examples, you can use this counter variable to great advantage in your loops.

Displaying a Counter Variable by Using the Print Method

A counter variable is just like any other variable in an event procedure. It can be assigned to properties, used in calculations, or displayed in a program. One of the handiest techniques for displaying a counter variable is to use the Print method, a special statement that displays output on a form or prints output on an attached printer. The Print method has the following syntax:

The Print method sends output to a form or a printer.

```
Print expression
```

where *expression* is a variable, property, text value, or numeric value in the procedure. In the following exercise, you'll use the Print method to display the output of a For...Next loop on a form.

Display information by using a For...Next loop

1 Start Microsoft Visual Basic.

If Visual Basic is already running, on the File menu, click the New Project command.

CommandButton control

Properties button

2 Use the CommandButton control to create a command button in the bottom center of the form.

3 Click the Properties button on the toolbar, and then set the Caption property of the command button to "Loop".

4 Open the object drop-down list box at the top of the Properties window, and then click the Form1 object name.

The properties for the form appear in the Properties window.

5 Change the Font property to Times New Roman.

The Font property controls how text is displayed on the form. You can use any font on your system with the form, but TrueType fonts work the best because they can be displayed in many sizes and because they look the same on screen as they do in print.

6 Double-click the Loop button on the form.

The Command1_Click event procedure appears in the Code window.

7 Type the following program statements in the procedure:

```
For i = 1 To 10
    Print "Line"; i
Next i
```

This For...Next loop uses the Print method to display the word *Line*, followed by the loop counter, 10 times on the form. The semicolon (;) in the Print statement directs Visual Basic to display the counter variable next to the string "Line", with no additional spaces in between. (You will, however, see a space between "Line" and the counter variable when your program runs. When printing numeric values, the Print method reserves a space for a minus sign, even if the minus sign isn't needed.)

NOTE The Print method supports the semicolon (;) and comma (,) symbols to separate elements in an expression list. The semicolon places the elements side by side, and the comma places the elements one tab field apart. You can use any combination of semicolon and comma symbols to separate expression list elements.

The complete For Next Loop program is available on disk in the \Vb\Practice\Lesson 6 folder.

Now you're ready to run the program.

Start button

8 Click the Start button on the toolbar.

The program runs in the programming environment.

9 Click the Loop button.

The For...Next loop prints 10 lines on the form, as shown here:

10 Click the Loop button again.

The For...Next loop prints another 10 lines on the form (or as many as will fit). Each time a line is printed, the cursor moves down one line, until the cursor is below the edge of the form.

End button

11 Click the End button on the toolbar to stop the program.

12 Click the Save Project button on the toolbar. Save the form as **My For Next Loop.frm**, and then save the project as **My For Next Loop.vbp**.

Save the files in the \Vb\Practice\Lesson 6 folder.

Save Project button

Changing a Property in a For...Next Loop

The FontSize property changes the point size of fonts on a form.

Visual Basic lets you change properties and update key variables in a loop. In the following exercise, you'll modify the My For Next Loop program so that it changes the FontSize property in the For...Next loop. The FontSize property specifies the point size of the text on a form; you can use it as an alternative to changing the point size with the Font property.

Change the FontSize property

1 Open the Command1_Click event procedure if it is not already open.

The For...Next loop appears in the Code window.

2 Insert the following instruction directly below the For statement:

```
FontSize = 10 + i
```

This statement sets the FontSize property of the form to 10 points greater than the value of the loop counter. The first time through the loop, the font size will be set to 11 points, the next time to 12 points, and so on until the last loop, when the font will be enlarged to 20 points. When you've finished, your For...Next loop should look like the following:

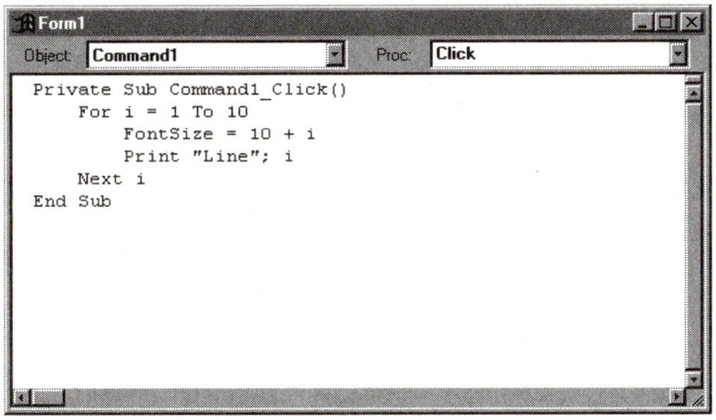

Start button

3 Click the Start button on the toolbar to run the program.

4 Click the Loop button.

The For...Next loop displays the following output on the form:

The complete Enlarge Font program is available on disk in the Lesson 6 folder.

Each time the loop counter was incremented, it caused the point size on the form to grow.

End button

5 Click the End button to stop the program.

The program stops, and the programming environment returns.

6 On the File menu, click the Save File As command. Save the modified form as **My Enlarge Font.frm**.

7 On the File menu, click the Save Project As command. Save the project as **My Enlarge Font.vbp**.

IMPORTANT A For...Next loop can save considerable space in a program. In the previous example, a For...Next loop four lines long processed the equivalent of 20 program statements.

Complex For...Next Loops

You can create a different sequence of numbers for your For...Next counter variable by using the Step keyword.

The counter variable in a For...Next loop can be a powerful tool in your programs. With a little imagination, you can use it to create several useful sequences of numbers in your loops. To create a loop with a counter pattern other than 1, 2, 3, 4, and so on, you can specify a different value for *start* in the loop and then use the Step keyword to increment the counter at different intervals. For example, the loop

```
For i = 5 To 25 Step 5
    Print i
Next i
```

would print the following sequence of numbers on a form:

```
5
10
15
20
25
```

You can use the Step keyword with decimal values.

You can also specify decimal values in a loop. For example, the For...Next loop

```
For i = 1 To 2.5 Step 0.5
    Print i
Next i
```

would print the following numbers on a form:

```
1
1.5
2
2.5
```

In addition to displaying the counter variable, you can use the counter to set properties, calculate values, or process files. The following exercise shows how you can use the counter to open Visual Basic icons that are stored on disk in files that have numbers in their names. The program also demonstrates how you can use a For...Next loop to work with several image objects as a group. To organize the image objects so that they can be processed efficiently, you'll place them in a container called a control array.

Open files by using a For...Next loop

1 On the File menu, click the New Project command.

Image control

2 Click the Image control in the toolbox, and then create a small, square image box near the upper left corner of the form.

3 On the Edit menu, click the Copy command.

A copy of the image box is placed on the Microsoft Windows Clipboard. You'll use this copy to create three additional image boxes on the form.

4 On the Edit menu, click the Paste command.

You create a control array by copying and pasting objects.

Visual Basic displays a message asking whether you want to create a control array in your program. A *control array* is a collection of identical interface objects. Each object in the group shares the same object name, so the entire group can be selected and defined at once. However, the objects in a control array can also be referenced individually, giving you complete control over each of the items in your user interface. To reference an individual array object, you identify the object by using its Index property. The first object in an array has an index of 0, the second has an index of 1, and so on throughout the array. However, you can change the index of one or more objects in a control array if that makes the elements easier to work with.

5 Click Yes to create a control array.

Visual Basic creates a control array of image boxes and pastes the second image box in the upper left corner of the form. The new image box is selected.

6 Drag the second image box to the right of the first image box.

NOTE After you select an object, you can drag it to any location on the form.

---

7 On the Edit menu, click the Paste command, and then drag the third image box to the right of the second image box.

8 Click the Paste command again, and then place the fourth image box to the right of the third image box.

When you've finished pasting, your screen should look like the one shown on the following page.

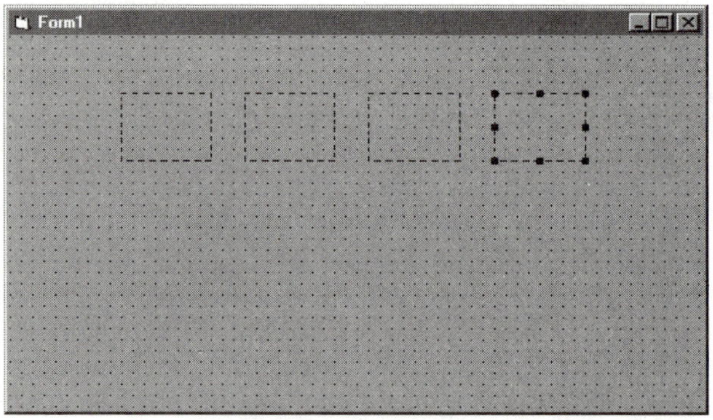

CommandButton control

You work with all the objects in a control array by selecting them as a group.

9 Click the CommandButton control in the toolbox, and then create a command button at the bottom of the form.

Now set the properties of the objects on the form. First you'll set the properties of the image boxes in the control array as a group.

10 Click the first image box, hold down the SHIFT key, and then click the second, third, and fourth image boxes.

The image boxes in the control array appear selected on the form.

11 Click the Properties button on the toolbar, and then set the following properties. (After you set the image box properties, click the command button to set its property.)

Object	Property	Setting
Image1 control array	BorderStyle	1 - Fixed Single
	Stretch	True
Command1	Caption	"Display icons"

12 Double-click the Display Icons button on the form to display the event procedure for the command button object.

The Command1_Click event procedure appears in the Code window.

13 Type the following loop to load the icons from disk:

```
For i = 1 To 4
    Image1(i - 1).Picture = _
      LoadPicture("c:\vb\practice\lesson 6\misc0" & i & ".ico")
Next i
```

NOTE In this event procedure, the LoadPicture Function is too long to be printed on one line in this book, so I broke it into two lines by using the Visual Basic line continuation character (_). You can use this character anyplace in your program code except within a string expression.

The loop uses the LoadPicture function to load four icon files from the \Vb\Practice\Lesson 6 folder on your hard disk. (You'll also find these files in the \Program Files\Microsoft Visual Basic\Icons\Misc folder.) The tricky part of the loop is the statement

```
Image1(i - 1).Picture = _
  LoadPicture("c:\vb\practice\lesson 6\misc0" & i & ".ico")
```

which loads the files from your hard disk. The first part of the statement,

```
Image1(i - 1).Picture
```

accesses the Picture property of each image box in the control array. Control array items are referenced by their index values, so you would refer to the individual image boxes in this example as Image1(0), Image1(1), Image1(2), and Image1(3). The number in parentheses is the index value in the array; in this example, the correct index value is calculated by subtracting 1 from the counter variable.

The filename is created by using the counter variable and the concatenation operator you learned about in the previous lesson. The code

```
LoadPicture("c:\vb\practice\lesson 6\misc0" & i & ".ico")
```

combines a pathname, a filename, and the .ico extension to create four valid filenames of icons on your hard disk. In this example, the files you're loading into the image boxes are Misc01.ico, Misc02.ico, Misc03.ico, and Misc04.ico. This statement works because several files in the \Vb\Practice\Lesson 6 folder have the filename pattern Misc*xx*.ico. Recognizing the pattern let you build a For...Next loop around the filenames.

Save Project button

14 Click the Save Project button on the toolbar.

Save the form to disk as **My Control Array.frm**, and then save the project to disk as **My Control Array.vbp.**

Start button

15 Click the Start button on the toolbar to start the program, and then click the Display Icons button.

The For...Next loop loads the icons from disk into the image boxes.

The complete Control Array program is available on disk in the Lesson 6 folder.

NOTE If Visual Basic displays an error message, check your program code for typos and then verify that the icon files are in the path you specified in the program. If you installed the Step by Step practice files in a folder other than the default folder, or if you moved your icon files after installation, the pathname in the event procedure might not be correct.

The program displays the following output:

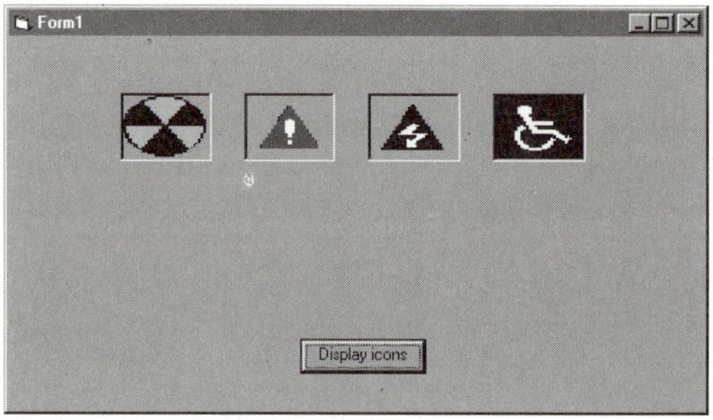

16 Click the Close button on the title bar to quit the program.

The program stops, and the programming environment returns.

Using the Step Keyword in the My Control Array Program

Imagine that the \Vb\Practice\Lesson 6 folder is full of files that have the filename pattern Misc*xx*.ico, and try using the Step keyword to display a few more icons in the image boxes. (You can also do this exercise using the \Program Files\Microsoft Visual Basic\Icons\Misc folder, which really is full of icon files.) To load filenames that follow a different pattern, you simply need to change the numbers that appear after the For statement and touch up the code that creates the control array index and the icon filename. You also need to change the image box indexes to match the new counter values you'll be using.

Modify the My Control Array program

Properties button

1 Click the first image box object on the form, and then click the Properties button on the toolbar.

The properties for the Image1(0) image box appear in the Properties window.

2 Change the Index property to 22.

The first item in a control array usually has an index value of 0, but you can change the index value to a different number if that makes the control array easier to use. In this exercise, the files you want to open are Misc22.ico, Misc24.ico, Misc26.ico, and Misc28.ico, so changing the object indexes to 22, 24, 26, and 28 will make the objects easier to reference.

3 Open the object drop-down list box in the Properties window, and then click the Image1(1) object name.

4 Change the Index property of the second image box to 24.

5 Open the object drop-down list box, and then click the Image1(2) object name.

6 Change the Index property of the third image box to 26.

7 Open the object drop-down list box, and then click the Image1(3) object name.

8 Change the Index property of the fourth image box to 28.

Now change the code in the For...Next loop.

9 Double-click the Display Icons button on the form.

The Command1_Click event procedure appears in the Code window.

10 Change the For statement to the following:

```
For i = 22 To 28 Step 2
```

This code sets the counter variable to 22 in the first loop, 24 in the second loop, and 26 and 28 in subsequent loops. Now update the LoadPicture function in the loop.

11 Change the control array index from Image1(i – 1) to Image1(i).

Since the index now matches the loop and image object names exactly, no calculating is needed to determine the index.

12 Remove the 0 (zero) from the pathname inside the LoadPicture function.

The Misc*xx*.ico filenames no longer contain zeroes. When you've finished, your event procedure should look like the following:

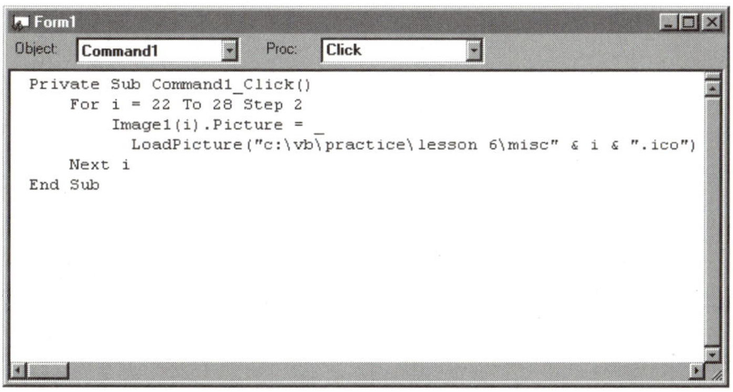

The complete Step Loop program is located on disk in the Lesson 6 folder.

13 Click the Start button on the toolbar, and then click the Display Icons button.

The For...Next loop loads four new icons in the image boxes. Your screen should look like the following:

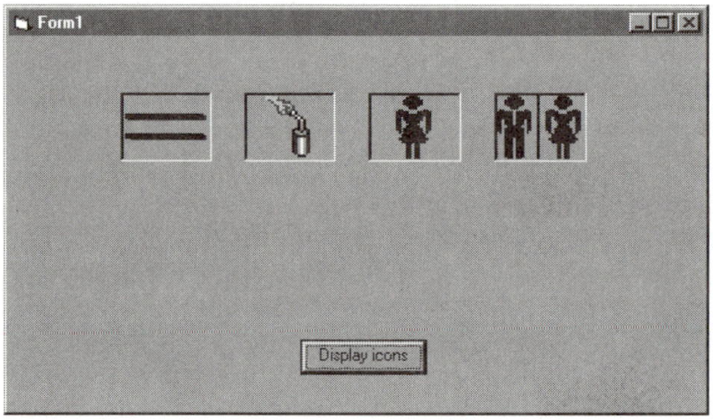

NOTE The \Program Files\Microsoft Visual Basic\Icons\Misc folder contains dozens of interesting icons like the ones shown above. Feel free to use them as buttons or artwork in your programs.

14 Click the Close button on the title bar.

The program stops, and the programming environment returns.

15 Save the revised form and project to disk under the name **My Step Loop**.

Exit For Statements

An Exit For statement allows you to exit a For...Next loop before the loop has finished executing. This allows you to respond to a specific event that occurs before the loop runs the preset number of times. For example, in the following For...Next loop

```
For i = 1 To 10
    InpName = InputBox("Enter your name or type Done to quit.")
    If InpName = "Done" Then Exit For
    Print InpName
Next i
```

the loop prompts the user for 10 names and prints them on the form, unless the word *Done* is entered (in which case, the program jumps to the first statement following the Next statement). Exit For statements are usually used with If statements. You'll find them useful for handling special cases that come up in a loop.

Writing Do Loops

Do loops execute code until a specific condition is met.

As an alternative to a For...Next loop, you can write a Do loop that executes a group of statements until a certain condition is True in the loop. Do loops are valuable because often you can't know in advance how many times a loop should repeat. For example, you might want to let the user enter names in a database until the user types the word *Done* in an input box. In that case, you could use a Do loop to cycle indefinitely until the text string "Done" was entered.

A Do loop has several formats, depending on where and how the loop condition is evaluated. The most common syntax is

```
Do While condition
    block of statements to be executed
Loop
```

For example, the following statements are a Do loop that will process input until the word *Done* is entered:

```
Do While InpName <> "Done"
    InpName = InputBox("Enter your name or type Done to quit.")
    If InpName <> "Done" Then Print InpName
Loop
```

The placement of the conditional test affects how a Do loop runs.

The conditional statement in this loop is InpName <> "Done", which the Visual Basic compiler translates to mean "loop as long as the InpName variable doesn't contain the word *Done*." This brings up an interesting fact about Do loops: if the condition at the top of the loop is not True when the Do statement is first evaluated, the Do loop is never executed. In this example, if the InpName variable did contain the text string "Done" before the loop started (perhaps from an earlier assignment in the event procedure), Visual Basic would skip the loop altogether and continue with the line below the Loop keyword. Note that this type of loop requires an extra If...Then structure to prevent the exit value from being displayed when the user types it.

If you want the loop to always run at least once in a program, put the conditional test at the bottom of the loop. For example, the loop

```
Do
    InpName = InputBox("Enter your name or type Done to quit.")
    If InpName <> "Done" Then Print InpName
Loop While InpName <> "Done"
```

is essentially the same as the Do loop shown above, but the loop condition is tested after a name is received from the InputBox function. This has the advantage of updating the InpName variable before the conditional test in the loop, so a preexisting "Done" value won't cause the loop to be skipped. Testing the loop condition at the bottom ensures that your loop will be executed at least once, but you'll often need to add a few extra statements to process the data.

Avoiding an Endless Loop

Be sure that each loop has a legitimate exit condition.

Because of the relentless nature of Do loops, it is very important to design your test conditions so that each loop has a true exit point. If a loop test never evaluates to False, the loop will execute endlessly and your program will no longer respond to input. Consider the following example:

```
Do
    Number = InputBox("Enter a number to square.  Type -1 to quit.")
    Number = Number * Number
    Print Number
Loop While Number >= 0
```

In this loop, the user enters number after number and the program squares each number and prints it on the form. Unfortunately, when the user has had enough, he or she can't quit because the advertised exit condition doesn't work. When the user enters –1, the program squares it and the Number variable is assigned the value 1. (The problem can be fixed by setting a different exit condition.) Endless loops are a good thing to watch for when you're writing Do loops. Fortunately, they're pretty easy to spot if you test your programs thoroughly.

The following exercise shows how you can use a Do loop to convert Fahrenheit temperatures to Celsius temperatures. The simple program prompts the user for input by using the InputBox function, converts the temperature, and displays the output in a message box. The program also demonstrates how you can hide a form by setting its Visible property to False.

Convert temperatures by using a Do loop

1. On the File menu, click the New Project command.

   Visual Basic displays a new form in the programming environment.

Properties button

2. Click the Properties button on the toolbar.

   The property settings for the Form1 object appear in the Properties window.

You make a form invisible at runtime by setting its Visible property to False.

3. Set the Form1 Visible property to False by using the Properties window.

   When you set a form's Visible property to False, Visual Basic hides the form when you run the program. This essentially makes the entire user interface invisible at runtime—no objects can be displayed. You probably won't want to do this very often, but it's a useful technique when you want part or all of your program to work on a task in the background. Since this program only receives Fahrenheit temperatures and spits back Celsius temperatures, hiding its form is a good idea. You can handle the input by using the InputBox function and the output by using the MsgBox function.

4. Double-click the form.

The Form_Load event procedure is executed when a program starts running.

The Form_Load event procedure appears in the Code window. In this program, this is where all the code goes.

5 Type the following program statements:

```
Prompt = "Enter a Fahrenheit temperature."
Do
    FTemp = InputBox(Prompt, "Fahrenheit to Celsius")
    If FTemp <> "" Then
        Celsius = Int((FTemp + 40) * 5 / 9 - 40)
        MsgBox (Celsius), , "Temperature in Celsius"
    End If
Loop While FTemp <> ""
End
```

These nine lines handle the calculations for the utility. The first line assigns a text string to the Prompt variable, which is then used to display a message of instruction in the input box. The Do loop repeatedly prompts the user for a Fahrenheit temperature, converts the number to Celsius, and then displays it on the screen by using the MsgBox function. The loop executes until the user clicks the Cancel button, which returns an empty, or *null,* value to the Ftemp variable. The loop checks for the null value by using a While conditional test at the bottom of the loop. Finally, the program statement

```
Celsius = Int((FTemp + 40) * 5 / 9 - 40)
```

handles the conversion from Fahrenheit to Celsius in the program. The statement employs a standard conversion formula, but it uses the Int function to return to the Celsius variable a value that contains no decimal places. (Everything to the right of the decimal point is discarded.) This cutting sacrifices accuracy, but it helps you avoid long, unsightly numbers, such as 21.1111111111111, the Celsius value for 70 degrees Fahrenheit.

Now try running the program.

Start button

6 Click the Start button on the toolbar.

The program starts, and the InputBox function prompts you for a Fahrenheit temperature. (The form is invisible.) Your screen should look like the following:

The complete Celsius program is available on disk in the Lesson 6 folder.

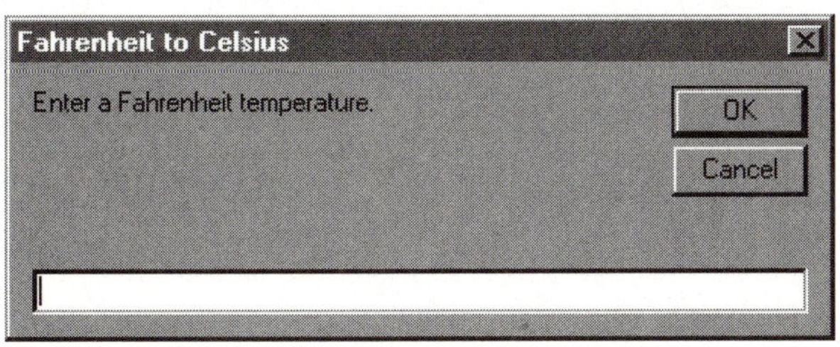

7 Type **32** and click OK.

The temperature 32 degrees Fahrenheit is converted to 0 degrees Celsius, as shown in the following message box:

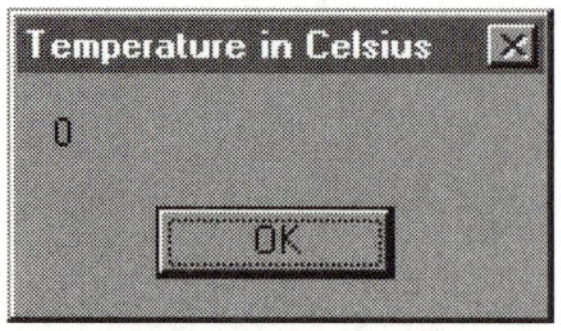

8 Click OK. Type **72** in the input box and click OK.

The temperature 72 degrees Fahrenheit is converted to 22 degrees Celsius.

9 Click OK, and then quit the program by clicking Cancel in the input box.

The program quits, and the programming environment returns.

Save Project button

10 Save the form and project to disk under the name **My Celsius**.

Using the Until Keyword in Do Loops

The Do loops you have worked with so far have used the While keyword to execute a group of statements as long as the loop condition remained True. Visual Basic also lets you use the Until keyword in Do loops to cycle *until* a certain condition is True. The Until keyword can be used at the top or bottom of a Do loop to test a condition, just like the While keyword. For example, the following Do loop uses the Until keyword to loop repeatedly until the user enters the word *Done* in an input box:

```
Do
    InpName = InputBox("Enter your name or type Done to quit.")
    If InpName <> "Done" Then Print InpName
Loop Until InpName = "Done"
```

As you can see, a loop that uses the Until keyword is very similar to a loop that uses the While keyword, except that the test condition usually contains the opposite operator—the = (equal to) operator versus the <> (not equal to) operator, in this case. If using the Until keyword makes sense to you, feel free to use it with test conditions in your Do loops.

Using Timer Objects

A timer object is like an invisible stopwatch in a program.

Visual Basic lets you execute a group of statements for a specified *period of time* by using a timer object. A timer object is an invisible stopwatch that gives you access to the system clock from your programs. It can be used like an egg timer to count down from a preset time, it can be used to cause a delay in a program, or it can be used to repeat an action at prescribed intervals. A timer object is accurate to 1 millisecond, or 1/1000 of a second. Although timers aren't visible at runtime, each timer is associated with an event procedure that runs every time the timer's preset *interval* has elapsed. You set a timer's interval by using the Interval property, and you activate a timer by setting the timer's Enabled property to True. Once a timer is enabled, it runs constantly—executing its event procedure at the prescribed interval—until the user stops the program or the timer is disabled.

Creating a Digital Clock by Using a Timer Object

The Interval property sets the tick rate of a timer.

One of the most practical uses for a timer object is in a digital clock. In the following exercise, you'll create a simple digital clock that keeps track of the current time down to the second. In the example, you'll set the Interval property for the timer to 1000, directing Visual Basic to update the clock time every 1000 milliseconds, or once a second. Since the Windows operating system is a multitasking environment and other programs will also require processing time, Visual Basic might not always get a chance to update the clock each second, but it will always catch up if it gets behind. To keep track of the time at other intervals (such as once every tenth of a second), simply adjust the number in the Interval property.

Create the Digital Clock program

1. On the File menu, click the New Project command.
2. Resize the form to a small window.

   You don't want the clock to take up much room.

Timer control

3. Click the Timer control in the toolbox.
4. Create a small timer object on the right side of the form.

   When you finish creating the timer, Visual Basic resizes it to a standard size. A timer object can be only one size.

Label control

5. Click the Label control in the toolbox.
6. In the center of the form, create a label that fills most of the form.

You'll use the label to display the time in the clock. Your form should look like the following:

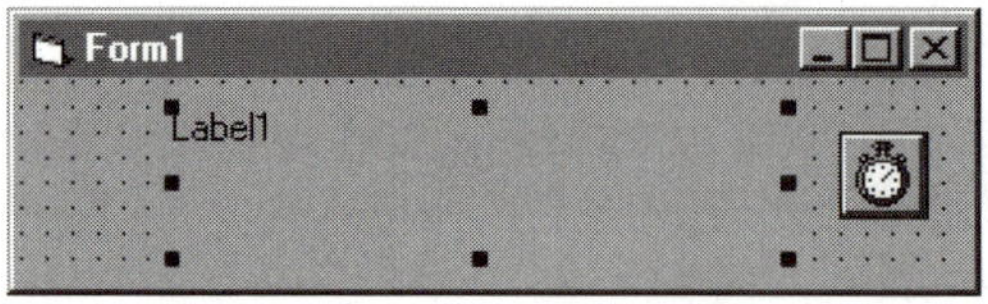

Properties button

The Caption property of a form controls the name displayed in the program's title bar.

7 Click the Properties button on the toolbar.

The Properties window appears.

8 Set the following properties in the program. To give the Digital Clock program a name that appears in its title bar, set the Caption property of the Form1 object to "Digital Clock".

Object	Property	Setting
Label1	Caption	(Empty)
	Font	Times New Roman, Bold, 28-point
	Alignment	2 - Center
Timer1	Interval	1000
	Enabled	True
Form1	Caption	"Digital Clock"

NOTE If you would like to put some artwork in the background of your clock, set the Picture property of the Form1 object to the pathname of a graphics file.

Now write the program code for the timer.

9 Double-click the timer object on the form.

The Timer1_Timer event procedure appears in the Code window.

10 Type the following statement:

The complete Digital Clock program is available on disk in the Lesson 6 folder.

```
Label1.Caption = Time
```

This statement gets the current time from the system clock and assigns it to the caption property of the Label1 object. Only one statement is required in this program because you set the Interval property for the timer by using the Properties window. The timer object handles the rest.

Start button

11 Close the Code window, and then click the Start button on the toolbar to run the clock.

The clock appears, as shown here:

12 Watch the clock for a few moments.

Visual Basic updates the time every second.

13 Click the Close button in the title bar to stop the clock.

Clicking the Close button is an alternative to using the End button to stop the program. This is the method a user would use to close the clock if he or she was running it as a stand-alone program.

Save Project button

14 Save the form and project to disk under the name **My Digital Clock**.

Your little clock is quite handy, and you might want to compile the My Digital Clock program into an executable file so that you can use it now and then on your computer. Feel free to customize it by using your own artwork, text, and colors.

One Step Further: Using a Timer Object to Set a Time Limit

Another interesting implementation of a timer object is to use it to wait for a set period of time and then to either enable or prohibit an action. This is a little like setting an egg timer in your program—you set the Interval property with the delay you want, and then you start the clock ticking by setting the Enabled property to True. The following exercise shows how you can use this idea to set a time limit for entering a password. The program uses a timer to close its own program if a valid password is not entered in 15 seconds. (Normally a program like this would be part of a larger application.) The password for this program is "secret". You can also use this timer technique to display a welcome message or a copyright message on the screen, or you can use it to repeat an event at a set interval, such as saving a file to disk every 10 minutes.

Set a password time limit

1 On the File menu, click the New Project command.

2 Resize the form to a small rectangular window about the size of an input box.

TextBox control

3 Click the TextBox control in the toolbox.

4 Create a rectangular text box in the middle of the form.

Label control

5 Click the Label control in the toolbox, and then create a long label above the text box.

CommandButton control

Timer control

6 Click the CommandButton control in the toolbox, and then create a command button below the text box.

7 Click the Timer control in the toolbox.

8 Create a timer object in the lower left corner of the form.

9 Set the following properties for the program:

Object	Property	Setting
Text1	Text PasswordChar	(Empty) *
Label1	Caption	"Enter your password in 15 seconds."
Command1	Caption	"Try Password"
Timer1	Interval Enabled	15000 True
Form1	Caption	"Password"

The PasswordChar setting will display asterisk (*) characters in the text box when the user enters a password. Setting the timer Interval property to 15000 will give the user 15 seconds to enter his or her password and click the Try Password button. Setting the Enabled property to True (the default) will start the timer running when the program starts. (You could also disable this property and then enable it in an event procedure if your timer was not needed until later in the program.)

Your form should look like the following:

10 Double-click the timer object on the form, and then type the following statements:

```
MsgBox ("Sorry, your time is up.")
End
```

The first statement displays a message indicating that the time has expired, and the second statement stops the program. Visual Basic executes this event procedure if the timer interval reaches 15 seconds and a valid password has not been entered.

11 Click the Command1 object in the Code window drop-down list box, and then type the following statements in the Command1_Click event procedure:

```
If Text1.Text = "secret" Then
    Timer1.Enabled = False
    MsgBox ("Welcome to the system!")
    End
Else
    MsgBox ("Sorry, friend, I don't know you.")
End If
```

This program code tests whether the password entered in the text box is "secret". If it is, the timer is disabled, a welcome message is displayed, and the program ends. (A more useful program would continue working rather than ending here.) If the password entered is not a match, the user is notified with a message box and is given another chance to enter the password. But the user had better be quick—he or she has only 15 seconds!

Start button

The complete Timed Password program is available on disk in the Lesson 6 folder.

12 Close the Code window, and then click the Start button to run the program.

The program starts, and the 15-second clock starts ticking.

13 Type **open** in the text box, and then click the Try Password button.

The following dialog box appears on the screen, noting your incorrect response:

14 Click OK, and then wait patiently until the sign-on period expires.

The program displays the following message:

15 Click OK to end the program.

The Visual Basic programming environment appears.

16 Save the form and project to disk under the name **My Timed Password.**

Save Project button

If you want to continue to the next lesson

➤ Keep Visual Basic running, and turn to the Part 2 Review & Practice section or to Lesson 7.

If you want to quit Visual Basic for now

➤ On the File menu, click Exit.

If you see a Save dialog box, click Yes.

Lesson Summary

To	Do this	Button

Execute a group of program statements a set number of times	Insert the statements between For and Next statements in a loop. For example:
	`For i = 1 To 10`
	`    MsgBox ("Press OK already!")`
	`Next i`	

Display one or more lines of output on a form	Use the Print method. For example:
	`For Cnt = 1 To 5`
	`    Print "The current count is"; Cnt`
	`    Print "So far, so good."`
	`Next Cnt`	

Use a specific sequence of numbers with statements	Insert the statements in a For...Next loop and use the To and Step keywords to define the sequence of numbers. For example:
	`For i = 2 To 8 Step 2`
	`    Print i; "...";`
	`Next i`
	`Print "Who do we appreciate?"`	

Exit a For...Next loop prematurely	Use the Exit For statement. For example:
	`For i = 1 To 10`
	`    InpName = InputBox("Name?")`
	`    If InpName = "Trotsky" Then Exit For`
	`    Print InpName`
	`Next i`	

Execute a group of program statements until a specific condition is met	Insert the statements between Do and Loop statements. For example:
	`Do While Query <> "Yes"`
	`    Query = InputBox("Trotsky?")`
	`    If Query <> "Yes" Then Print Query`
	`Loop`	

To	Do this	Button
Avoid an endless Do loop	Be sure the loop has a test condition that can evaluate to False.	

Loop until a certain condition is True	Use a Do loop with the Until keyword. For example:
	`Do`
	`    GiveIn = InputBox("Say 'Uncle'")`
	`Loop Until GiveIn = "Uncle"`	

Loop for a specific period of time in your program	Use a timer object.	
Place a name in an application's title bar	Set the Caption property of the Form1 object to the name you want to use.	

For online information about	On the Visual Basic Help menu, click Search For Help On, and then
For...Next loops	Type **For**
Do loops	Type **Do**
The Print method	Type **Print**
Timer objects	Type **timer**

For more information on	In the Visual Basic *Programmer's Guide*, see
For...Next and Do loops	Chapter 5, "Programming Fundamentals"
Displaying one or more lines of output on a form	Chapter 16, "Displaying and Printing Information"
Timer objects	Chapter 17, "Interacting with the Environment"

Preview of the Next Lesson

The next section in this book is the Review & Practice exercise for Part 2. You can work through this Review & Practice section to review what you learned in Part 2. In Lesson 7, "Working with Forms, Printers, and Error Handlers," you'll learn more about creating the user interface of your program. You'll learn how to add additional forms, how to send program output to the printer, and how to process unexpected events by using event handlers.

Part

2

Review & Practice

You will review and practice how to:

- Create the interface for an appointment alarm.
- Check the time periodically by using a timer object.
- Watch for a specified time by using an If...Then decision structure.
- Display output by using the MsgBox function.

Estimated time

30 min.

Before you move on to Part 3, which focuses on adding advanced features to your user interfaces, you can practice the skills you learned in Part 2 by solving the programming problem in this Review & Practice section. You will use a timer object, an If...Then decision structure, and several programming statements to create a personal appointment alarm that you can use in your daily work.

Scenario

If you're like most people, you have several commitments to keep each day. Whether you spend your time at home, at school, or at the office, you've probably developed your own techniques for remembering daily appointments and special events. You might use a desk calendar, a personal planner, or even those little yellow sticky notes (my favorite) to avoid missing important meetings. Now and then, however, everyone misses a scheduled appointment. It's not that we're lazy—we just lose track of time, right? Fortunately, our computers are a lot better at keeping track of information than we are. Each personal computer contains a built-in clock that maintains the current date and time. You can use this information in a Microsoft Visual Basic program to remind you when it's time to do something.

In this Review & Practice, your programming problem is to create a Visual Basic utility that reminds you when it's time for your next appointment. Your program should contain a text box for the time of your next appointment and a text box for a brief description of the event. The utility should let you set a reminder alarm, and then the utility should wait patiently as a task on the taskbar until it's time for your appointment. (You'll learn how to minimize a form and place it on the taskbar in Step 2.) When the appointment time comes, the program should use a message box to display an appropriate reminder, and then the program should disable the alarm. As always, the program should have appropriate title bars, labels, and command buttons.

If you like, you can try solving the problem before looking at the following practice steps. This will give you some "real world" experience at using Visual Basic to create a utility on your own, without any help. Or you can solve the problem by following these steps carefully and reviewing the related sections in Parts 1 and 2 when the need arises. The solution to the problem is available in the \Vb\Practice\Review folder, in the project file named Problem 2.vbp.

Step 1: Create the Interface for the Appointment Alarm

The first step in building your program is designing the user interface. You might want to sketch the appointment alarm on paper before you get started. As you create the program, try to design each element so that it can be used by a person who has never seen your program or talked to you about it. Your program should contain two text boxes, two command buttons, several descriptive labels, a timer, and (optionally) an image box containing a clock.

1. Start Visual Basic.
2. Resize the form so that it is the size of a medium-size dialog box.
3. Use the Label control to create a wide label along the top edge of the form.
4. Use the TextBox control to create two text boxes in the center of the form.
5. Use the Label control to create descriptive labels above both of the text boxes.
6. Use the Image control to create a small image box to the right of the text boxes.
7. Use the CommandButton control to place two buttons along the bottom edge of the form.
8. Use the Timer control to place a timer in the lower left corner of the form.
9. Set the following form and object properties:

Object	Property	Setting
Label1	Caption Font ForeColor	"My Own Appointment Reminder" Times New Roman, Bold, 14-point Dark purple
Text1	Text	(Empty)
Text2	Text	(Empty)
Label2	Caption Font	"Alarm time (00:00 - 23:59)" Bold
Label3	Caption Font	"Message" Bold
Image1	Picture	"c:\vb\practice\review\clock01.ico"
Command1	Caption	"Set Alarm and Minimize"
Command2	Caption	"Quit"
Timer1	Interval Enabled	15000 False
Form1	Caption Icon	"Personal Alarm" "c:\vb\practice\review\clock01.ico"

NOTE The Icon property, introduced here for the first time, specifies a custom icon for the form that appears when the form is minimized and placed on the taskbar. Specifying a custom icon is not necessary, but it gives your program a finished look.

Your user interface should look similar to the following:

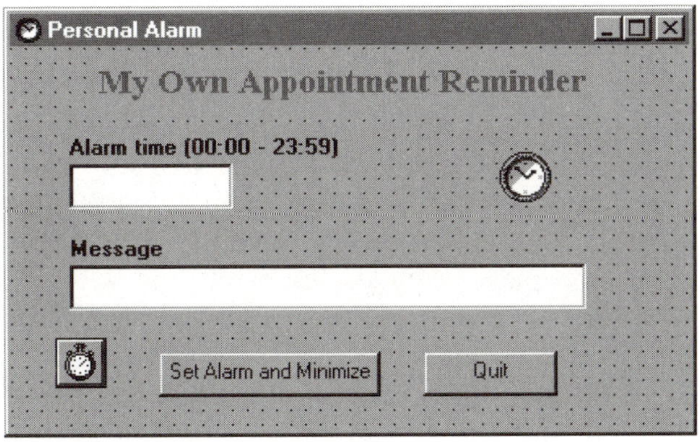

10 Save the form to disk under the name **My Alarm.frm**, and save the project to disk under the name **My Alarm.vbp**. Specify the \Vb\Practice\Review folder.

For more information on	See
Using basic controls	Lessons 1 and 2
Using timer objects	Lesson 6
Setting properties	Lessons 1 and 2

Step 2: Write the Program Code

The next step in building the program is writing the program code associated with the objects in the user interface. To complete the My Alarm program, you need to write code for the event procedures associated with the Timer1, Command1, and Command2 objects.

1. Double-click the Set Alarm And Minimize button (the Command1 object) on the form.
2. Type the following program statements in the Command1_Click event procedure:

The WindowState property is used to minimize the form.

```
Form1.WindowState = 1  'Minimize form
Timer1.Enabled = True  'Start timer
```

The first statement uses the WindowState property to minimize the form when the user sets the alarm. This handy trick is optional in your program, but it adds a nice touch if you want to get the form out of the way for a while. The second statement starts the timer running. Every 15 seconds the timer will check the system time to see whether it matches the alarm time entered by the user.

3. Open the Object drop-down list box in the Code window, and then click the Command2 object in the list box.
4. Type the following statement in the Command2_Click event procedure:

```
End
```

The statement ends the program when the user clicks Quit.

5. Open the Object drop-down list box, and then click the Timer1 object in the list box.
6. Type the following statements in the Timer1_Timer event procedure:

```
CurrentTime = Format(Time, "hh:mm")
If CurrentTime = Text1.Text Then
     Beep
     MsgBox (Text2.Text), , "Personal Alarm"
     Timer1.Enabled = False
     Form1.WindowState = 0 'Restore form
End If
```

This event procedure is executed every 15 seconds after the alarm is set. (Fifteen seconds is the delay you specified with the timer Interval property.) Checking the system clock every 15 seconds guarantees that the program won't miss your appointment if Microsoft Windows is working on some other application and gets behind on its timer updates. The first statement uses two functions—Format and Time—to create a text string that has the format *hh:mm*, where *hh* is the current hour (in 24-hour, military-style notation) and *mm* is the current minute. This string is then assigned to the CurrentTime variable and compared to the time the user entered in the text box. This strategy is safer than using only the Time function in the comparison because the Time function includes seconds and *AM* or *PM* in its format. The decision structure displays a message if the times match and then disables the timer and restores the form to its original size.

NOTE To learn more about the Format and Time functions, check the Visual Basic online Help.

7 Click the Save button on the toolbar.

For more information on	See
Using variables and the & operator	Lesson 4
Writing decision structures	Lesson 5
Using the MsgBox function for output	Lesson 5
Using time in your programs	Lessons 3 and 6

Step 3: Run and Compile the Program

After the program is complete, you need to run it in the programming environment and test the alarm to verify that it is working correctly. Use the clock on the taskbar to check the system time before you run the program. (Set the alarm for a few minutes later.) The My Alarm program will usually activate in the first 15 seconds of the minute you specified in the Alarm text box.

1 Click the Start button on the toolbar.

2 Type a time in the format *hh:mm* in the Alarm Time text box. Specify a time one or two minutes after the current system time. Be sure to use 24-hour, military-style notation when specifying the time. (One o'clock in the afternoon is 13:00, for example.)

3 Press TAB, and then type a reminder message, such as **Late lunch meeting with Gerry.**, in the Message text box.

Your screen will look similar to the following:

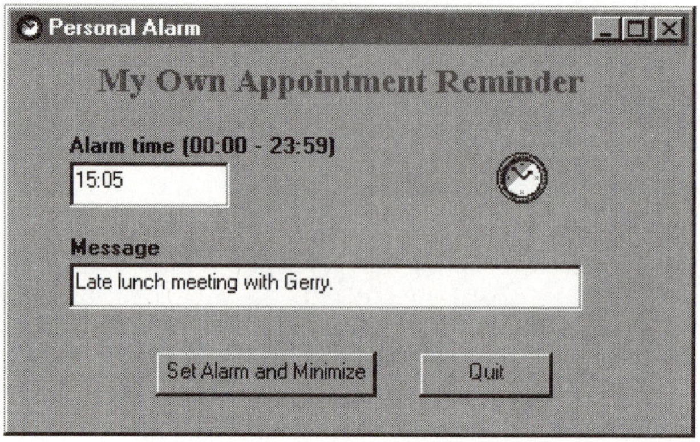

4 Click the Set Alarm And Minimize button.

The form shrinks to a small button on the taskbar when it is minimized.

5 Do some other work with your computer until My Alarm displays its reminder dialog box. (You can work in a different application—the alarm will notify you with a beep.) When the reminder message appears, click OK to close the dialog box, and then click Quit to stop the program.

6 If you want to use this program in your daily work, use the Make EXE File command on the File menu to create an executable version of the file.

For more information on	See
Running a clock program	Lesson 6
Creating an executable file	Lesson 1

Part

3

Creating the Perfect User Interface

Lesson

7

Working with Forms, Printers, and Error Handlers

In this lesson you will learn how to:

Estimated time **45 min.**

- Add new forms to a program.
- Send output to a printer.
- Process runtime errors by using error handlers.

In Part 2, you learned how to use a variety of Microsoft Visual Basic statements, functions, and control structures to do useful work in your programs. In Part 3, you'll focus again on the user interface, and you'll learn how to create impressive effects and bulletproof applications. In this lesson, you'll learn how to add more forms to an interface to handle input, output, or special messages. You'll also learn how to send the output of a program to an attached printer and how to use error handlers to process unexpected results.

Adding New Forms to a Program

Each new form has a unique name and its own set of objects, properties, and event procedures.

Each program you have written so far has used only one form for input and output. In many cases, one form will be sufficient for communication with the user. But if you would like to add more screens of information to a program, Visual Basic lets you add one or more extra forms to it. Each new form is considered an object and maintains its own objects, properties, and event procedures. The first form in a program is named Form1, and subsequent forms are named Form2, Form3, and so on. You create new forms by clicking the Form command on the Insert menu or by clicking the Form button on the toolbar. The table on the following page lists several practical uses for extra forms in your programs.

Form or forms	Description
Introductory screen	A screen that displays a welcome message, artwork, or copyright information when the program starts
Program instructions	A screen that displays information and tips about how the program works
Dialog boxes	Custom dialog boxes that accept input and display output in the program
Document contents and artwork	A screen that displays the contents of one or more files used in the program

How Forms Are Used

New forms can be modal or nonmodal.

In Visual Basic, you have significant flexibility when using forms. You can make all of the forms in a program visible at the same time, or you can load and unload forms as they are needed by the program. If you display more than one form at once, you can allow the user to switch between the forms or you can control the order in which the forms are used. A form that must be used when it is displayed on the screen is known as a *modal* form—the form retains the focus until the user clicks OK, clicks Cancel, or otherwise dispatches it. A form that the user can switch away from is known as a *nonmodal,* or *modeless,* form. Most applications for Microsoft Windows use nonmodal forms when displaying information because they give the user more flexibility, so nonmodal is the default when you create a new form. You can also independently set any property on a form, including the form's caption, form size, border style, foreground and background colors, display font, and background picture.

Form Statements in Program Code

After you create a new form in the programming environment, you can load it into memory and access it by using specific statements in event procedures. The statement you use to load a new form has the syntax

The Load statement brings a new form into memory.

```
Load formname
```

where *formname* is the name of the form you want to load. For example, the statement

```
Load Form2
```

would load the second form in a program into memory, when the statement was executed by Visual Basic. After you have loaded a form, you can use it from any event procedure in the program and you can access any property or method you want to use with it. For example, to set the Caption property of the second form in your program to "Sorting Results", you could type the following program statement in any event procedure:

```
Form2.Caption = "Sorting Results"
```

The Show method displays a loaded form.

When you are ready to display a loaded form, you call it by using the Show method and note whether it is modal or nonmodal. The syntax for the Show method is

```
formname.Show mode
```

The default for a new form is nonmodal.

where *formname* is the name of the form and *mode* is 0 for nonmodal (the default) or 1 for modal. For example, to display Form2 as a nonmodal form (the default), you could use the Show method without specifying a mode:

```
Form2.Show
```

To display Form2 as a modal form, you would type this statement:

```
Form2.Show 1
```

NOTE If you use the Show method before using the Load statement, Visual Basic will load and display the specified form automatically. Visual Basic provides a separate Load statement to let programmers preload forms in memory so that the Show method works quickly and users don't notice any performance lag. It's a good idea to preload your forms, especially if they contain several objects or pieces of artwork.

Hiding and Unloading Forms

The Hide method makes a form invisible.

The Unload statement removes a form from memory.

You can hide forms by using the Hide method, and you can unload forms by using the Unload statement. These keywords are the opposites of Show and Load, respectively. Hiding a form makes the form invisible but keeps it in memory for use later in the program. (Hiding a form is identical to making it invisible by using the Visible property.) Unloading a form removes the form from memory. This frees up the RAM used to store the objects and graphics on the form, but it doesn't free up the space used by the form's event procedures. These are always in memory. You could use the Hide and Unload keywords to hide and unload Form2 in the following manner:

```
Form2.Hide
Unload Form2
```

IMPORTANT After you unload a form, its runtime values and properties are lost. If you reload the form, it will contain the original values set in the program code.

You can minimize a form (place it on the taskbar) or maximize a form (expand it to fill the screen) by using the WindowState property. For example, the following statement would minimize Form1 in a program:

```
Form1.WindowState = 1
```

To maximize Form1, you would use the following statement:

```
Form1.WindowState = 2
```

To return Form1 to its normal, default view, you would use:

```
Form1.WindowState = 0
```

The Part 2 Review & Practice exercise demonstrates how the WindowState property works.

Adding Preexisting Forms to a Program

Visual Basic lets you reuse your forms in new programming projects. This is the reason you have been saving your forms as separate .frm files while using this book. To add a preexisting form to a programming project, click the Add File command on the Visual Basic File menu. The Add File command displays a dialog box that lists all the forms in your Visual Basic home folder (typically C:\Program Files\Microsoft Visual Basic). To add an existing form, double-click the form filename in the dialog box. Visual Basic adds the specified form to the project, and you can view the form and modify its event procedures by clicking the View Form and View Code buttons in the Project window. You can specify the startup form in your program by clicking the Options command on the Tools menu and choosing the appropriate form on the Project tab of the Options dialog box.

Working with Multiple Forms: The Italian Program

The following exercises demonstrate how you can use a second form to display graphics and text in a foreign-language vocabulary program named Italian. Right now the program uses a MsgBox function to display a definition for each word, but you'll modify the program so that it uses a second form to display the information.

Run the Italian program

1. Start Visual Basic.
2. Click the Open Project button on the toolbar.

Open Project button

3. Open the Italian project in the \Vb\Practice\Lesson 7 folder.

   The project files appear in the Project window.
4. Click the View Form button in the Project window.

   The user interface for the program appears. Try running the utility now.
5. Click the Start button on the toolbar.

Start button

   A list of Italian verbs appears in the list box on the form. I wrote this program to learn a new group of Italian verbs each week, but you can modify it to help you memorize any type of information. To get the definition for a word, you double-click the word in the list box.

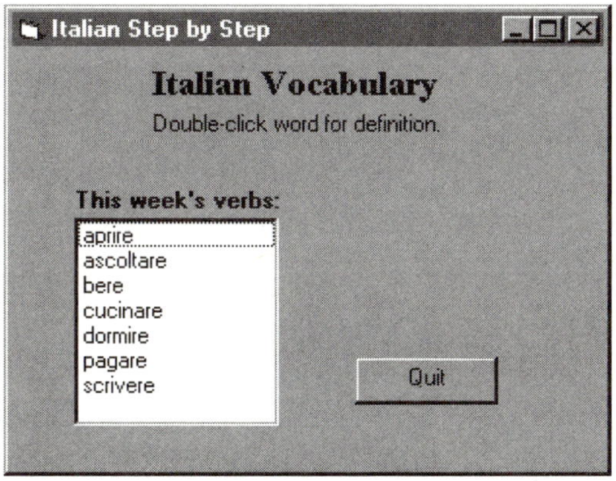

6 Double-click *dormire.*

A definition for the word *dormire* appears in a message box:

The output is displayed by the MsgBox function in an effective but rather plain dialog box.

7 Click OK to close the dialog box.

The dialog box closes, and the main form returns.

8 Click Quit to quit the program.

The programming environment returns.

Now you'll remove the MsgBox function and replace it with an extra form used to display the information. You'll use the Form button on the toolbar to create the new form in the program.

Create a second form in the program

Form button

1 Click the Form button on the toolbar to add a second form to the program.

A blank form appears in the programming environment. The new form is the same size as the original Form1 and is named Form2.

2 Resize the second form so that it's about the size and shape of a small, rectangular dialog box.

Image control

3 Click the Image control in the toolbox, and then create a medium-size image box on the left side of the form.

Label control

TextBox control

CommandButton control

You'll use this image box to hold a bit map of the Italian flag.

4 Click the Label control, and then create a label in the top middle of the form.

5 Click the TextBox control, and then create a large text box below the label in the middle of the form.

6 Click the CommandButton control, and then create a command button on the right side of the form.

7 Set the following properties for the objects on your new form:

Object	Property	Setting
Image1	Picture Stretch	"c:\vb\practice\lesson 7\flgitaly.ico" True
Label1	Font	Times New Roman, Bold, 14-point
Text1	TabStop	False
Command1	Caption	"Close"
Form2	Caption	"Definition"

> **NOTE** Setting the TabStop property of the text box to False keeps the text box from getting the focus when the user presses the TAB key. If you don't set this property, the cursor will blink in the text box when the form appears.

When you've finished setting properties, your form should look similar to the following:

Now save the new project and the new form to disk. As you know, Visual Basic requires that each form be saved under its own filename. However, more than one project can share a form. Before you save Form2, be sure that it is the active, or selected, form in the programming environment.

8 On the File menu, click the Save File As command.

The Save File As dialog box appears.

9 Save Form2 to disk under the name **My Definition.frm**. Store the form in the \Vb\Practice\Lesson 7 folder.

The second form is saved to disk and is registered in the Project window. You can switch back and forth between the forms by clicking the forms or by highlighting a form name in the Project window and then clicking the View Form button.

10 Save Form1 to disk under the name **My Word List.frm**.

Now changes you make to Form1 won't be reflected in the Italian project.

11 On the File menu, click the Save Project As command, and then save the project to disk under the name **My Italian Forms.vbp**.

Now you'll modify the Text1_DblClick event procedure to display the new form.

Access the second form in an event procedure

1 Click the first form, and then double-click the List1 object on the form.

The List1_DblClick event procedure appears in the Code window. In this event procedure, I placed a Select Case decision structure that uses a MsgBox function to display the definition of the selected Italian word. The decision structure determines the list box pick and then assigns the appropriate definition to the Def variable. Take some time to examine the decision structure if you like, and then continue.

2 Scroll to the bottom of the event procedure in the Code window.

The following MsgBox function appears:

```
MsgBox (Def), , List1.Text
```

3 Delete the MsgBox function, and then type the following program statements in its place:

The object name Form2 identifies the new form in the program.

```
Load Form2
Form2.Label1 = List1.Text
Form2.Text1 = Def
Form2.Show
```

The first statement loads Form2 into memory. (You could also preload the form in the Form_Load event procedure.) After bringing the form into memory, you can change the form's properties and get it ready for viewing. The second line puts a copy of the selected Italian word into the first label on Form2. The third line assigns the Def variable (containing the word's definition) to the text box on the new form. You're using a text box to support longer definitions in the program. If the definition fills the text box, scroll bars will appear to provide access to the whole string. Finally, the Show method displays the completed form on the screen.

Now you'll add a statement to the Close button on Form2 to close the form when the user is through with it.

4 Close the Code window, click Form2 (or display it by using the Project window), and then double-click the Close button.

Objects on different forms can have the same name.

The Command1_Click event procedure appears in the Code window. This is the event procedure associated with the first button on Form2—not the first button on Form1. Objects on different forms can have the same name, and Visual Basic has no trouble keeping them separate. However, if similar or identical names make it hard for you to tell the objects apart, you can change their names by using the Properties window.

NOTE To change an object name, select the object on the form and then use the Properties window to change the object's Name property. The Name property holds the title that Visual Basic uses to identify the object, so if you change an object name, be sure to change it everywhere in your program code. An object name should be logical so that you can easily remember what the object does. Object names, like variables, should also carry identifying prefixes. For example, a command button used to quit a program might be named cmdQuit.

5 Type the following program statement in the event procedure:

The Hide method makes your new form invisible when the user clicks Close.

```
Form2.Hide
```

This statement uses the Hide method to make Form2 invisible when the user clicks the Close button. Because Form2 was displayed in a nonmodal state, the user is free to switch between Form1 and Form2 while the program runs. The user can close Form2 by clicking the Close button.

Save Project button

Start button

6 Click the Save Project button to save your revised project to disk.

7 Click the Start button to run the program.

8 Double-click the verb *cucinare* in the list box.

The program displays the definition for the word on the second form, as shown in the following illustration:

The complete Italian Forms program is available on disk in the Lesson 7 folder.

Now practice switching back and forth between the forms.

9 Click the first form, and then double-click the word *scrivere.*

The program displays the definition for *scrivere* (to write) on the second form. Because the forms are nonmodal, you can switch between them as you wish.

10 Click Close on the second form.

The program hides the form.

11 Click Quit on the first form.

The program stops, and Visual Basic unloads both forms. The programming environment returns.

MDI Forms: Windows That Have a Parent-Child Relationship

In most of the programs you'll write, you will probably create a standard "home" form where the user does most of his or her work, and then you'll add special-purpose forms to handle the input and output of a program. However, Visual Basic also lets you set up a *hierarchy,* which is a special relationship among forms in a program that work best as a group. These special forms are called MDI (Multiple Document Interface) forms, and they are distinguished by their roles as *parent* and *child* forms. You create an MDI parent form by clicking the MDI Form command on the Insert menu, and you create an MDI child form by clicking the Form command on the Insert menu and then setting the form's MDIChild property to True. MDI forms perform like regular forms at runtime, with the following exceptions:

- All child forms are displayed within their parent form's window space.
- When a child form is minimized, it shrinks to a small title bar on the MDI form instead of appearing as a button on the taskbar.
- When the parent form is minimized, the parent and all its children appear as one button on the taskbar.
- All child menus are displayed on the parent form's menu bar. When a child form is maximized, its caption is displayed in the parent's title bar.
- You can display all the child forms of a parent form by setting the AutoShowChildren property of the parent form to True.

Parent and child forms are especially useful in so-called *document centered applications,* in which many windows are used to display or edit a document. To learn more about MDI forms and their applications, see Chapter 14, "Multiple-Document Interface (MDI) Applications," in the Visual Basic *Programmer's Guide.*

Sending Program Output to a Printer

The Printer object controls printing.

Visual Basic lets you send output to an installed printer by using the Print method. You learned about the Print method in Lesson 6 when you used it, in a loop, to display text on a form. To send output to an attached printer, you use the Print method with the Printer object. For example, the following line sends the text string "Mariners" to the Windows default printer:

```
Printer.Print "Mariners"
```

Before printing, you can also use the Printer object to adjust certain font characteristics. For example, the following code prints "Mariners" in 14-point type:

```
Printer.FontSize = 14
Printer.Print "Mariners"
```

In all, the Printer object has several dozen properties and methods that you can use to control different aspects of printing. Unlike with forms and objects you create by using controls in the toolbox, though, you can't set Printer properties by using the Properties window. Each property must be set with program code at runtime. (The Form_Load event procedure is a good place to put standard settings that you'll use every time your program runs.) However, many of the properties and methods for the Printer object are similar to keywords you've already been using with forms and objects created by using toolbox controls. The following tables list some of the more useful Printer properties and methods.

> **NOTE** For a complete listing of Printer properties and methods, search for *Printer* in the Visual Basic online Help. You can also use properties to determine the capabilities of your printer.

Property	Description
FontName	Sets the font name for the text
FontSize	Sets the font size for the text
FontBold	True sets the font style to bold
FontItalic	True sets the font style to italic
Page	Contains the page number that is being printed

Method	Description
Print	Prints the specified text on the printer
NewPage	Starts a new page in the print job
EndDoc	Signals the end of a printing job
KillDoc	Terminates the current print job

In the following exercise, you'll add basic printing support to the My Italian Forms program you created earlier in this lesson. You'll use the FontName, FontSize, and FontBold properties to change the style of the text, the Print method to send definitions to the printer, and the EndDoc method to signal the end of the printing job.

The complete Italian Forms project is available on disk in the Lesson 7 folder.

Add printer support to the My Italian Forms program

1. Open the My Italian Forms project file if it is not already open.

   If you didn't create My Italian Forms.vbp, you can load Italian Forms.vbp from disk.

2 Display the second form in the project (My Definition.frm, or Definition.frm if you're using Italian Forms.vbp).

This is the form that displays the definition for the Italian word the user double-clicks in the list box. You'll add a Print button to this form to give the user the option of printing out a copy of the definition.

CommandButton control

3 Click the CommandButton control in the toolbox, and then create a command button to the left of the Close button.

You may need to make room for the button by moving the Close button or by adjusting the size of the Label1 object. When you've finished, your revised form should look similar to the following:

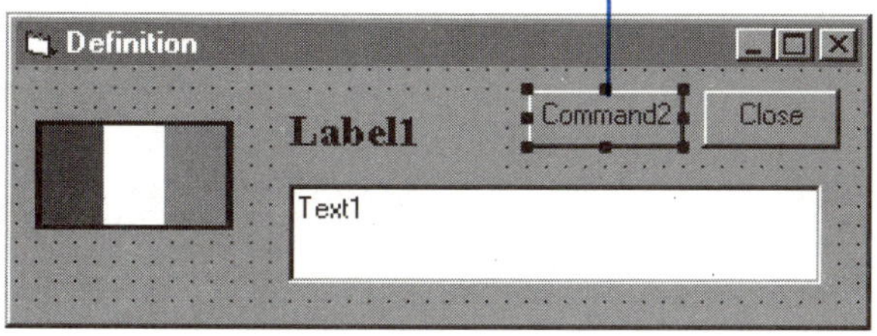

4 Change the caption of the button to "Print" by using the Properties window.

5 Double-click the new Print button to edit its event procedure.

The Command2_Click event procedure appears in the Code window.

6 Type the following printing statements in the event procedure:

```
Printer.FontName = "Arial"
Printer.FontSize = 14
Printer.FontBold = True
Printer.Print Label1.Caption
Printer.FontBold = False
Printer.Print Text1.Text
Printer.EndDoc
```

Using one of the TrueType fonts that was supplied with Windows will make your program compatible with most printers.

The purpose of each of these statements is pretty straightforward. The first three statements set the FontName, FontSize, and FontBold properties of the Printer object to settings supported by the default printer. The Arial font is supplied with most versions of Windows, and since Arial is a TrueType font, you can use it to display information on the screen and to send information to the printer. You're not limited to the printer's built-in fonts. The fourth statement uses the Print method to send the Italian word stored in the Label1.Caption property to the printer. It prints the word in bold on the first line of the current page and then instructs the printer to move to the beginning of the second line. The printer font is then set to normal, and the word definition is printed. Finally, the EndDoc method terminates the print job.

NOTE If you want to allow the user to print several word definitions on one page, you might want to postpone using the EndDoc method until the user clicks Quit to end the program.

7 On the File menu, click the Save File As command, and then save the second form as **My Print Button.frm**. This will preserve the original My Definition.frm form on disk.

8 On the File menu, click the Save Project As command, and then save the new project as **My Printer Support.vbp**.

Since you didn't save My Word List.frm under a new name, its form and code will be shared by the My Printer Support.vbp project and the My Italian Forms.vbp project. Whenever you make a change to the My Word List.frm file (on the form or in the event procedures), the change will be reflected in both projects.

The complete Printer Support project is located on disk in the Lesson 7 folder.

Now run the program if you have a printer attached to your system. Your application will use the default printer specified in the Windows Printers folder, so the device can be a local printer, a network printer, or a fax modem program. Verify that the printer is online and ready to go.

Start button

9 Click the Start button on the toolbar.

The program runs in the programming environment.

10 Double-click the Italian word *bere* in the list box.

The following definition appears:

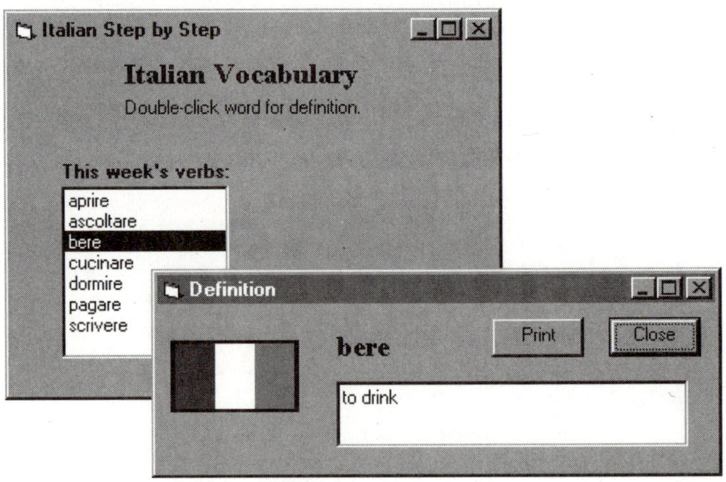

11 Click the Print button on the form to print the definition on paper.

Visual Basic sends your document to the default printer. After a few moments, the definition emerges.

WARNING If your printer is not ready to print, Windows could return an error to Visual Basic that your program is not ready to handle. This could result in a runtime error, or program crash. You'll learn how to handle runtime errors associated with disk drives, printers, and other devices later in this lesson.

12 Click Close to close the definition window, and then click Quit to end the program.

The program stops, and the programming environment returns.

Printing an Entire Form by Using the PrintForm Method

As an alternative to printing individual lines by using the Print method, you can send the entire contents of one or more forms to the printer by using the PrintForm method. This technique lets you arrange the text, graphics, and user interface elements you want on a form and then send the entire form to the printer. You can use the PrintForm keyword by itself to print the current form, or you can include a form name to print a specific form. For example, to print the contents of the second form in a program, you could enter the statement

```
Form2.PrintForm
```

in any event procedure in the program.

The following example shows how the PrintForm method can be used to print a form containing both text and graphics. In most situations, PrintForm is the easiest way to send artwork to a printer.

NOTE The PrintForm method prints your form at the current resolution of your display adapter, typically 96 dots per inch.

Use PrintForm to print text and graphics

Label control

CommandButton control

1 On the File menu, click the New Project command.
2 Click the Label control, and then create a medium-size label near the center of the form.
3 Click the CommandButton control, and then create a button in the lower right corner of the form.

4 Set the following properties for the objects in the program:

Object	Property	Setting
Label1	Caption	"Quarterly Report"
	BackStyle	0 - Transparent
	Font	MS Sans Serif, Bold, 14-point
Command1	Caption	"Print this!"
Form1	Picture	"c:\vb\practice\lesson 7\prntout2.wmf"

5 Double-click the Print This! button to open its event procedure.

6 Type the following program statement:

```
Form1.PrintForm
```

Save Project button

7 Click the Save Project button on the toolbar to save the form and the project to disk. Type **My Print Form** for the form name and for the project name.

8 Click the Start button on the toolbar to run the program.

The program displays the following output:

The complete Print Form project is located on disk in the Lesson 7 folder.

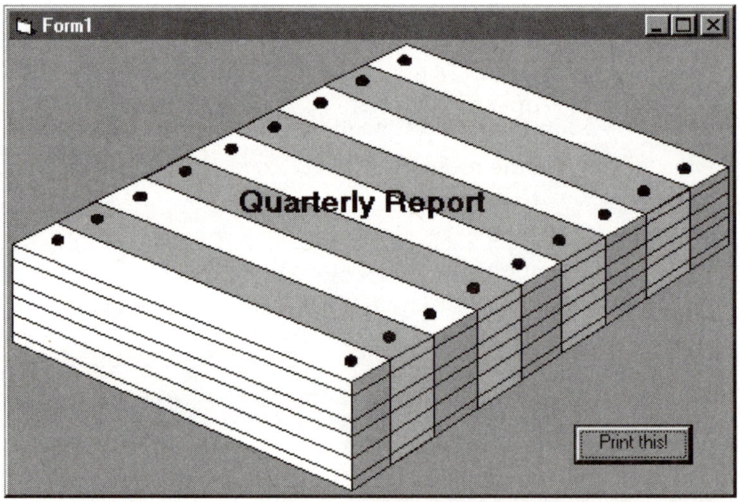

9 Click the Print This! button to print the contents of the form.

Visual Basic sends the entire contents of the form (label, Windows metafile, and command button) to the printer. While the document prints, you might see the following Visual Basic dialog box:

The PrintForm method prints all visible objects on a form.

In a few moments, the output of the program emerges from the printer.

10 Click the Close button on the form to end the program.

IMPORTANT The PrintForm method prints only the objects that are currently visible on the form. To remove unwanted objects from a printout (such as the Print This! button in the last example), set the Visible property of the objects to False before calling the PrintForm method. After you have sent the form to the printer, you can make the objects visible again.

Processing Errors by Using Error Handlers

Have you experienced a runtime error in a Visual Basic program yet? A *runtime error,* or *program crash,* is an unexpected event that happens while your program is running and that Visual Basic can't recover from. You may have experienced your first program crash in this lesson when you were trying to print, if something didn't work right. (Perhaps the printer was out of paper or was turned off and you received a printer error message from Visual Basic or Windows.) A runtime error happens anytime Visual Basic executes a statement that for some reason can't be completed "as dialed." It's not that Visual Basic isn't tough enough to handle the glitch; it's just that the compiler hasn't been told what to do when something goes wrong.

An error handler helps your program recover from runtime errors.

Fortunately, you don't have to live with occasional errors that cause your programs to crash. Visual Basic lets you write special routines, called *error handlers,* to respond to runtime errors. An error handler handles a runtime error by telling the program how to continue when one of its statements doesn't work. Error handlers are placed in the same event procedures that the potentially unstable statements are in, and they handle, or *trap,* a problem by using a special error handling object named Err. Err has a Number property that identifies the error and lets your program respond to it. For example, if a floppy disk causes an error, your error handler might display a custom error message and then disable disk operations until the user fixes the problem.

When to Use Error Handlers

Most runtime errors are caused by external events.

You can use error handlers in any situation in which an unexpected action might result in a runtime error. Typically, error handlers are used to process external events that influence a program—for example, events caused by a failed network drive, an open floppy drive door, or a printer that is offline. The table on the following page lists potential problems that can be addressed by error handlers.

Problems	Description
Network problems	Network drives or resources that fail, or "go down," unexpectedly
Floppy disk problems	Unformatted or incorrectly formatted disks, open drive doors, or bad disk sectors
Offline printers	Printers that are offline, out of paper, or otherwise unavailable
Overflow errors	Printing or drawing too much information on a form
Out-of-memory errors	Running out of application or resource space in Windows
Clipboard problems	Problems with data transfer or the Windows Clipboard
Logic errors	Syntax or logic errors undetected by the compiler and previous tests (such as an incorrectly spelled filename)

Setting the Trap: The On Error Statement

The On Error statement identifies the error handler.

The program statement used to detect a runtime error is On Error. You place On Error in an event procedure, right before you use the statement you're worried about. The On Error statement sets, or *enables,* an event trap by telling Visual Basic where to branch if it encounters an error. The syntax for the On Error statement is

```
On Error GoTo label
```

where *label* is the name of your error handler.

Error handlers are typed near the bottom of an event procedure, following the On Error statement. Each error handler has its own label, which is followed by a colon (:) for identification purposes—for example, ErrorHandler: or PrinterError:. An error handler usually has two parts. The first part typically uses the Err.Number property in a decision structure (such as If...Then or Select Case) and then displays a message or sets a property based on the error. The second part is a Resume statement that sends control back to the program so that the program can continue. In the Resume statement, you can use the Resume keyword alone, use the Resume Next keywords, or use the Resume keyword with a label you'd like to branch to, depending on which part of the program you want to continue with.

Resume, Resume Next, and Resume label *return control to the program.*

The Resume keyword returns control to the statement that caused the error (in hopes that the error condition will be fixed or won't happen again). Using the Resume keyword is a good strategy if you're asking the user to fix the problem, for example by closing the floppy drive door or tending to the printer. The Resume Next keywords return control to the statement *following* the one that caused the error. Using the Resume Next keywords is the strategy to take if you want to skip the command and continue working. You can also follow the Resume keyword with a label you'd like to branch to. This gives you the flexibility of moving to any place in the event procedure you want to go. A typical location to branch to is the last line of the procedure.

The following example shows how you can create an error handler to recover from errors associated with floppy disk drives. You'll add the error handler to a program that attempts to load a Windows metafile from a disk in drive A. You can use the same technique to add error handling support to any Visual Basic program—just change the error numbers and messages.

NOTE The following program uses an error number (from the Err.Number property) to diagnose a runtime error. To see a complete listing of error numbers, search for *error codes* in the Visual Basic online Help.

Create a disk drive error handler

1 Open the Error Handler project file.

The Error Handler form appears in the Project window.

2 Click the View Form button, and then double-click the Check Drive button on the form.

The event procedure for the Command1_Click object appears in the Code window.

This event procedure loads a Windows metafile named Prntout2.wmf from the root folder of drive A, but it currently generates an error if the file does not exist or if the floppy drive door is open.

3 Type the following statement at the top of the event procedure:

This error handler handles floppy drive problems.

```
On Error GoTo DiskError
```

This statement enables the error handler in the procedure and tells Visual Basic where to branch if a runtime error occurs. Now you'll add the DiskError error handler to the bottom of the event procedure.

4 Move one line below the LoadPicture statement, and then type the following program code:

```
Exit Sub  'exit procedure

DiskError:
If Err.Number = 71 Then  'if DISK NOT READY
    MsgBox ("Please close the drive latch."), , _
      "Disk Not Ready"
    Resume
Else
    MsgBox ("I can't find prntout2.wmf in A:\."), , _
      "File Not Found"
    Resume StopTrying
End If
StopTrying:
```

The conditional expression in the error handler's If...Then statement tests the Err.Number property to see if it contains the number 71, the error code that is returned whenever a disk drive is not functioning. If a disk error has occurred, the program gives the user the opportunity to fix the problem (either by closing the drive latch or by inserting a new disk) and then continue with the loading operation. (The LoadPicture function is attempted again with the Resume keyword.) If the error was not related to the disk drive, the program assumes that the disk was valid but that the file could not be located in the root folder. Then the error handler branches to the StopTrying: label at the bottom of the procedure. In either case, the error handler prints a message for the user and stops the program from being prematurely terminated. You could add more ElseIf statements and error numbers to the error handler to give the user more specific and useful information about the disk problem.

You can use the Exit Sub statement to skip over an error handler in a procedure.

If the program encounters no disk problems or if the user fixes an initial problem, the program proceeds until the Exit Sub statement ends the event procedure. Exit Sub is a general-purpose statement that you can use to exit any Visual Basic procedure before the End Sub statement is executed. In this case, Exit Sub prevents the error handler from running after the program successfully loads the Windows metafile.

5 On the File menu, click the Save File As command, and then save the form as **My Final Handler**.

6 On the File menu, click the Save Project As command, and then save the project as **My Final Handler**.

7 Use Windows Explorer to copy the file Prntout2.wmf from the C:\Vb\Practice\Lesson 7 folder to a floppy disk in drive A. (You need a spare floppy disk to complete this step.)

Be sure to copy the file to the root folder on the disk (A:\).

8 Remove the floppy disk from drive A, or open the drive latch.

The complete Final Handler program is available on disk in the Lesson 7 folder.

9 Click the Start button to run the program.

10 Click the Check Drive button on the form.

Visual Basic generates a runtime error, and the error handler displays the error message shown in the illustration on the facing page:

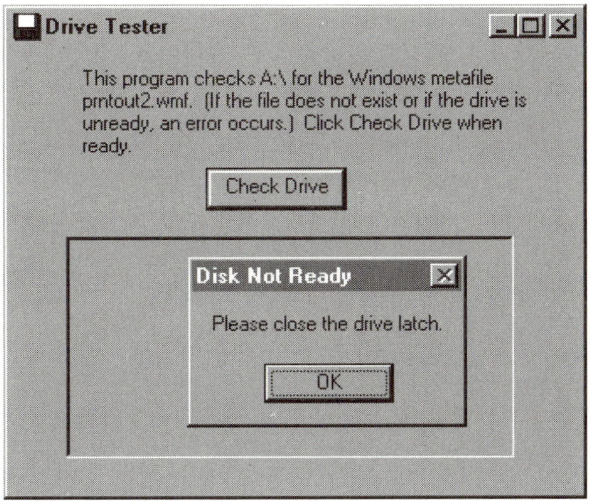

11 Insert the floppy disk that has the Windows metafile on it, or close the drive door.

12 Click OK to close the error handler and retry the loading operation.

After a few moments, the Prntout2.wmf Windows metafile is displayed on the form, as shown in the following illustration:

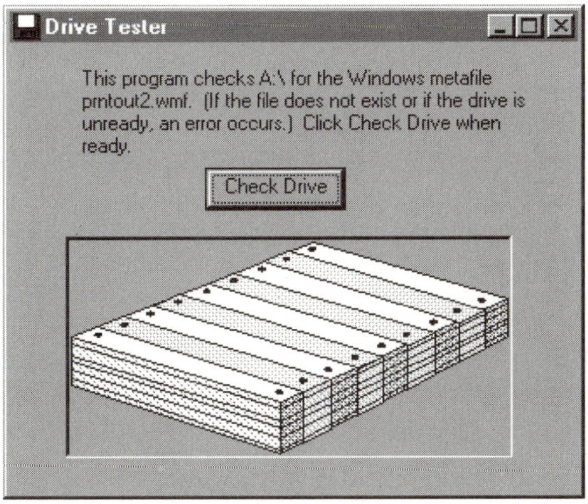

NOTE If an error message still appears, you may have a different error in your program. Try stepping through your program code by using the Debug window. Errors are easy to spot by using watch expressions, and the process shows you graphically how error handlers work.

13 Click the Close button on the form to end the program.

One Step Further: More Techniques for Error Handlers

The Err.Description property contains an explanation of a runtime error.

The Err object contains a few other properties that you might want to use to display additional information in your error handlers. The Err.Description property contains the error message returned to Visual Basic when a runtime error occurs. You can use this message as an additional source of information for the user, whether or not you plan to respond to the error programatically. For example, the following error handler uses the Description property to display an error message if an error occurs when you are loading artwork from a floppy disk.

```
On Error GoTo DiskError
Image1.Picture = LoadPicture("a:\prntout2.wmf")
Exit Sub                       'exit procedure

DiskError:
MsgBox (Err.Description), , "Loading Error"
Resume                         'try LoadPicture function again
```

You can use this technique to trap floppy disk problems such as unformatted disks, missing files, or an open drive door. The error handler uses the Resume statement to try the loading operation again when the user fixes the problem and clicks OK in the message box. When the file eventually loads, the Exit Sub statement ends the event procedure.

NOTE If you get stuck in an error loop and can't get out, press CTRL+BREAK.

Specifying a Retry Period

Another strategy you can use in an error handler is to try an operation a few times and then jump over the problem if it isn't resolved. For example, the following error handler uses a counter variable named Retries to track the number of times an error message has been displayed, and then the program skips the loading statement if it fails twice:

```
Retries = 0                 'initialize counter variable
On Error GoTo DiskError
Image1.Picture = LoadPicture("a:\prntout2.wmf")
Exit Sub                    'exit the procedure

DiskError:
MsgBox (Err.Description), , "Loading Error"
Retries = Retries + 1       'increment counter on error
If Retries >= 2 Then
    Resume Next
Else
    Resume
End If
```

This is a useful technique if the error you're handling is a problem that can occasionally be fixed by the user. The important thing to remember here is that Resume retries the statement that caused the error and that Resume Next skips the statement and moves on to the next line in the event procedure. When you use Resume Next, be sure that the next statement really is the one you want to execute, and when you continue, make sure that you don't accidentally run the error handler again. A good way to skip over the error handler is to use the Exit Sub statement; or you can use Resume Next with a label that directs Visual Basic to continue executing below the error handler.

If you want to continue to the next lesson

➤ Keep Visual Basic running, and turn to Lesson 8.

If you want to quit Visual Basic for now

➤ On the File menu, click Exit.

If you see a Save dialog box, click Yes.

Lesson Summary

To	Do this	Button
Add new forms to a program	Click the Form button on the toolbar. *or* On the Insert menu, click Form.	
Load a form into memory	Use the Load statement. For example, `Load Form2`	
Display a loaded form	Use the Show method. For example, `Form2.Show`	

To	Do this	Button
Create a modal form	Include a 1 when displaying a form. For example, `Form2.Show 1`	
Hide a form	Use the Hide method. For example, `Form2.Hide`	
Remove a form from memory	Use the Unload statement. For example, `Unload Form2`	
Change the name of an object	Change the Name property for the object in the Properties window.	
Create an MDI parent form	On the Insert menu, click the MDI Form command.	
Create an MDI child form	On the Insert menu, click the Form command, and then set the MDIChild property of the form to True.	
Send a line of text to the printer	Use the Printer object and the Print method. For example, `Printer.Print "Mariners"`	
Change printing options	Set properties of the Printer object at runtime.	
End a printing job	Use the EndDoc method. For example, `Printer.EndDoc`	
Print an entire form	Use the PrintForm method. For example, `Form2.PrintForm`	
Detect runtime errors in your programs	Enable error handling by using the statement `On Error GoTo` *`label`* where *label* is the name of the error handler.	
Process runtime errors	Create an error handling routine (usually consisting of If...Then...Else or Select Case statements) beneath a label identifying the error handler. Typical error handlers set properties and display messages to the user by using the MsgBox function.	

To	Do this	Button
Continue after an error	Use Resume, Resume Next, or Resume *label*.	
Exit a procedure before an End Sub statement	Use the Exit Sub statement.	

For online information about	On the Visual Basic Help menu, click Search For Help On, and then
Working with forms	Type **forms**
Using MDI forms	Type **MDI**
Using the Printer object	Type **Printer**
The Print method	Type **Print**
The PrintForm method	Type **PrintForm**
The Err object	Type **Err**
Visual Basic error codes	Type **error codes**

For more information on	In the Visual Basic *Programmer's Guide*, see
Using a new form as a custom dialog box	Chapter 11, "Dialogs"
Using MDI parent and child forms	Chapter 14, "Multiple-Document Interface (MDI) Applications"
Printing text and graphics	Chapter 16, "Displaying and Printing Information"
Writing an error handler	Chapter 21, "Handling Run-Time Errors"

Preview of the Next Lesson

In the next lesson, "Adding Artwork and Special Effects," you'll learn how to add special shapes and graphical buttons to your user interface. You'll also learn how to support drag-and-drop commands, work with sound, and create simple animation in your programs.

Lesson

8

Adding Artwork and Special Effects

Estimated time

55 min.

In this lesson you will learn how to:

- Use the Line and Shape controls to add artwork to a form.
- Use the Image control to create graphical command buttons.
- Add drag-and-drop support to your programs.
- Change the shape of the mouse pointer.
- Create special effects with animation.

For most developers, adding artwork and special effects to an application is the most exciting—and addicting—part of programming. Fortunately, creating impressive and useful graphical effects with Microsoft Visual Basic is both satisfying and easy. In this lesson, you'll learn how to add interesting "bells and whistles" to your programs. You'll learn how to create compelling artwork on a form, build graphical command buttons, and change the shape of the mouse pointer. You'll also learn how to add drag-and-drop support to your programs and how to create simple animation by using image and timer objects. When you've finished, you'll have the skills you need to create the ultimate user interface.

Adding Artwork by Using the Line and Shape Controls

The Line and Shape controls let you create geometric images.

You've already learned how to add bit maps, icons, and Windows metafiles to a form by creating picture box and image objects. Adding premade artwork to your programs is easy in Visual Basic, and you've had practice doing it in almost every lesson. Now you'll learn how to create original artwork on your forms by using the Line and Shape controls. These handy tools are located in the toolbox, and you can use them to build a variety of images of different shapes, sizes, and colors. The objects you create by using these controls do have a few limitations—they can't receive the focus at runtime, and they can't appear on top of other objects—but they are powerful, fast, and easy to use.

The Line Control

Line control

You can use the Line control to create a straight line on a form. You can then set a variety of properties to change the appearance of the line object you create, just as you can for other objects. The most important line object properties are BorderWidth, BorderStyle, BorderColor, and Visible. The BorderWidth property adjusts the thickness of the line on your form. This is especially useful when you are creating an underline or a line that separates one object from another. The BorderStyle property lets you make the line solid, dotted, or dashed, and the BorderColor property lets you set the color of the line to any of Visual Basic's standard colors. Finally, the Visible property lets you hide or display the line as it becomes necessary in your program.

You'll get a chance to work with the Line control after you learn a little about the Shape control.

The Shape Control

Shape control

You can use the Shape control to create rectangles, squares, ovals, and circles on your forms. You use the Shape control to draw the image you want, and then you use the Properties window to adjust the image characteristics. The Shape property controls the shape of the image; you can select a rectangle, rounded rectangle, square, rounded square, oval, or circle shape after you create the object. You can build complex images by drawing several shapes and lines. Other important shape object properties include FillColor, which lets you specify the object's color; FillStyle, which lets you specify a pattern for the fill color; and BorderColor, which lets you specify a separate color for the shape's border. A shape object also has a Visible property, which lets you hide or display your artwork as necessary.

The following exercise gives you hands-on practice using the Line and Shape controls. You'll use the controls to create an introductory welcome screen used by a fictitious business named Northwest Window Screens. The welcome screen will look like this:

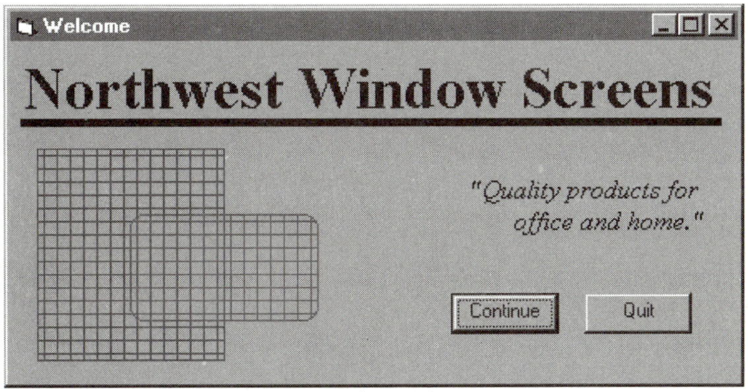

Use the Line and Shape controls

1. Start Visual Basic.

   If Visual Basic is already running, click the New Project command on the File menu.

Label control

2. Click the Label control in the toolbox, and then create a long label across the top of the form.
3. Click the Properties button on the toolbar, and then set the Caption property of the label to "Northwest Window Screens".

Properties button

4. Set the Font property of the label to Times New Roman, Bold, 26-point. Set the ForeColor property to Dark blue.

   Your label should now take up most of the width of the screen. Adjust the label width and height, if necessary, so that the business name fits on one line.

Line control

Selection handles help you resize existing lines and shapes.

5. Click the Line control in the toolbox, and then create a line under the business name. Make the line stretch across most of the form, just like the label does.

   The Line control places selection handles on either side of the line after you create it. You can use these handles to resize the line, if necessary.
6. Click the Properties button to display the Properties window, and then set the following properties for the line object:

Object	Property	Setting
Line1	BorderWidth	5
	BorderColor	Dark blue

The name of your new line object is Line1. The BorderWidth setting changes the width of the line to five twips. (A twip is 1/20 point, or 1/1440 inch.) The BorderColor setting changes the color of the line to dark blue.

Now create two window screen images on the form.

Shape control

7 Click the Shape control in the toolbox, and then create a rectangle on the left side of the form.

This rectangle is the outline of the first window screen. You'll set the FillStyle property of this object a little later to make the rectangle look like a screen.

8 Click the Shape control again, and then create a second rectangle on the left side of the form, partially overlapping the first rectangle.

The Shape control works a lot like a general-purpose drawing tool in an art program. The control creates the basic shape, and then you set properties to refine that shape.

9 Click the Properties button, and then set the following properties for the two shapes:

Object	Property	Setting
Shape1	Shape	Rectangle
	FillColor	Dark yellow
	FillStyle	6 - Cross
	BorderColor	Dark yellow
Shape2	Shape	Rounded rectangle
	FillColor	Light blue
	FillStyle	6 - Cross
	BorderColor	Light blue

10 Create a label on the right side of the form, and then set the following properties. Create a fairly narrow label so that the label caption wraps over two lines.

Object	Property	Setting
Label2	Caption	""Quality products for office and home.""
	Font	Times New Roman, Italic, 12-point
	Alignment	1 - Right Justify

CommandButton control

11 Click the CommandButton control in the toolbox, and then create a command button in the lower right corner of the form. Create a second command button to the left of the first button.

12 Set the following properties for the command buttons:

Object	Property	Setting
Command1	Caption	"Quit"
Command2	Caption	"Continue"

13 Double-click the Quit command button, type **End** in the Command1_Click event procedure, and then close the Code window.

The welcome form you are creating is intended to be a gateway to the program, but if the user wants to quit without moving on to the rest of the program, the Quit button gives him or her a way out. Since the welcome screen is the only part of this program that exists now, you'll also use the Quit button to end the program.

14 Change the Caption property of the form to "Welcome", and then resize the objects and the form so that the screen looks well proportioned.

When you've finished, your form should look similar to the following:

You can use a welcome form like this for any program you write. Its purpose is to welcome the user to the program gracefully and then let the user continue or exit as he or she sees fit. When the user clicks the Continue button, the program should hide the welcome form and then display the main form of the application.

Start button

The complete Welcome Form program is available on disk in the \Vb\Practice\Lesson 8 folder.

15 Click the Start button on the toolbar.

The Welcome form appears, as shown in the following illustration:

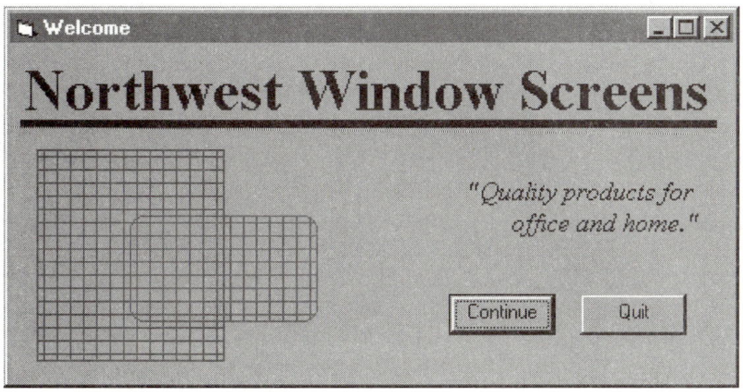

The line and shape objects appear immediately on the form and add to the general character of the welcome screen. Line and shape objects always appear faster than artwork loaded from disk does.

16 Click the Quit button to end the program.

Save Project button

17 Click the Save Project button on the toolbar, and then save your form in the Lesson 8 folder as **My Welcome Form.frm**. Save the project file as **My Welcome Form.vbp**.

Using Graphics Methods to Create Shapes

Visual Basic supports several method keywords for adding artwork to your programs. You can use these graphics methods to create special visual effects. Graphics methods are commands you use in event procedures to create images on a form or send images to a printer. The disadvantage of graphics methods is that they take considerable planning and programming to use. You need to learn the syntax of the commands, understand the coordinate system used on your form, and refresh the images if they become covered by another window. However, you can use graphics methods to create some visual effects that you can't create by using the Line control or the Shape control, such as arcs and individually painted pixels. The most useful graphics methods are Line, which creates a line, rectangle, or solid box; Circle, which creates a circle, ellipse, or "pie slice"; and PSet, which sets the color of an individual pixel on the screen.

To learn more about graphics methods and the coordinate system used on your form, see Chapter 15, "Creating Graphics for Applications," in the Visual Basic *Programmer's Guide*.

Creating Graphical Command Buttons

You can use the Image control to create toolbar-style command buttons.

You've used command buttons throughout this book to give the user an intuitive method for issuing commands. As you've learned, you create a command button by using the CommandButton control, and then you set the caption property of the button to a word that describes the command the button executes. As an alternative to creating text-based buttons, Visual Basic lets you use the Image control to create graphical buttons in your programs. A graphical button contains artwork that is a visual representation of the command executed by the button. For example, a button containing a floppy disk icon could represent a command that saves information to disk. Graphical buttons can be placed individually in programs, or they can be grouped in collections called *toolbars*. The Visual Basic toolbar is an example of this type of button grouping. In this section, you'll learn how to create authentic graphical command buttons that "push in" and "pop out" when you click them, just like the buttons you've seen in other applications for Windows.

Detecting a MouseDown Event

The MouseDown event detects the first half of a mouse button click.

To give your graphical buttons a realistic look and "feel," you'll want your program to respond as soon as the user places the mouse pointer over a graphical button and holds down the mouse button. So far you've been using the Click event to take action in your programs, but in this case Click is not good enough. Your program needs to respond when the user first *presses* the button, not after the button is released. You can track mouse activity in Visual Basic by using the MouseDown event. MouseDown is a special event that executes an event procedure whenever the user places the mouse pointer over an object on the form and then holds down the mouse button. If you write a special event procedure for the MouseDown event (such as Image1_MouseDown), your program can take action whenever the user holds down the mouse button while the mouse pointer is over the object. When you're creating graphical command buttons, you'll want your program to change the picture in the button when the user clicks, to give the button that "pushed in" look, and then execute the specified command in the program.

NOTE In addition to recognizing MouseDown events, your programs can recognize MouseUp events (generated whenever the user releases the mouse button) and MouseMove events (generated whenever the user moves the mouse).

Swapping Out Buttons

So how do you make graphical command buttons look pushed in and popped out when they are clicked in a program? As you may suspect, the icon pictures aren't modified on the screen when the user clicks the icons; the icons are replaced by other icons, or are *swapped out,* by a MouseDown event procedure. As the following illustration shows, each graphical command button has three states: up, down, and disabled.

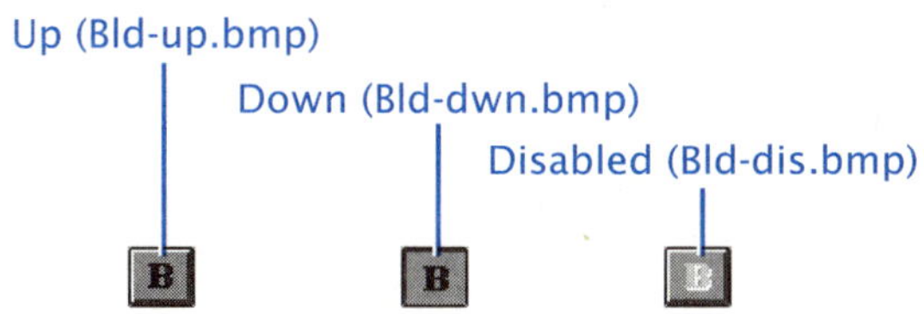

Up is the normal, or popped out, state—the appearance of the button when it is in its at rest, or default, position. Down is the selected, or pushed in, state—the appearance of the button when it has been selected or is active. Disabled is an optional state that is used when a button is not currently available for use in the program. Some graphical command buttons never use this state.

You can update button states by using the MouseDown event procedure.

In a Visual Basic program, button states are controlled by swapping icons in and out of the image object used to hold the button. The MouseDown event procedure associated with the image object handles the swapping. For the event procedure to work correctly, it must read the current state of the button (up, down, or disabled), change to the requested state, and then execute the requested command (such as changing text to boldface). The button icons can be loaded at runtime by using the LoadPicture function, or they can be swapped on the form by using assignment statements. Some programmers put all three button states on the form to make the updating quicker. If you have Visual Basic Professional Edition, you can find a large collection of useful buttons in the \Program Files\Microsoft Visual Basic\Bitmaps folder on your hard disk. (You might use the Browser program you created in Lesson 2 to view them.) The \Program Files\Microsoft Visual Basic\Bitmaps\Toolbar3 folder has an especially good collection of toolbar icons you can use to create buttons that have different states.

NOTE You can create graphical buttons and toolbars on any Visual Basic form, but MDI forms have special built-in properties that make working with collections of buttons easier. For more information about using toolbars with MDI forms, see Chapter 14, "Multiple-Document Interface (MDI) Applications," in the Visual Basic *Programmer's Guide*.

In the following exercise, you'll create a program that uses three graphical command buttons (Bold, Italic, and Underline) to format text on a form. The program uses six icons from the Lesson 8 folder to display the buttons on the form, and it uses three MouseDown event procedures to update the buttons and format the text. The following illustration shows the form you'll build.

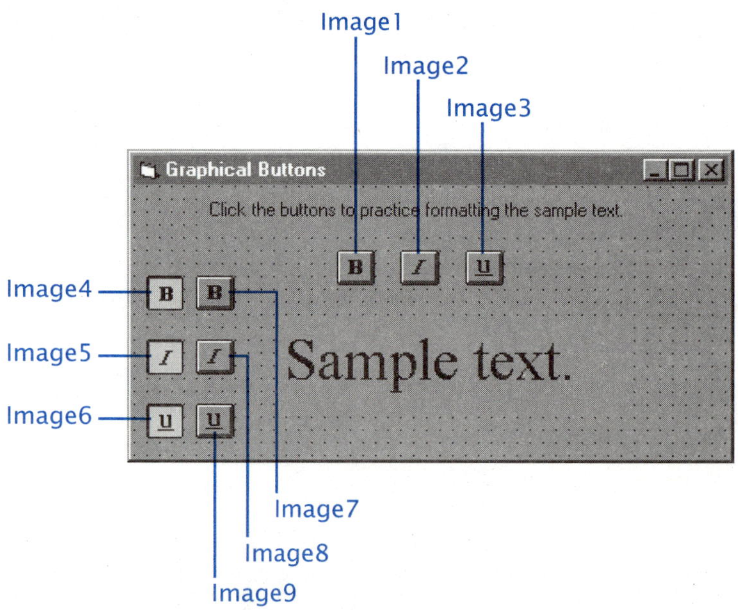

Practice creating Bold, Italic, and Underline buttons.

Label control

Image control

Create toolbar buttons

1. On the File menu, click the New Project command.
2. Resize the form so that it is the size of a medium-size dialog box.
3. Click the Label control, and then create a long label along the top edge of the form.
4. Click the Image control, and then create three small image boxes centered below the label on the form.

   These image boxes will hold the Bold, Italic, and Underline buttons you'll use in the program.
5. Create six image boxes on the left side of the form. See the previous illustration for the suggested placement of these objects.

   These image boxes will hold the six button states you'll be swapping in and out of the first three image boxes. (Alternatively, you could load these buttons from disk or store some of the states in global variables, but keeping them all on the form is fast and convenient for this example.)
6. Create a large label in the middle of the form, to hold the sample text.

   This is the label you'll format by using the toolbar buttons. You'll adjust the text by using the FontBold, FontItalic, and FontUnderline properties in the MouseDown event procedures.

   Now set the properties for the objects on the form. First, make the six swapping icons invisible on the form, and then change and format the text in the labels. Next, record the opening button states in a special image box property called *Tag*. Tag is a property you can use to include descriptive notes in an object you're working with. Tag is often used to store the name of the object, but in this case you'll use it to store the button state "Up" or "Down".

The Tag property lets you place an identification note, or tag, in an object.

7. Set the following properties for the objects.

NOTE When you set the Picture property, the image boxes adjust to the size of the toolbar icon.

Object	**Property**	**Setting**
Label1	Caption	"Click the buttons to practice formatting the sample text."
Label2	Caption Font	"Sample text." Times New Roman, 28-point
Form1	Caption	"Graphical Buttons"
Image1	Picture Tag	"c:\vb\practice\lesson 8\bld-up.bmp" "Up"

Object	Property	Setting
Image2	Picture Tag	"c:\vb\practice\lesson 8\itl-up.bmp" "Up"
Image3	Picture Tag	"c:\vb\practice\lesson 8\ulin-up.bmp" "Up"
Image4	Picture Visible	"c:\vb\practice\lesson 8\bld-dwn.bmp" False
Image5	Picture Visible	"c:\vb\practice\lesson 8\itl-dwn.bmp" False
Image6	Picture Visible	"c:\vb\practice\lesson 8\ulin-dwn.bmp" False
Image7	Picture Visible	"c:\vb\practice\lesson 8\bld-up.bmp" False
Image8	Picture Visible	"c:\vb\practice\lesson 8\itl-up.bmp" False
Image9	Picture Visible	"c:\vb\practice\lesson 8\ulin-up.bmp" False

When you've finished, your form should look similar to the following:

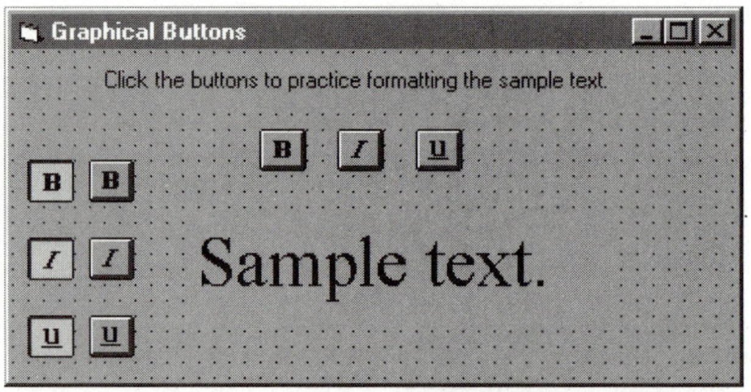

Now enter the code for the three MouseDown event procedures.

8 Double-click the Image1 object (the Bold button above the sample text) on the form.

The Image1_Click event procedure appears in the Code window. This time you'll write code for the MouseDown event rather than for the Click event. To open a different event procedure for an object, you click the event in the Proc drop-down list box.

9 Open the Proc drop-down list box in the Code window.

The drop-down list box displays the events that can be recognized by the image object.

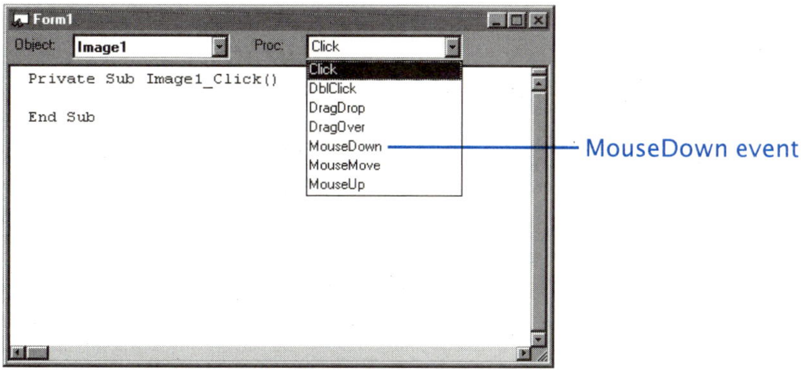

The MouseDown event procedure supplies four variables you can use in your programs.

10 Click the MouseDown event in the list box.

The Image1_MouseDown event procedure appears in the Code window. This event procedure receives four pieces of information about the MouseDown event: the mouse button pressed; the combination of ALT, CTRL, and SHIFT keys being held down (if any); the x (horizontal) screen coordinate of the mouse pointer; and the y (vertical) screen coordinate of the mouse pointer. These values are returned, or *passed,* to the event procedures in variables that you can use in your code. Although you won't use event procedure variables, or *parameters,* in this program, they can be useful tools, and many event procedures provide them. You'll learn a little about using parameters in the Drag and Drop program later in this lesson.

11 Type the following program statements in the Image1_MouseDown event procedure:

The FontBold property controls boldface formatting.

```
If Image1.Tag = "Up" Then
    Image1.Picture = Image4.Picture
    Label2.FontBold = True
    Image1.Tag = "Down"
Else
    Image1.Picture = Image7.Picture
    Label2.FontBold = False
    Image1.Tag = "Up"
End If
```

This simple If decision structure processes the two types of Bold button clicks the user can perform in the program. If the Bold button is currently in the up state, the procedure replaces the Bld-up.bmp icon with the Bld-dwn.bmp icon, changes the text to boldface, and sets the image box tag to "Down". If the button is currently in the down state, the procedure replaces the Bld-dwn.bmp icon with the Bld-up.bmp icon, cancels the boldface setting, and sets the image box tag to "Up". Whichever state the button is in, the decision structure changes it to the opposite state.

12 Open the Object drop-down list box in the Code window, and then select the Image2 object. Open the Proc drop-down list box, and then select the MouseDown event.

The Image2_MouseDown event procedure appears.

13 Type the following program statements:

The Tag property is used to determine the current button state.

```
If Image2.Tag = "Up" Then
    Image2.Picture = Image5.Picture
    Label2.FontItalic = True
    Image2.Tag = "Down"
Else
    Image2.Picture = Image8.Picture
    Label2.FontItalic = False
    Image2.Tag = "Up"
End If
```

This decision structure controls the operation of the Italic button in the program. The code is almost identical to the Image1_MouseDown procedure. The only differences are the names of the image boxes and the use of the FontItalic property instead of the FontBold property.

14 Open the Object drop-down list box, and then select the Image3 object. Open the Proc drop-down list box, and then select the MouseDown event. When the Image3_MouseDown event procedure appears, type the following program statements:

The Picture property is used to switch the buttons.

```
If Image3.Tag = "Up" Then
    Image3.Picture = Image6.Picture
    Label2.FontUnderline = True
    Image3.Tag = "Down"
Else
    Image3.Picture = Image9.Picture
    Label2.FontUnderline = False
    Image3.Tag = "Up"
End If
```

Save Project button

This decision structure controls the operation of the Underline button. It is nearly identical to the two previous procedures. You've finished building the program, so save it to disk.

15 Click the Save Project button on the toolbar. Specify the Lesson 8 folder, and then save your form as **My Graphical Buttons.frm**. Save your project as **My Graphical Buttons.vbp** in the same folder.

The complete Graphical Buttons program is available on disk in the Lesson 8 folder.

Now run the program.

Run the program and test the buttons

Start button

1 Click the Start button on the toolbar.

The My Graphical Buttons program runs, as shown in the following illustration:

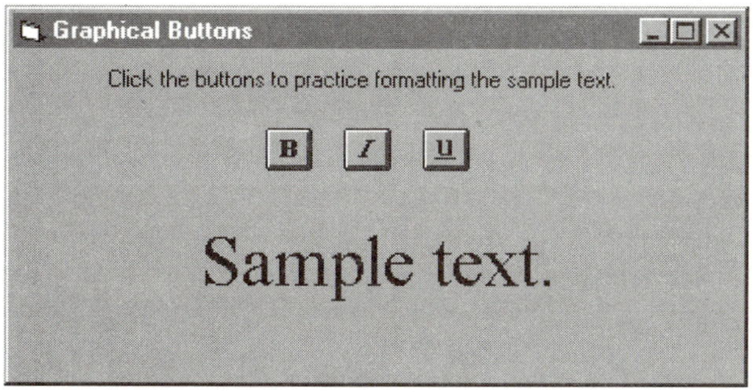

The instructions, toolbar buttons, and sample text appear on the form. You can use the three buttons in any order and as many times as you like.

2 Click the Italic button.

As soon as you hold down the mouse button, the button "pushes in" and the sample text is italicized.

3 Click the Underline button.

Your screen should look like this:

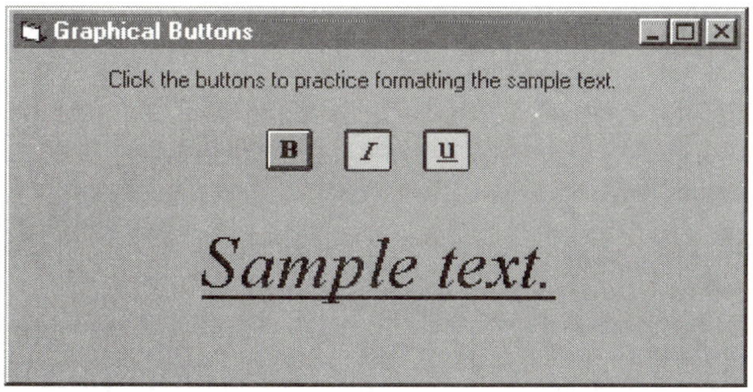

NOTE If you wanted to wait until the mouse button was released to format the text, you could still handle the icon swap in the MouseDown procedure but you could use a MouseUp event to change the font. As the programmer, you have complete control over how the buttons are used.

4 Click the Italic and Underline buttons again.

The buttons "pop out," and the text returns to normal.

5 Experiment with the Bold button to see how it works. Try using different buttons in different combinations.

End button

6 When you've finished testing the buttons, click the End button on the toolbar.

The program stops, and the programming environment returns.

Adding Drag-and-Drop Support to Your Programs

Drag-and-drop support can make your user interface more intuitive and easier to use.

In applications for Windows, users execute many commands by clicking menus and buttons with the mouse. Visual Basic lets you provide another way to perform some actions in your programs—you can allow users to use a mouse motion called *drag and drop*. Drag and drop means holding down the mouse button, dragging an object from one location to another, and then releasing the mouse button to relocate the object or to issue a command. One application of drag and drop would be to move text from one location to another in a word processing program. Another would be dragging unwanted items to a "trash can" to remove them from the screen.

The DragDrop event procedure recognizes when an object has been dropped.

You can use several properties and two event procedures to control drag-and-drop operations. You can set an object's DragMode property to 1 to allow the user to drag the object. You can also use the DragIcon property to specify that the mouse pointer appears as a picture of the dragged object while the object is being dragged. When the user drops an object on the form, Visual Basic responds to the event by executing the DragDrop event procedure for the object on which the icon was dropped. When one object is dragged over another object on the form, Visual Basic executes the DragOver event procedure for the object over which the object being dragged is located.

Drag and Drop Step by Step

To add drag-and-drop support to a program, you need to follow three general steps.

1. Enable drag and drop for the object. Visual Basic requires that you enable objects on your form for drag and drop individually. To add drag-and-drop support to an object, you set its DragMode property to 1 by using program code or the Properties window.

2. Select a drag icon. Visual Basic uses a rectangle to represent an object being dragged, but you can substitute a different drag icon if you want to. To specify a different icon, set the DragIcon property of the object to the bit map or icon you want by using program code or the Properties window.

3. Write a DragDrop or DragOver event procedure for the target object. Write an event procedure for the object that is the target, or *destination,* object of the dragging motion. Visual Basic executes the event procedure for the object onto which the dragged object is dragged or dropped. The event procedure should perform some appropriate action, such as relocating or hiding the object being dragged, executing a command, or changing the destination object in some way. You open the event procedure by clicking the destination object on the form, opening the Code window, and then clicking the DragDrop or DragOver event in the Proc drop-down list box.

The following illustration shows the three programming steps visually:

Form_Load
① Image1.Picture = LoadPicture("c:\vb\practice\lesson 8\face03.ico")
② Image1.DragMode = 1
③ Image1.DragIcon = LoadPicture("c:\vb\practice\lesson 8\face01.ico")

Image2_DragDrop
④ Image1.Visible = False

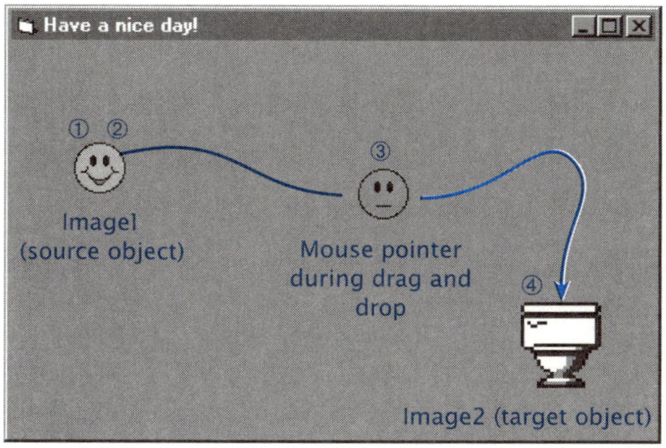

The Drag and Drop Program

The burn barrel in the Drag and Drop program gives users a place to toss unwanted items.

The following program shows you how to add drag-and-drop functionality to your applications. The program lets the user drag three items to a burn barrel on the form and then drop in a match and torch the items. The burn barrel is similar in some ways to the Windows 95 Recycle Bin or a Macintosh-style trash can. You can use the burn barrel in your programs to let the users dispose of a variety of objects, including unwanted documents, files, artwork, electronic mail, network connections, screen elements, and so on. The program uses image boxes for the screen elements, and it hides objects by setting their Visible properties to False.

Use drag and drop to create a burn barrel

1. On the File menu, click the New Project command.
2. Resize the form so that it is the size of a medium-size dialog box.
3. Click the Label control in the toolbox, and then create a long label across the top of the form.

   Label control

   This label will contain the program instructions for the user.
4. Click the Image control, and create the six image boxes shown in the illustration on the following page. Be sure to create the image boxes in the order indicated. (Create Image1 first, Image2 second, and so on.) This will ensure that when you set the image box properties in the next step, the correct icon will be placed in each image box.

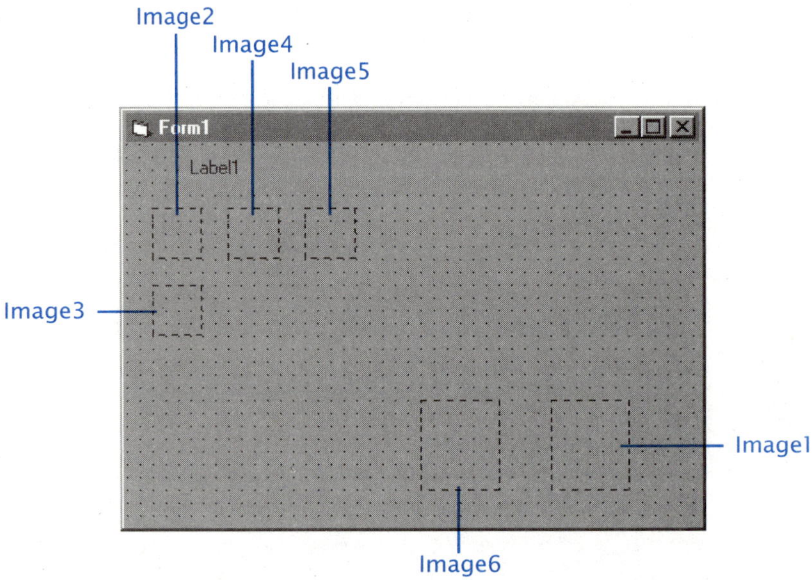

5 Set the following properties for the objects in the program. As you do, note the "Fire" setting for the Image3 Tag property. You'll use this tag to identify the match when the user drops it in the burn barrel.

Object	Property	Setting
Label1	Caption	"Throw everything away, and then drop in the match."
	Font	Times New Roman, Bold, 10-point
Form1	Caption	"Burn Barrel"
Image1	Picture	"c:\vb\practice\lesson 8\trash02a.ico"
	Stretch	True
Image2	Picture	"c:\vb\practice\lesson 8\cdrom02.ico"
	DragIcon	"c:\vb\practice\lesson 8\cdrom02.ico"
	DragMode	1 - Automatic
Image3	Picture	"c:\vb\practice\lesson 8\fire.ico"
	DragIcon	"c:\vb\practice\lesson 8\fire.ico"
	DragMode	1 - Automatic
	Tag	"Fire"
Image4	Picture	"c:\vb\practice\lesson 8\gaspump.ico"
	DragIcon	"c:\vb\practice\lesson 8\gaspump.ico"
	DragMode	1 - Automatic

The "Fire" tag will help you identify the match icon.

Object	Property	Setting
Image5	Picture	"c:\vb\practice\lesson 8\point11.ico"
	DragIcon	"c:\vb\practice\lesson 8\point11.ico"
	DragMode	1 - Automatic
Image6	Picture	"c:\vb\practice\lesson 8\trash02b.ico"
	Stretch	True
	Visible	False

When you've finished setting the properties, your form should look similar to the following:

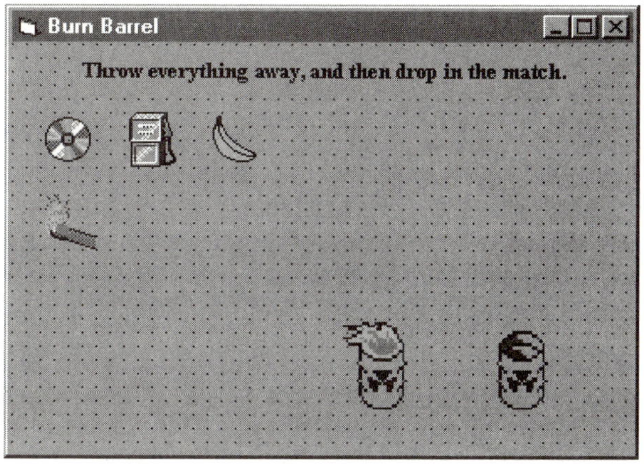

6 Double-click the Image1 object (the empty burn barrel) on the form.

The Image1_Click event procedure appears in the Code window.

7 Open the Proc drop-down list box in the Code window, and then click the DragDrop event in the list box.

The DragDrop event procedure returns three parameters that you can use in your program.

The Image1_DragDrop event procedure appears. The Sub statement of the procedure lists three parameters that are returned when an object is dropped: Source, X, and Y. The Source parameter identifies the source object that was dragged in the program. You'll use this parameter to hide the source object on the form to make it look like the object has been thrown away. You won't use the X and Y parameters in this procedure.

8 Type the following program statements in the event procedure:

```
Source.Visible = False
If Source.Tag = "Fire" Then
    Image1.Picture = Image6.Picture
End If
```

The Source variable identifies the object dropped in the burn barrel.

These are the only program statements in the program. The first line uses the Source variable and the Visible property to hide the object that was dragged and dropped. This makes it look like the item was thrown into the burn barrel. The remaining lines check whether the object thrown away was the match icon. Remember that when you set the properties for this program, you set the Tag property of the Image3 object to "Fire" to identify it as the match that would light the burn barrel. The If...Then decision structure uses Tag now to check whether the match is being thrown into the barrel. If it is, the decision structure "lights the fire" by copying the burning barrel icon over the empty barrel icon.

Save Project button

9 Click the Save Project button on the toolbar. Specify the Lesson 8 folder, and then save your form as **My Drag and Drop.frm**. Save your project as **My Drag and Drop.vbp** in the same folder.

Now run the program.

Start button

10 Click the Start button on the toolbar.

The My Drag and Drop program appears, as shown here:

The complete Drag and Drop program is available on disk in the Lesson 8 folder.

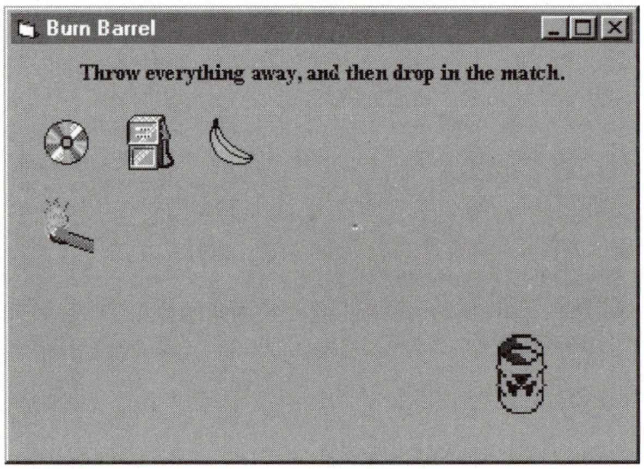

11 Drag the CD-ROM icon into the burn barrel, and then release the mouse button.

Drag icons appear as you drag objects.

As you drag the icon, the mouse pointer changes to a gray outline of the original CD-ROM icon (the DragIcon property at work). When you release the mouse button over the burn barrel, the mouse pointer changes back to its original shape and the original CD-ROM icon disappears.

12 Drag and drop the gas pump icon and the banana icon into the burn barrel.

The mouse pointer changes to the gray drag icons as you drag the elements. (The gas pump will really get the fire going.)

13 Now drop in the match.

As soon as you release the mouse button, the burn barrel starts burning, as shown in the following illustration.

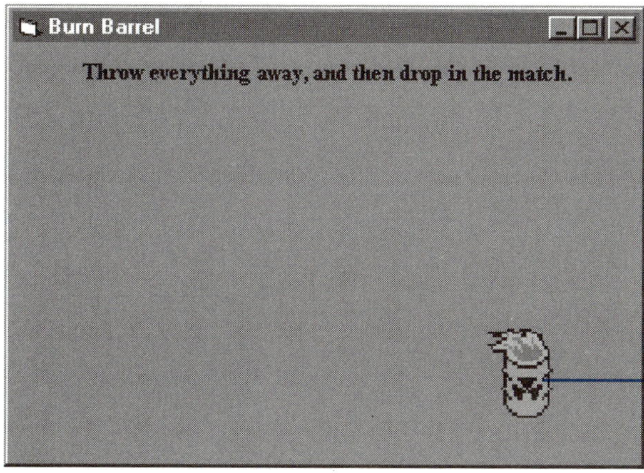

NOTE This general drag-and-drop technique has several applications. Consider using it whenever you want to give users visual feedback when the program is processing or deleting an object. For example, you could change the barrel icon to another shape and use drag and drop to process artwork, print files, send faxes and electronic mail, work with databases, or organize resources on a network. You'll find a number of interesting icons to help you with these and other tasks in the \Program Files\Microsoft Visual Basic\Icons folder.

14 Click the Close button to stop the program.

The burn barrel stops burning, and the programming environment returns.

Changing the Mouse Pointer

In the Drag and Drop program, you learned how to use the DragIcon property to change the mouse pointer during a drag-and-drop operation. You can also change the mouse pointer to one of 12 predefined pointers by using the MousePointer property, or you can load a custom pointer by using the MouseIcon property. Predefined mouse pointers let the user know graphically how the mouse should be used. You can change mouse pointers at any time in a program. If you set the MousePointer property for an object on the form, the mouse pointer will change to the specified shape when the user moves the mouse pointer over that object. If you set the MousePointer property for the form itself, the mouse pointer will change to the shape you specify unless it is over another object that has a predefined shape.

The table on the following page lists a few of the pointer shapes you can select by using the MousePointer property. (You can check the Properties window for a complete list.) If you specify shape 13 (Custom), Visual Basic uses the MouseIcon property to set the pointer shape.

Pointer	MousePointer setting	Description
	2	Crosshairs pointer for drawing
	3	Insertion pointer for text-based applications
	5	Sizing pointer. (Pointers that have the arrows pointing in other directions are available)
	11	Hourglass pointer, which indicates that the user needs to wait
	12	No-drop pointer, which indicates that the action the user is attempting to perform can't be performed

Adding Animation to Your Programs

Animation makes objects "come alive" in a program.

Switching icons and dragging objects adds visual interest to a program, but for programmers, the king of graphical effects has always been animation. *Animation* is the simulation of movement produced by rapidly displaying a series of related images on the screen. In a way, drag and drop is a "poor man's animation" because it lets you move images from one place to another on a form. Real animation involves moving objects programmatically, and it often involves changing the size or shape of the images along the way. In this section, you'll learn how to add simple animation to your programs. You'll learn how to use the Move method, update a picture box's Top and Left properties, and control the rate of animation by using a timer object.

Using a Form's Coordinate System

The Visual Basic coordinate system is a grid of rows and columns on the form.

A common trait of animation routines is that they move images in relation to a predefined coordinate system on the screen. In Visual Basic, each form has its own coordinate system. The coordinate system's starting point, or *origin,* is in the upper left corner of a form. The default coordinate system is made up of rows and columns of device-independent twips. (A twip is 1/20 point, or 1/1440 inch.) In the Visual Basic coordinate system, rows of twips are aligned to the x-axis (horizontal axis) and columns of twips are aligned to the y-axis (vertical axis). You define locations in the coordinate system by identifying the intersection of a row and column with the notation (*x*, *y*). Although you can change the coordinate system to a scale other than twips, the (*x*, *y*) coordinates of the upper left corner of a form are always (0, 0). The following illustration shows how an object's location is described in the Visual Basic coordinate system:

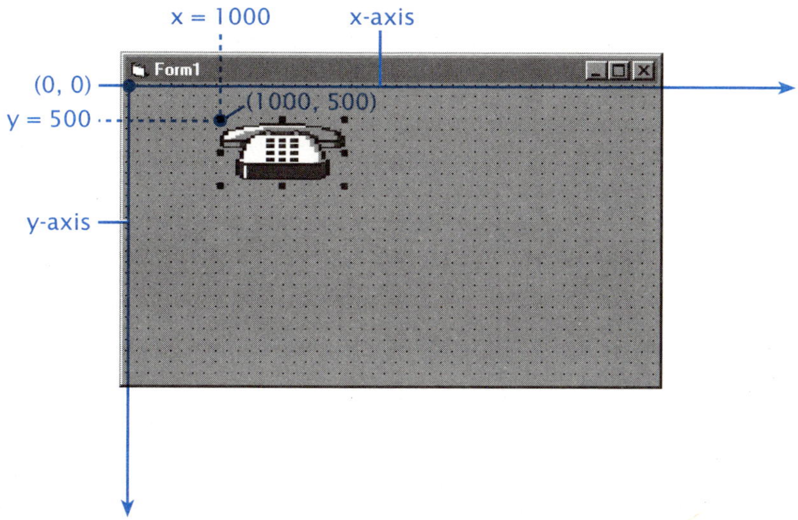

Moving Objects in the Coordinate System

The Move method moves objects.

Visual Basic includes a special method named Move that lets you move objects in the coordinate system. The basic syntax for the Move method is

```
object.Move left, top
```

where *object* is the name of the object on the form that you want to move, and *left* and *top* are the screen coordinates of the new location for the object, measured in twips. The *left* measurement is the distance between the left edge of the form and the object, and the *top* measurement is the distance between the top edge of the form and the object. (The Move method also lets you adjust the height and width of an object. See the One Step Further section toward the end of this lesson for an example.)

The Visual Basic statement

```
Picture1.Move 1440, 1440
```

moves the Picture1 object to the location (1440, 1440) on the screen, or exactly 1 inch from the top edge of the form and 1 inch from the left edge of the form. You can also use the Move method to specify a relative movement. A relative movement is the distance the object should move from its *current location.* When specifying relative movements, you use the Left and Top properties of the object (values that maintain its x-axis and y-axis location) and a + (plus) or – (minus) operator. For example, the statement

Relative movements are specified with the Left and Top properties of the object.

```
Picture1.Move Picture1.Left - 50, Picture1.Top - 75
```

moves the Picture1 object from its current position on the form to a location 50 twips closer to the left edge and 75 twips closer to the top edge.

NOTE A picture box object is usually used with the Move method because it creates less flicker on the screen than an image box object.

Creating Animation by Using the Move Method and a Timer Object

A timer object sets the pace of movement in a program.

The trick to creating animation in a program is placing one or more Move methods in a timer event procedure so that at set intervals the timer will cause one or more objects to drift across the screen. In Lesson 6, you learned to use a timer object to update a simple clock utility every second so that it displayed the correct time. When you create animation, you set the Interval property of the timer to a much faster rate—1/5 second (200 milliseconds), 1/10 second (100 milliseconds), or less. The exact rate you choose depends on how fast you want the animation to run. Another trick is to use the Top and Left properties to "sense" the top edge and the left edge of the form. Using these values in an event procedure will let you stop the animation (disable the timer) when an object reaches the edge of the form. You can also use the Top property or the Left property, or both, in an If...Then or Select Case decision structure to make an object appear to bounce off one or more edges of the form.

Adding a Smoke Cloud to the Drag and Drop Program

You can create animation by using the Move method.

The following exercise demonstrates how you can animate a picture box in a program by using the Move method and a timer object. In this exercise, you'll add a smoke cloud to the Drag and Drop program. The smoke cloud is made visible when the user drops the match in the burn barrel. Using the Move method and a timer object, the program makes the smoke cloud appear to gently drift in the wind until it flies off the form.

Create smoke animation

1. On the File menu, click the Save File As command, and then save the Drag and Drop form as **My Smoking Barrel.frm**.
2. On the File menu, click the Save Project As command, and then save the Drag and Drop project as **My Smoking Barrel.vbp**.

   Saving the form and project in new files will preserve the original Drag and Drop program on your disk.

PictureBox control

3. Click the PictureBox control in the toolbox, and then draw a small rectangle above the empty burn barrel on the form.

   You'll place a cloud icon in this picture box when you set properties.

Timer control

4. Click the Timer control in the toolbox, and then draw a timer object in the lower left corner of the form.

   The timer object (Timer1) resizes itself on the form.

5 Set the following properties for the picture box and timer:

Object	Property	Setting
Picture1	Appearance	0 - Flat
	BorderStyle	0 - None
	Picture	"c:\vb\practice\lesson 8\cloud.ico"
	Visible	False
Timer1	Enabled	False
	Interval	65

After you set these properties, your form will look similar to the following:

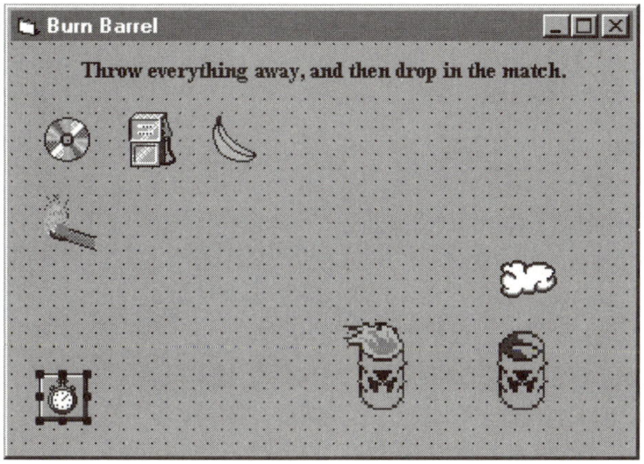

6 Double-click the empty burn barrel (the Image1 object) to edit its event procedure.

The Image1_DragDrop event procedure appears in the Code window.

7 Update the event procedure so that it looks like the one below. (The fourth and fifth lines are new.)

```
Source.Visible = False
If Source.Tag = "Fire" Then
    Image1.Picture = Image6.Picture
    Picture1.Visible = True
    Timer1.Enabled = True
End If
```

The new statements make the cloud icon visible when the barrel lights, and they start the timer running to get the cloud moving. Because you've already set the timer interval to 65 milliseconds, the timer is ready to go. You only need to add the Move method.

8 Open the Object drop-down list box in the Code window, and then click the Timer1 object.

The Timer1_Timer event procedure appears in the Code window.

9 Type the following program statements:

```
If Picture1.Top > 0 Then
    Picture1.Move Picture1.Left - 50, Picture1.Top - 75
Else
    Picture1.Visible = False
    Timer1.Enabled = False
End If
```

As long as the timer is enabled, this If...Then decision structure is executed every 65 milliseconds. The first line in the procedure checks whether the smoke cloud has reached the top of the form. If it hasn't (if its Top property is still positive), the procedure uses a relative Move method to move the cloud 50 twips closer to the left edge of the form and 75 twips closer to the top edge of the form. As you'll see when you run the program, this movement gives the cloud animation a gentle drift quality. To make the cloud drift to the right, you would simply add a positive value to the Left property. To make the cloud move down, you would add a positive value to the Top property. When the cloud reaches the top of the form, the Else clause in the Timer1_Timer procedure makes the picture invisible and disables the timer. Disabling the timer ends the animation.

To make the cloud drift to the right or down, use a positive operator with the Move method.

10 Close the Code window, and click the Save Project button to save your changes.

Save Project button

Now run the program.

11 Click the Start button on the toolbar to run the program.

The My Smoking Barrel program runs in the programming environment.

The complete Smoking Barrel program is available on disk in the Lesson 8 folder.

12 Drag and drop the CD-ROM, gas pump, and banana into the burn barrel, and then drop in the match.

The burn barrel lights, and the smoke cloud starts moving, as shown in the following illustration:

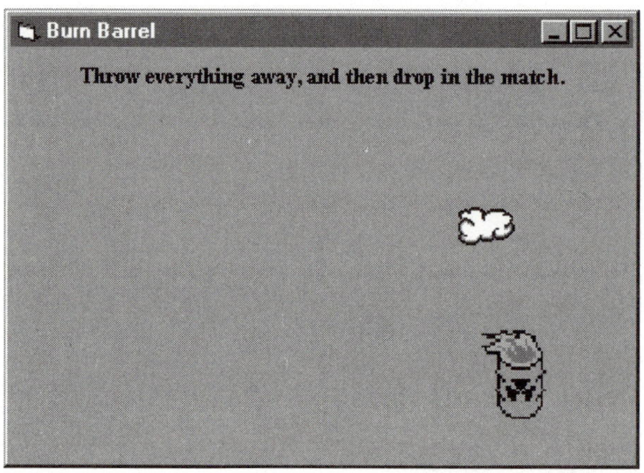

The animation stops when the cloud reaches the top of the form.

After a few moments, the cloud drifts off the edge of the screen and the animation stops.

13 Click the End button to stop the program.

Congratulations! You've added animation—and a number of other useful programming skills—to your graphics repertoire. Feel free to continue to experiment on your own with Visual Basic graphics. You'll learn a lot about programming in the process, and your users will appreciate the results.

NOTE For another example of animation with the Move method, load and run the Step Up program in the \Vb\Practice\Lesson 1 folder. The Step Up program bounces a stick of dynamite down a few steps and then displays a smoke cloud when the dynamite explodes. (The animation code is in the timer event procedures.) You might remember Step Up as the welcome program you ran in the first lesson. You've certainly come a long way since then!

Expanding and Shrinking Objects While a Program Is Running

The Height and Width properties let you expand and shrink an object.

Interested in one last special effect? In addition to maintaining a Top property and a Left property, Visual Basic maintains a Height property and a Width property for most objects on a form. You can use these properties in clever ways to expand and shrink objects while a program is running. The following exercise shows you how to do it.

Expand a picture box at runtime

Image control

1 On the File menu, click the New Project command.

2 Click the Image control in the toolbox, and then draw a small image box near the upper left corner of the form.

3 Set the following properties for the image box and the form. When you set the properties for the image box, note the current values in the Height and Width properties. (You can set these at design time too.)

Object	Property	Setting
Image1	Picture Stretch	"c:\vb\practice\lesson 8\earth.ico" True
Form1	Caption	"Approaching Earth"

4 Double-click the Image1 object on the form.

The Image1_Click event procedure appears in the Code window.

5 Type the following program code in the event procedure:

```
Image1.Height = Image1.Height + 200
Image1.Width = Image1.Width + 200
```

Increasing the Height and Width properties of the Earth icon makes the Earth icon grow.

These two lines increase the height and width of the Earth icon by 200 twips each time the user clicks the picture box. If you let your imagination run a little, watching the effect makes you feel like you're approaching the Earth in a spaceship.

The complete Zoom program is available on disk in the Lesson 8 folder.

6 Close the Code window, and then click the Start button to run the program.

The Earth icon appears alone on the form, as shown here:

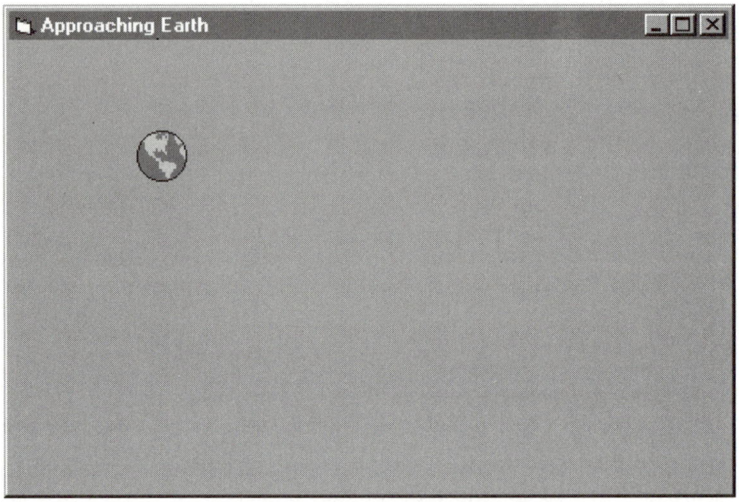

7 Click the Earth icon several times to expand it on the screen.

After 11 or 12 clicks, your screen should look similar to the following:

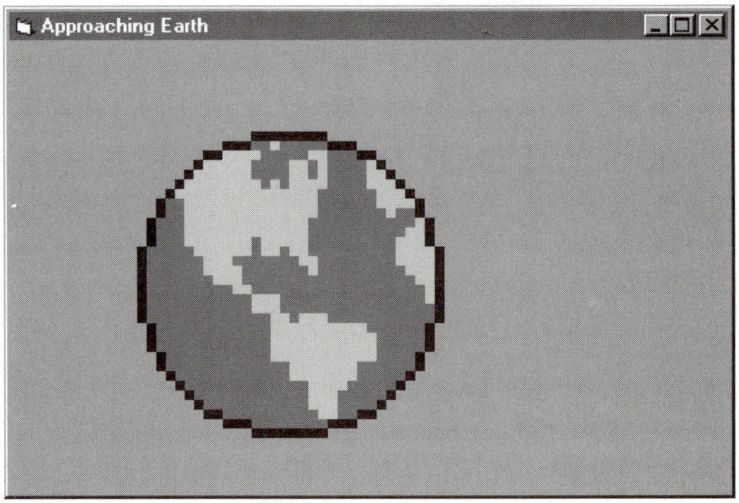

"Standard orbit, Mr. Data."

8 When you get close enough to establish a standard orbit, click the Close button to quit the program.

The program stops, and the programming environment returns.

9 Click the Save button, and then save the form to disk as **My Zoom.frm**. Save the project to disk as **My Zoom.vbp**.

One Step Further: Naming Objects in a Program

Naming interface objects helps you identify them in the program code.

Earlier in this lesson, you created the My Graphical Buttons program, which demonstrated how graphical command buttons are created and processed in a Visual Basic program. The program contains nine image box objects (Image1 through Image9) and three event procedures that display and process the buttons. In addition to showing how graphical buttons are used in a program, the exercise demonstrated the inadequacy of using the default object names to manage objects of the same type in a program. If you or another programmer revisits the My Graphical Buttons program in a few weeks, it will probably take you some time to figure out which object is doing what in the program code.

You can assign intuitive, easy-to-remember object names by using the Name property. The name you give an object must begin with a letter, and it can be no longer than 40 characters.

The solution to the problem of object name ambiguity is to assign each object a unique name by using the Name property. Each object name (like any variable name) should clearly identify the purpose of the object in the program and the control that created the object. Unique and intuitive object names will help you identify objects on the form and in the program code. Because object names are included in event procedure names and property settings in the program code, you should set an object's Name property immediately after creating the object.

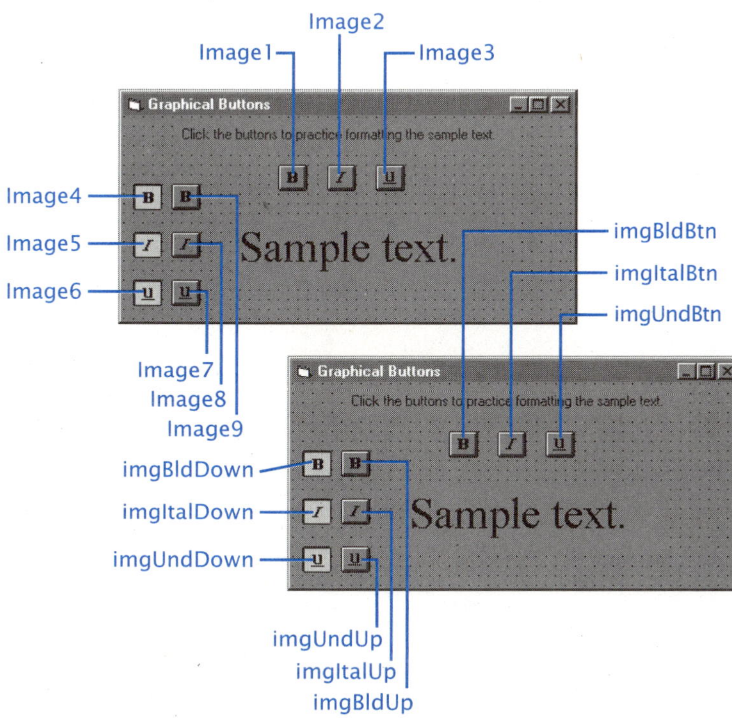

Object Naming Conventions

By convention, Visual Basic programmers use three-character prefixes to identify objects.

The Visual Basic community has agreed on a set of three-character prefixes that everyone can use in their object names. Using these standard prefixes helps programmers identify which control created an object. You can use these naming conventions for the objects you create to make your program code more descriptive and more easily understood by other Visual Basic developers. Learning the naming conventions will also help you understand the sample programs that are included with Visual Basic. In addition, the naming conventions cause objects to be listed alphabetically in groups in the Object list box in the Code window.

The following table lists the object naming conventions and includes an example of each. You'll get a chance to practice using the conventions in the next exercise.

Object	Prefix	Example
combo box	cbo	cboEnglish
check box	chk	chkReadOnly
command button	cmd	cmdCancel
common dialog	dlg	dlgOpen
data	dat	datBiblio
data-bound combo box	dbc	dbcEnglish
data-bound list box	dbl	dblPolicyCode
directory list box	dir	dirSource
drive list box	drv	drvTarget
file list box	fil	filSource
frame	fra	fraLanguage
form	frm	frmPrintForm
horizontal scroll bar	hsb	hsbVolume
image	img	imgEmptyBarrel
label	lbl	lblInstructions
line	lin	linUnderline
list box	lst	lstPeripherals
menu	mnu	mnuFileOpen
OLE	ole	oleObject1
option button	opt	optFrench
picture box	pic	picSmokeCloud
shape	shp	shpWireScreen
text box	txt	txtGetName
timer	tmr	tmrRunAnimation
vertical scroll bar	vsb	vsbTemperature

Use the Name property to change object names

1 On the File menu, click the New Project command.

Label control

2 Use the Label control to create two label objects in the center of the form, one near the top edge of the form and one in the middle.

Properties button

3 Click the Properties button on the toolbar, and then set the following properties for the label and form objects. Use the naming conventions, as indicated.

Object	Property	Setting
Label1	Caption	"Welcome to the program!"
	Name	lblWelcome
Label2	Caption	"To exit the program, click Quit."
	Name	lblInstructions
Form1	Caption	"Naming Conventions"
	Name	frmMainForm

When you set the Name properties, the names of the objects change both in the Properties window and internally in the program. The *lbl* or *frm* prefix identifies each object as a label or a form, and the rest of each object name identifies the object's purpose in the program.

CommandButton control

4 Use the CommandButton control to create a command button below the lblInstructions object.

Properties button

5 Click the Properties button on the toolbar, and then set the following properties for the command button:

Object	Property	Setting
Command1	Caption	"Quit"
	Name	cmdQuit

The *cmd* prefix identifies the object as a command button, and *Quit* describes the purpose of the button in the program.

6 Double-click the cmdQuit button to open the object's event procedure.

The event procedure cmdQuit_Click appears in the Code window. Visual Basic is using the name you entered as the official name of the object.

7 Open the Object drop-down list box in the Code window.

The list of object names appears in the list box, as shown on the following page.

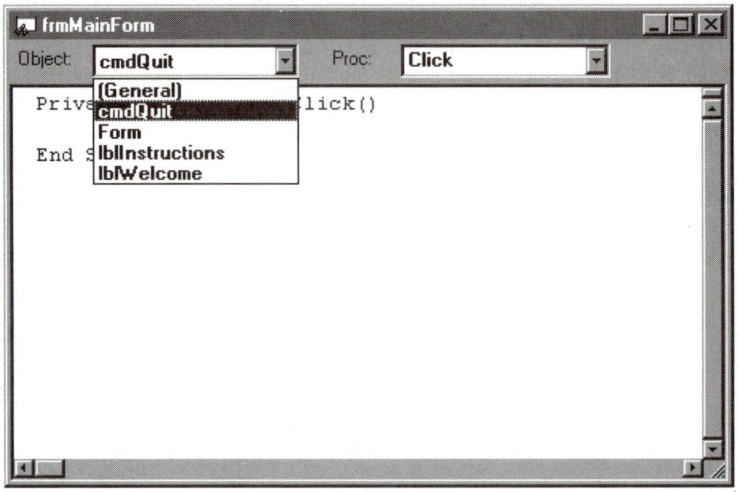

Here the value of the object naming you've done becomes immediately apparent. It's easy to recognize which object does what in the program, and other programmers will benefit from your new names too.

8 Press ESC to close the Object list box, and then type **End** in the cmdQuit_Click event procedure.

Start button

The complete Naming Conventions program is available on disk in the Lesson 8 folder.

9 Close the Code window, and then click the Start button on the toolbar to run the program.

Your screen should look similar to the following:

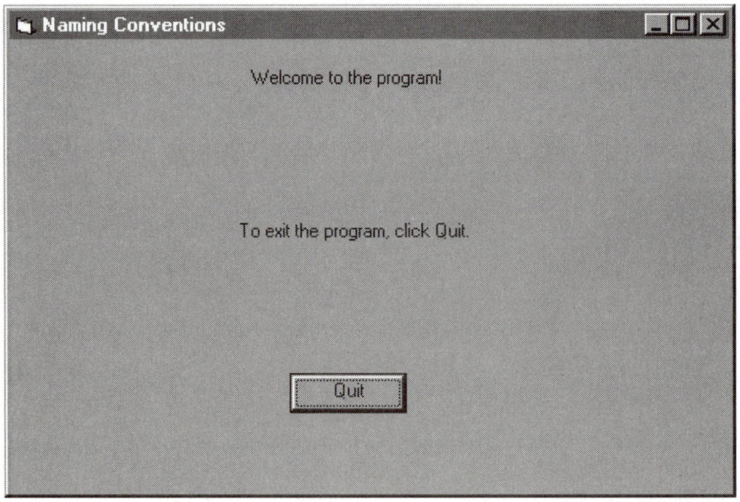

10 Click the Quit button to stop the program.

The program stops, and the programming environment returns.

Save Project button

11 Click the Save Project button on the toolbar, and then save the form as **My Naming Conventions.frm** in the Lesson 8 folder. Save the project file as **My Naming Conventions.vbp**.

IMPORTANT Assigning intuitive names to objects will really pay off when you start to write longer programs or work in a group with other programmers. In general, it's a good idea to use the naming conventions if you have more than two objects of the same type on a form.

If you want to continue to the next lesson

- Keep Visual Basic running, and turn to the Part 3 Review & Practice section or to Lesson 9.

If you want to quit Visual Basic for now

- On the File menu, click Exit.

Lesson Summary

To	Do this	Button
Create straight lines on a form	Use the Line control in the toolbox.	
Create rectangles, squares, ovals, and circles on a form	Use the Shape control in the toolbox. Set the Shape property of the object to set the shape type and characteristics.	
Create graphical command buttons	Place one or more image boxes on a form, and load bit-mapped icons into them. Put code that processes mouse clicks in MouseDown event procedures associated with the image boxes.	
Support drag and drop in a program	Enable an object for drag and drop by setting its DragMode property to 1. You can select a drag icon for the object if you want to. Write a DragDrop or DragOver event procedure for the object on which the source object will be dragged or dropped.	
Change the mouse pointer to a predefined shape	Set the MousePointer property of the form and of any related objects to one of the 12 pointer styles.	

To	Do this	Button
Specify a custom mouse pointer	Set the MousePointer property to 13, and then specify the custom pointer by using the MouseIcon property.	
Move an object on a form	Relocate the object by using the Move method. For example: `Picture1.Move 1440, 1440`	
Animate an object	Place one or more Move methods in a timer event procedure. Animation speed is controlled by the timer's Interval property.	
Expand or shrink an object at runtime	Change the object's Height property or Width property.	
Name an object	Specify a unique name in the Name property. Use the appropriate naming conventions so that the object can be identified.	

For online information about	On the Visual Basic Help menu, click Search For Help On, and then
The Line control	Type **Line**
The Shape control	Type **Shape**
Graphics methods	Type **graphics methods**
Creating graphical command buttons	Type **Image**
Drag and drop	Type **DragDrop**
Moving an object	Type **Move**

For more information on	In the Visual Basic *Programmer's Guide*, see
Line and Shape controls	Chapter 15, "Creating Graphics for Applications"
Graphics methods	Chapter 15, "Creating Graphics for Applications"
Creating graphical command buttons	Chapter 14, "Multiple-Document Interface (MDI) Applications"
Adding drag-and-drop support to programs	Chapter 12, "Responding to Mouse Events"
Changing the mouse pointer	Chapter 12, "Responding to Mouse Events"
Animation and moving objects	Chapter 15, "Creating Graphics for Applications"

Preview of the Next Lesson

The next section of this book is the Review & Practice exercise for Part 3. You can work through this Review & Practice section to review what you learned in Part 2. In Lesson 9, "Working with Text Files and Databases," you'll learn how to open and read text files in a program and how to organize your hard disk by using file system commands. You'll also learn how to open and manipulate databases by using the Visual Basic Data control.

Part

3

Review & Practice

You will review and practice how to:

- Drag and drop bit maps.
- Use the Image and Label controls.
- Use a second form for printing.
- Trap errors by using an error handler.

Estimated time
30 min.

Before you move on to Part 4, which focuses on programming techniques useful in larger development projects, you can practice the skills you learned in Part 3 by solving the programming problem in this Review & Practice section. You will use the Image control, the Label control, multiple forms, drag and drop, and an error handler to create a utility that magnifies and prints bit maps on your system.

Scenario

As an enterprising Microsoft Visual Basic programmer, you'll be anxious to find new and interesting bit maps to use for buttons and special effects in your programs. Bit map editors such as Paint let you view bit map files in their natural state, but they often don't let you examine the bit maps up close or compare different bit maps so that you can spot details. Looking at the dots, or *pixels,* of a bit map can be useful if you're interested in creating your own buttons, especially if you're curious about how the up, down, and disabled button states differ.

In this Review & Practice, your programming problem is to create a Visual Basic utility that lets you open existing bit maps on disk and view them in a magnification box. Your program should let you drag up to three bit maps from the magnification box to a scratch pad area that you can use to compare the bit maps in their natural, nonmagnified state. Your program should support drag and drop to and from the magnification box, and it should contain a print icon that prints bit maps when they are dropped on the icon. The printing routine should contain an error handler to recover from unexpected printing problems. As always, the program should have appropriate title bars, menus, and labels.

Bit Map Browser, from Part 1, will be the basis of the My Magnify utility.

An important skill for all programmers to learn is how to reuse code and forms from earlier programming projects. For this reason, the solution described here uses the Bit Map Browser program that you created in the Part 1 Review & Practice. Bit Map Browser uses menu commands and a common dialog object to open a bit map from disk and display it on the form. Bit Map Browser, with a few modifications, will be the basis of the My Magnify utility.

If you like, you can try solving this programming problem before looking at the following practice steps. Solving the problem on your own will give you some "real world" programming experience using Visual Basic and will let you express your own tastes and interests. You can also solve the problem by following the steps below carefully and reviewing the related sections in Part 3 when the need arises. The solution to the problem is available in the \Vb\Practice\Review folder, in a project file named Problem 3.vbp.

Step 1: Open the Bit Map Browser Program

The first step in building your program is designing the user interface. You'll get a head start by opening the Bit Map Browser program that you created in the Part 1 Review & Practice and using that program as the basis for your new program. Then you'll add the image box objects for the scratch pad area and the printer icon. You'll also replace the picture box object in the Bit Map Browser program with an image box object so that you can stretch the bit map that you open.

1. Start Visual Basic.
2. Open the Problem 1.vbp project in the \Vb\Practice\Review folder.
3. Click the View Form button to display the Bit Map Browser form.
4. On the File menu, click the Save File As command, and then save the form as **My Magnify.frm**. On the File menu, click the Save Project As command, and then save the project as **My Magnify.vbp**.
5. Delete the picture box object from the form, and replace it with a large, square image box object. This will be the magnification box. (An image box is required so that you'll be able to stretch, or magnify, the bit map when you open it.)
6. Use the Label control to create a label to the left of the magnification box. Set the caption for the label to "Bit map scratch pad". Then create a label to the right of the magnification box. Set the caption for the second label to "Printer drop area".

7 Use the Image control to create three icon-size image boxes below the Bit Map Scratch Pad label.

8 Use the Image control to create one icon-size image box below the Printer Drop Area label.

9 Use the Image control to create an extra icon-size image box in the lower right corner of the form.

The revised form should look similar to the following. (Note the arrangement of the image boxes.)

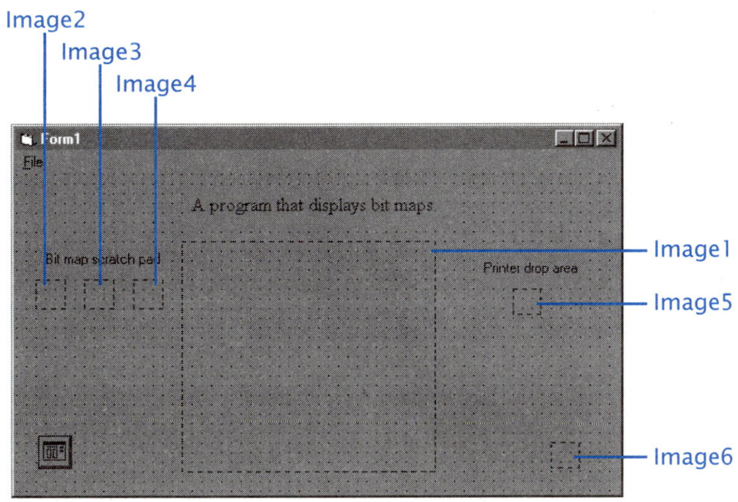

10 Set the following object properties in the program:

Object	Property	Setting
Label1	Caption	"A program that magnifies and prints bit maps."
Form1	Caption	"Bit Map Magnifier"
Image1	BorderStyle DragMode Stretch	1 - Fixed Single 1 - Automatic True
Image2	BorderStyle DragMode Stretch	1 - Fixed Single 1 - Automatic True
Image3	BorderStyle DragMode Stretch	1 - Fixed Single 1 - Automatic True

Object	Property	Setting
Image4	BorderStyle	1 - Fixed Single
	DragMode	1 - Automatic
	Stretch	True
Image5	Picture	"c:\vb\practice\review\prt-up.bmp"
Image6	Picture	"c:\vb\practice\review\prt-dis.bmp"
	Visible	False

11 Click the Save Project button to save your revised form and project to disk.

For more information on	See
Using the Label and Image controls	Lesson 2
Enabling drag and drop	Lesson 8
Using graphical command buttons	Lesson 8

Step 2: Create a Second Form for Printing

Now you'll create a second form for printing the bit maps in the program. The second form is a behind-the-scenes object that never appears when the program runs. Its sole purpose is to receive a bit map and to print it by using the PrintForm method. A simple label on this form identifies the selected bit map. The form is printed by the Image5_DragDrop event procedure.

1 Click the Form button on the toolbar.

2 Resize the new form so that it is a large rectangle, taller than it is wide.

3 Use the Label control to create a large label at the top of the form.

4 Use the Image control to create a large, square image box below the label.

5 Set the following properties for the objects on the form:

Object	Property	Setting
Label1	Caption	"Enlarged Bit Map"
	Font	Times New Roman, Bold, 20-point
Image1	Stretch	True

The completed form should look similar to the following:

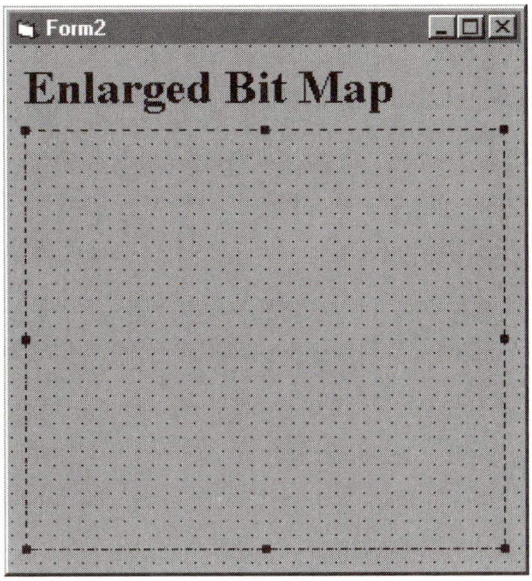

6 On the File menu, click the Save File As command, and save the form as **My Print.frm**.

For more information on	See
Adding new forms to a project	Lesson 7
Using the PrintForm method	Lesson 7

Step 3: Write the Program Code

The next step in building the program is writing the program code associated with the objects in the user interface. To complete the My Magnify program, you need to change Form1's Picture1 object name to Image1 in the mnuOpenItem_Click and mnuClose-Item_Click event procedures, and then you need to write DragDrop event procedures for Form1's image boxes Image1 through Image5.

1 Close Form2, and then open Form1 if it is not already open.

2 Click the File menu on the My Magnify menu bar, and then click the Open command.

3 Change the object name in the third line of the mnuOpenItem_Click event procedure from Picture1 to Image1.

4 Open the Object drop-down list box in the Code window, and then click the mnuCloseItem object. In the mnuCloseItem_Click event procedure, change the Picture1 object name to Image1.

5 Open the Object drop-down list box in the Code window, and then click the Image1 object. Open the Proc drop-down list box, and then click the DragDrop procedure.

The Image1_DragDrop event procedure appears in the Code window.

6 Type the following program statements:

```
Image1.Picture = Source.Picture
mnuCloseItem.Enabled = True
```

7 Open the Image2_DragDrop event procedure, and then type the following statement:

```
Image2.Picture = Source.Picture
```

8 Open the Image3_DragDrop event procedure, and then type the following statement:

```
Image3.Picture = Source.Picture
```

9 Open the Image4_DragDrop event procedure, and then type the following statement:

```
Image4.Picture = Source.Picture
```

10 Open the Image5_DragDrop event procedure, and then type the following statements:

Use the form name and a period when you want to set properties on a form other than the current form. In this case, you are using it to set properties on Form2 while Form1 is the current form.

```
Load Form2
Form2.Image1.Picture = Source.Picture
On Error GoTo PrinterError
Form2.PrintForm
Unload Form2
Exit Sub

PrinterError:
MsgBox (Err.Description), , "Printer Error"
MsgBox ("Printing feature disabled"), , "Bit Map Magnifier"
Image5.Enabled = False
Image5.Picture = Image6.Picture
Resume Next
```

This block of statements is responsible for printing bit maps that are dropped onto the printer icon in the program. The PrinterError error handler processes any printing errors that occur during the routine and disables printing if the user cannot fix the problem. (Windows 95 also includes an error handler that responds to common printing problems.) The drag-and-drop printing feature of the program is disabled in the error handler by setting the Enabled property of the Image5 object to False. You can use this technique to disable any object in a program. To let the user know that printing is disabled, the error handler displays an error message by using the MsgBox function and then switches the "up" printer icon (Image5.Picture) with the "disabled" printer icon (Image6.Picture) on the form.

NOTE You can delete unwanted empty event procedures from the Code window by selecting the empty event procedures and pressing DEL. Visual Basic automatically creates Click event procedures when you select objects that don't already have event procedures in the Object drop-down list box.

11 Click the Save Project button on the toolbar to save your program statements to disk.

For more information on	See
Writing code for drag-and-drop events	Lesson 8
Loading and programming forms	Lesson 7
Writing error handlers	Lesson 7
Swapping button icons	Lesson 8

Step 4: Run the Program

After the program is complete, you need to run it in the programming environment and test the drag-and-drop and printing features to verify that they are working correctly. When you've finished testing the program, you can compile it as an executable file if you wish.

1 Click the Start button on the toolbar.

2 On the File menu, click the Open command.

3 Open a bit map in the \Vb\Practice\Lesson 8 folder. The bit map should appear in the bit map magnification box.

4 Drag the bit map to one of the scratch pad boxes on the left.

5 Open a different bit map (perhaps a different state of the same graphical command button) by using the Open command, and then drag the bit map to one of the scratch pad boxes.

6 Open a third bit map, and drag it to the last scratch pad box.

Your screen should look similar to the following:

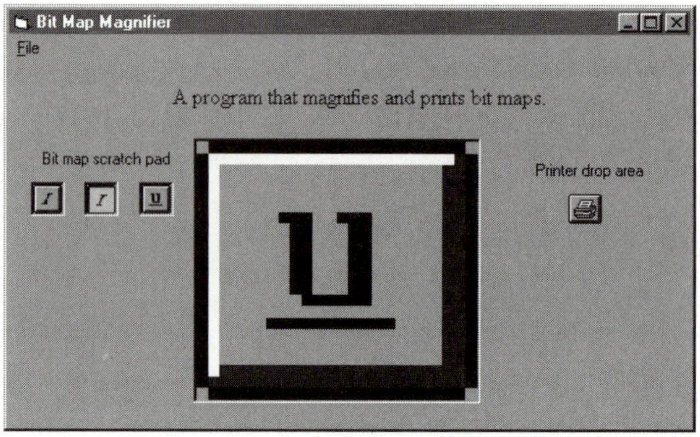

7 Turn your printer on, and verify that it is online and in working order.

8 Drag the bit map from the magnification box to the printer icon, and then drop it.

The message "Printing" appears in a dialog box, and the bit map is sent to the printer.

9 Test the drag-and-drop printing operation from each of the scratch pad boxes. If a printing error occurs, verify that the error handler properly displays a message and disables the printing icon. (If the printing error is detected by Windows 95 first, it will handle the error.)

10 When you've finished, click the Exit command on the My Magnify File menu.

For more information on	See
Testing a program containing an error handler	Lesson 7
Creating an executable file	Lesson 1

Part

4

Managing Corporate Data

Lesson

9

Working with Text Files and Databases

In this lesson you will learn how to:

Estimated time
50 min.

- Display a text file by using a text box object.
- Save notes in a text file.
- Create a database viewer by using the Data control.
- Search for information in a database.
- Add and delete database records.
- Back up files by using the FileCopy statement.

In this lesson you'll learn how to work with information stored in text files and databases on your system. You'll learn how to open a text file and display its contents by using a text box object, and you'll learn how to create a new text file on disk. You'll also learn how to open existing databases by using a data object, how to search for specific items, and how to add and delete database records. Microsoft Visual Basic was specifically designed to create custom interfaces, or *front-ends,* for existing databases, so if you'd like to customize or dress up data you've already created with another application, such as Microsoft Access, you can get started immediately.

Displaying Text Files by Using a Text Box Object

The simplest way to display a text file in a program is to use a text box object. You can create text box objects in a variety of sizes, and if the contents of the text file don't fit neatly in the text box, you can add scroll bars to the text box so that the user can examine the entire file. To load the contents of a text file into a text box, you need to use three statements and one function. These keywords are described in the following table and will be demonstrated in the first exercise in this lesson.

You can use four Visual Basic keywords with text files.

Keyword	Description
Open	Opens a text file for input or output
Line Input	Reads a line of input from the text file
EOF	Checks for the end of the text file
Close	Closes the text file

Opening a Text File for Input

Text files contain recognizable characters.

A text file consists of one or more lines of numbers, words, or characters. Text files are distinct from document files, which contain formatting codes, and from executable files, which contain instructions for the operating system. Typical text files on your system will be identified by Windows Explorer as "Text Documents" or will have the extension .txt, .ini, .dat, or .bat. Because text files contain only ordinary, recognizable characters, you can easily display them by using text box objects.

A common dialog object displays the Open common dialog box.

You can let the user decide which text file to open in a program by using a common dialog object to prompt the user for the file's pathname. Common dialog objects support the ShowOpen method, which displays the Open common dialog box on the screen. The pathname the user selects in the dialog box is returned to the program in the FileName property, and you can use this name to open the file. The common dialog object doesn't open the file; it just gets the pathname.

The Open Statement

After you get the pathname from the user, you open the file in the program by using the Open statement. The syntax for the Open statement is:

```
Open pathname For mode As #filenumber
```

where *pathname* is a valid Microsoft Windows pathname, *mode* is a keyword indicating how the file will be used (you'll use the Input and Output modes in this lesson), and *filenumber* is an integer from 1 through 255. The file number will be associated with the file when it is opened. You then use this file number in your code whenever you need to refer to the open file. There's nothing special about file numbers; Visual Basic just uses them to keep track of the different files you open in your program.

A typical Open statement using a common dialog object looks like this:

```
Open CommonDialog1.FileName For Input As #1
```

Here the CommonDialog1.FileName property represents the pathname, Input is the mode, and 1 is the file number.

> **NOTE** Text files that are opened by using this syntax are called *sequential files* because their contents must be worked with in sequential order. By contrast, you can access the information in a database file in any order.

The following exercise demonstrates how you can use a common dialog object and the Open statement to open a text file. The exercise also demonstrates how you can use the Line Input and EOF keywords to display the contents of a text file in a text box and how you can use the Close keyword to close a file.

Run the Text Browser program

1 Start Visual Basic if it is not already running.

2 Click the Open Project button on the toolbar.

Open Project button

3 Select the \Vb\Practice\Lesson 9 folder, and then double-click the filename Text Browser.

The Text Browser program loads into the programming environment.

The complete Text Browser program is located on disk in the Lesson 9 folder.

4 Click the View Form button in the Project window.

The Text Browser form appears, as shown in the following illustration:

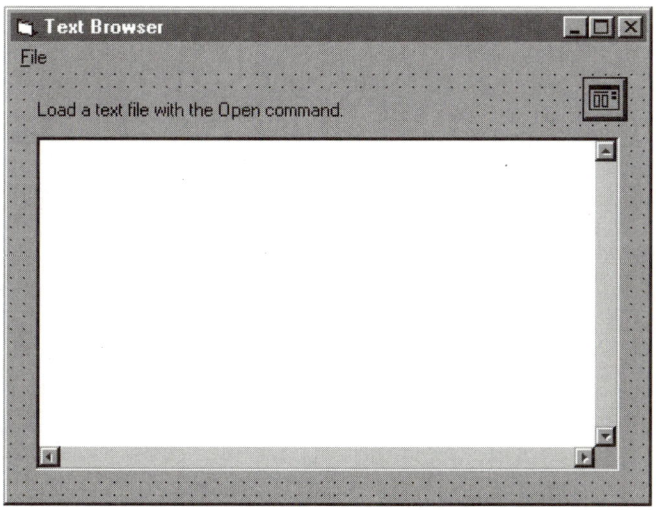

The form contains a large text box object that has scroll bars. It also contains a common dialog object, a label that provides operating instructions for the program, and a File menu containing Open, Close, and Exit commands. The following property settings have been made. Note especially the text box settings.

Object	Property	Setting
txtFile	Enabled	False
	Multiline	True
	Name	txtFile
	ScrollBars	3 - Both
	Text	(Empty)
mnuItemClose	Enabled	False
	Name	mnuItemClose
lblFile	Caption	"Load a text file with the Open command."
	Name	lblFile
Form1	Caption	"Text Browser"

Start button

5 Click the Start button on the toolbar.

The Text Browser program starts to run.

6 On the File menu, click the Open command.

The Open dialog box appears, as shown in the following illustration:

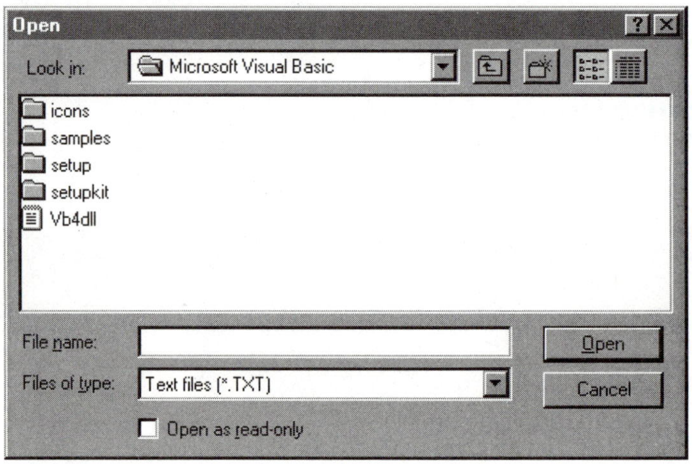

7 Select the \Vb\Practice\Lesson 9 folder, and then double-click the filename Badbills in the Open dialog box.

Badbills, a text file containing an article about counterfeit money written in 1951, appears in the text box:

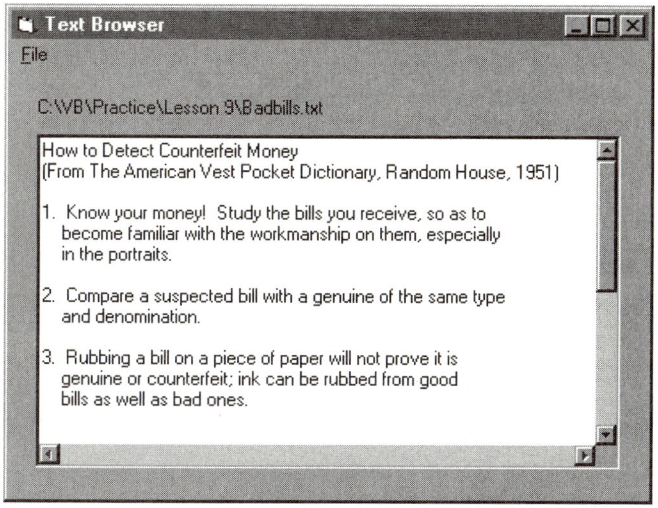

8 Use the scroll bars to view the entire document. Memorize step 5.

9 When you've finished, click the Close command on the File menu to close the file, and then click the Exit command to quit the program.

The program stops, and the programming environment returns. Now you'll take a look at two important event procedures in the program.

Examine the Text Browser program code

1 On the File menu, click the Open command.

The mnuItemOpen_Click event procedure appears in the Code window.

2 Click the Maximize button in the Code window to expand the Code window to its full size.

The Code window appears maximized, as shown in the illustration on the following page.

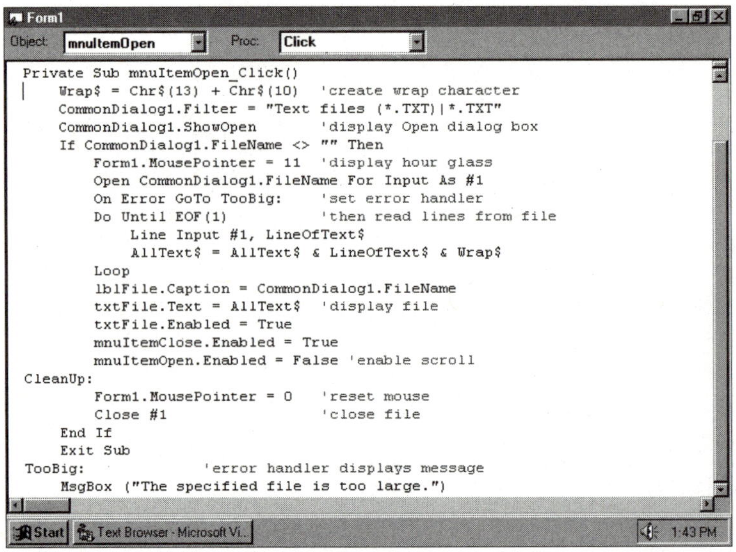

This event procedure performs the following actions. The Visual Basic statements used are shown in parentheses.

- Prompts the user for a pathname by using a common dialog object
- Opens the specified file for input (Open...For Input)
- Copies the file one line at a time into a string named AllText$ (Line Input)
- Copies lines until the end of the file is reached (EOF) or until there is no more room in the string. The AllText$ string has room for 64 KB of characters
- Displays the AllText$ string in the text box and enables the scroll bars
- Handles any errors that occur (On Error GoTo)
- Closes the file (Close) and updates the File menu commands and the mouse pointer

3 Take a moment to see how the statements in the mnuItemOpen_Click event procedure work—especially the Open, Line Input, EOF, and Close keywords.

For more information about these statements, check the Visual Basic online Help. The TooBig: error handler in the procedure displays a message and aborts the loading process if a file bigger than 64 KB has been selected by the user. This is necessary because of the 64-KB string size limitation of the text box object.

If you select a file that is several pages long, Visual Basic will take a few moments to load it. For this reason, I used the MousePointer property to change the pointer to an hourglass shape until the file is displayed on the screen. It's always a good idea to give users some visual feedback if they have to wait for more than a second or so for an action to occur.

4. Open the Object drop-down list box, and then click mnuItemClose to display the mnuItemClose_Click event procedure.

   This procedure runs when the Close menu command is executed. The procedure clears the text box, dims the Close command, enables the Open command, and disables the text box.

5. When you've finished looking at the Text Browser program code, close the Code window.

Now you can use this simple program as a template for more advanced utilities that process text files. In the next exercise you'll learn how to type your own text into a text box and how to save the text and text box to disk in a file.

Creating a New Text File on Disk

You use the keywords For Output in the Open statement when you want to create a new file on disk.

To create a new text file on disk by using Visual Basic, you'll use many of the objects and keywords you used in the last example. Creating new files on disk and saving data to them will be useful if you plan to generate custom reports or logs, save important calculations or values, or create a special-purpose word processor or text editor. Here's an overview of the steps you'll need to follow in the program:

1. Get input from the user or perform mathematical calculations, or both.
2. Assign the results of your processing to one or more variables. For example, you could assign the contents of a text box to a variable named InputForFile$.
3. Prompt the user for a pathname by using a Save As common dialog box. You use the ShowSave method of a common dialog object to display the dialog box.
4. Use the pathname received in the dialog box to open the file for output (Open...For Output).
5. Use the Print # statement to save one or more values to the open file (Print #).
6. Close the file when you've finished (Close).

The Print # statement sends output to the specified file.

The following exercise demonstrates how you can use text box and common dialog objects and the Open, Print #, and Close statements to create a simple note taking utility. You can use this tool to take notes at home or at work and then to stamp them with the current date.

Run the Quick Note program

Open Project button

1. Click the Open Project button on the toolbar.
2. Select the \Vb\Practice\Lesson 9 folder, and then double-click the project Quick Note.

   The Quick Note program loads into the programming environment.

3. Click the View Form button in the Project window.

The Quick Note form appears, as shown in the following illustration:

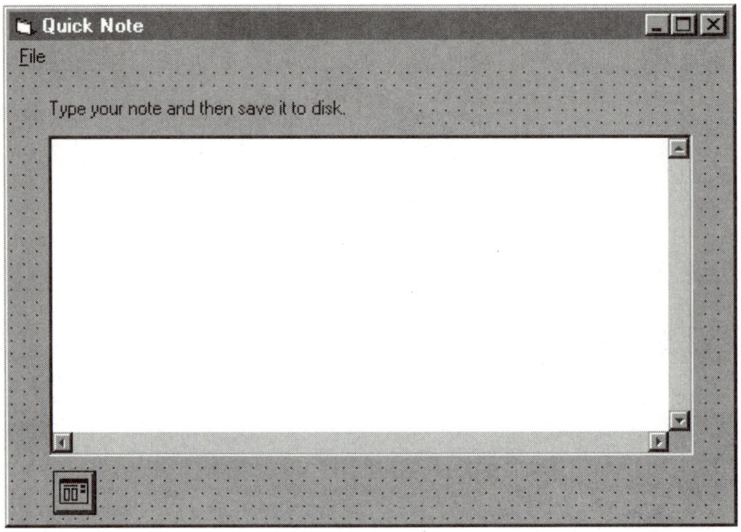

The form contains a large text box object that has scroll bars. It also contains a common dialog object, a label that provides operating instructions for the program, and a File menu containing Save As, Insert Date, and Exit commands. The following property settings have been made:

Object	Property	Setting
txtNote	Multiline	True
	Name	txtNote
	ScrollBars	3 - Both
	Text	(Empty)
Label1	Caption	"Type your note and then save it to disk."
Form1	Caption	"Quick Note"

Start button

4 Click the Start button on the toolbar.

The Quick Note program starts to run.

5 Type the following text, or some text of your own, in the text box:

```
How to Detect Counterfeit Coins

1.  Drop coins on a hard surface. Genuine coins have a bell-like
    ring; most counterfeit coins sound dull.
2.  Feel all coins. Most counterfeit coins feel greasy.
3.  Cut edges of questionable coins. Genuine coins are not easily cut.
```

When you've finished, your screen should look similar to the following:

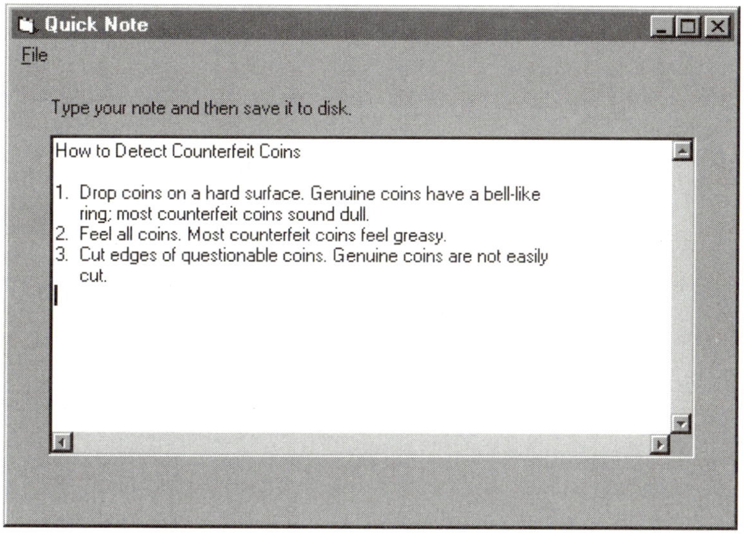

NOTE To copy text from the Windows Clipboard into the text box, press SHIFT+INS. To copy text from the text box to the Windows Clipboard, select the text by using the mouse and then press CTRL+C.

Now try using the commands on the File menu.

6 On the File menu, click the Insert Date command.

The current date appears as the first line in the text box:

Current date added to file

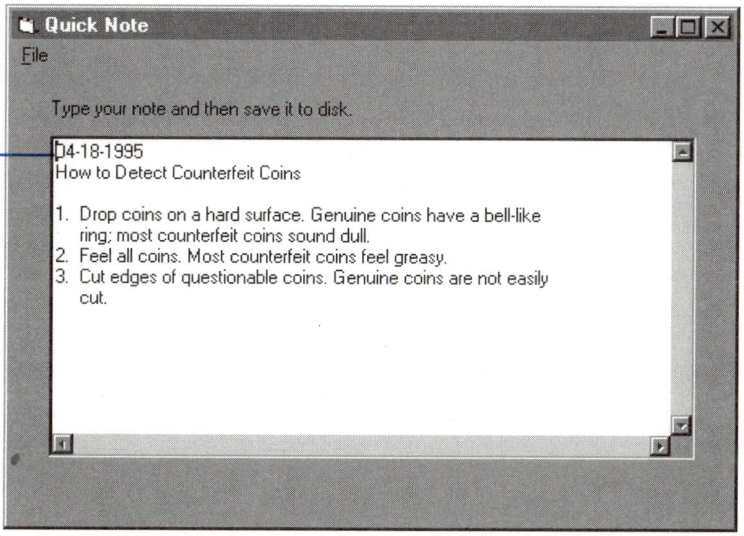

The Insert Date command provides a handy way to include the current date in a file. This is useful if you're creating a diary or a log book.

7 On the File menu, click the Save As command.

8 In the Save As dialog box, select the \Vb\Practice\Lesson 9 folder if it is not already selected. Then type **Badcoins.txt** in the File Name text box, and click Save.

The text of your document is saved to disk in the new text file Badcoins.txt. Now you'll quit the program.

9 On the File menu, click the Exit command.

The program stops, and the programming environment returns. Now you'll take a look at the event procedures in the program.

Examine the Quick Note program code

1 On the File menu, click the Insert Date command.

The mnuItemDate_Click event procedure appears in the Code window, as shown in the following illustration:

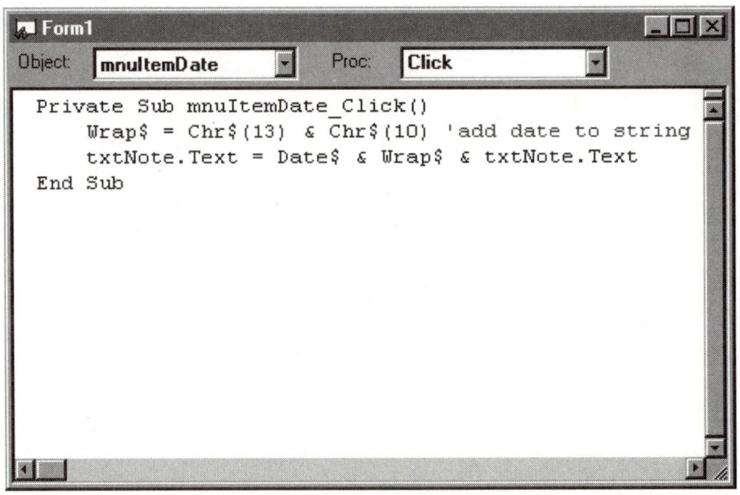

The Dates$ function retrieves the current date.

This event procedure adds the current date to the text box by linking together, or *concatenating,* the current date (generated by the Date$ function), a carriage return, and the Text property. You could use a similar technique to add the current time or any other information to the text in the text box.

2 Take a moment to see how the concatenation statements work, and then open the mnuItemSave_Click event procedure.

This block of statements uses a common dialog object to display a Save As common dialog box, opens the specified file for output as file number 1, writes the value in the txtNote.Text property to disk by using the Print # statement, and closes the text file. Note especially the statement

The Print # statement takes a file number as its first argument.

```
Print #1, txtNote.Text
```

which assigns the entire contents of the text box to the open file. Print # is similar to the Print method, except the output goes to the specified file rather than to the screen or the printer. The important thing to note here is that the entire file is stored in the txtNote.Text string.

3 Take a moment to review the Open, Print #, and Close statements, and then close the Code window.

You've finished with the Quick Note program. You've learned enough in these two examples to go a long way with text files. For more information about working with sequential files, consult the Visual Basic online Help.

Managing Databases

Visual Basic can read from and write to a variety of database formats.

As you learned in Lesson 2, a database is an organized collection of information stored electronically in a file. You can create powerful databases by using a variety of database products, including Microsoft Access, Microsoft FoxPro, Btrieve, Paradox, and dBASE. You can also use Open Database Connectivity (ODBC) client-server databases such as Microsoft SQL Server. If you regularly work with databases—especially the databases listed above—you should consider using Visual Basic as a powerful tool to enhance and display your data. Since Visual Basic implements the same database technology that is included with Microsoft Access (a database engine called Microsoft Jet), you can create basic custom database applications with just a few dozen lines of program code.

In this section, you'll learn how to use a Visual Basic data object to manage the Biblio.mdb database included with the Visual Basic software and within Access. Biblio.mdb is an Access database containing a bibliography of books about database programming. You'll learn how to display multiple records in a database, search for specific information in a database, add new records, delete unwanted records, and back up files. When you've finished, you'll be able to put these skills to work in your own database projects.

Creating Customized Database Applications

Customized database applications present personalized lists of database fields and records.

A customized database application is a program that takes the fields and records of a database and displays them in a way that is meaningful for a specific group of users. For example, a public library might create a customized version of its card catalog for a group of scientific researchers. Customized database applications typically present a variety of commands to their users. The commands allow users to use viewing filters; to search for, print, add, and delete records; and to make backup copies of the database. Because of the peculiarities of their design or subsequent evolution, some databases are organized in a way that makes them difficult to use in their original form or database environment. With Visual Basic, you can build a custom database application that displays just the information that your users want, and you can supply just the commands they need to process the data.

Using Bound Controls to Display Database Information

Bound controls process database information automatically.

Most objects you create by using the Visual Basic toolbox controls have the built-in ability to display database information. In database terminology, these objects are called *bound controls*. An object is bound to a database when its DataSource property is set to a valid database name and its DataField property is set to a valid table in the database. A *table* is a group of fields and records that you or someone else defined when the database was created. As you learned in Lesson 2, you can link your Visual Basic program to a database by using a data object. After the connection has been established, you can display database information by using objects created with any of the standard controls shown in the following table:

Control	Description
	CheckBox
	ComboBox
	DBCombo (data-bound combo box)
	DBList (data-bound list box)
	Image
	Label
	ListBox
	PictureBox
	TextBox

NOTE The third and fourth controls in the table on the facing page (DBList and DBCombo) are similar to the ListBox and ComboBox controls, but they contain additional properties that let them handle multiple tables of database data. For more information about these advanced controls, see Chapter 23 in the Visual Basic *Programmer's Guide*.

Using Text Box Objects to Display Data

The following program uses one data object and four text box objects to display four database fields from the Biblio.mdb database. It demonstrates how you can create a custom database application to view only the information you want. In this application, the ReadOnly property of the data object is set to True, so the information in the database can be viewed but can't be changed. To allow users to make changes to the Biblio.mdb database, set the ReadOnly property to False by using the Properties window.

NOTE To keep the original Biblio.mdb database unchanged, use Windows Explorer to make a backup copy of it before you complete the following exercises.

Run the Data Browser program

Open Project button

1. Click the Open Project button on the toolbar.
2. Select the \Vb\Practice\Lesson 9 folder, and then double-click Data Browser.vbp.

   The Data Browser program loads into the programming environment.
3. Click the View Form button in the Project window.

   The Data Browser form appears, as shown in the following illustration:

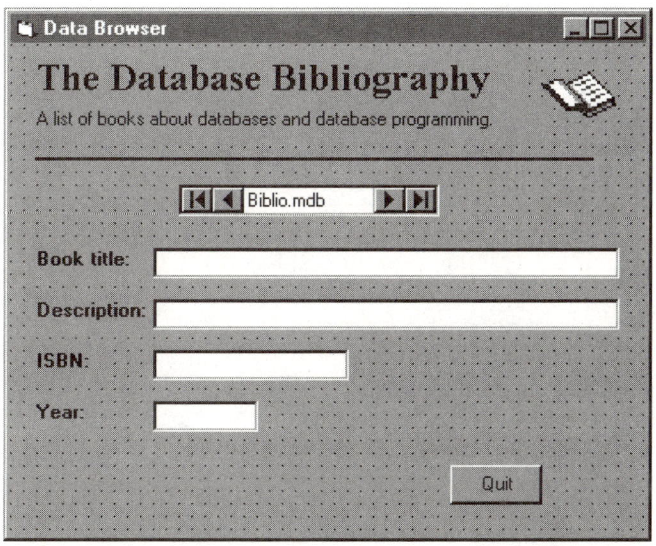

The form contains information about the program, artwork, a data object, several labels and text boxes, and a command button. The following property settings have been made for the data object and the text box objects, which are the objects involved with data transfer. To examine the property settings for the other objects, use the Properties window.

Object	Property	Setting
datBiblio	Caption	"Biblio.mdb"
	Connect	Access
	DatabaseName	"c:\program files\microsoft visual basic\biblio.mdb"
	Name	datBiblio
	ReadOnly	True
	RecordsetType	0 - Table
	RecordSource	Titles
txtTitle	DataField	Title
	DataSource	datBiblio
	Name	txtTitle
	Text	(Empty)
txtISBN	DataField	ISBN
	DataSource	datBiblio
	Name	txtISBN
	Text	(Empty)
txtYear	DataField	Year Published
	DataSource	datBiblio
	Name	txtYear
	Text	(Empty)

The data object has its RecordSource property set to Titles and its DatabaseName property set to "c:\program files\microsoft visual basic\biblio.mdb", and the three text boxes have identical DataSource properties (datBiblio) and individual field settings for the DataField properties. This establishes the basic link between the bibliography database on disk, the data object in the program, and the individual text fields on the form. The other properties fine-tune these basic settings.

NOTE If your copy of Biblio.mdb is not in the C:\Program Files\Microsoft Visual Basic folder (the default location), update the DataSource property of the data object to the correct pathname in your program.

Start button

4 Click the Start button on the toolbar.

The Data Browser program starts, and the first record of the Titles table in the Biblio.mdb database appears on the form.

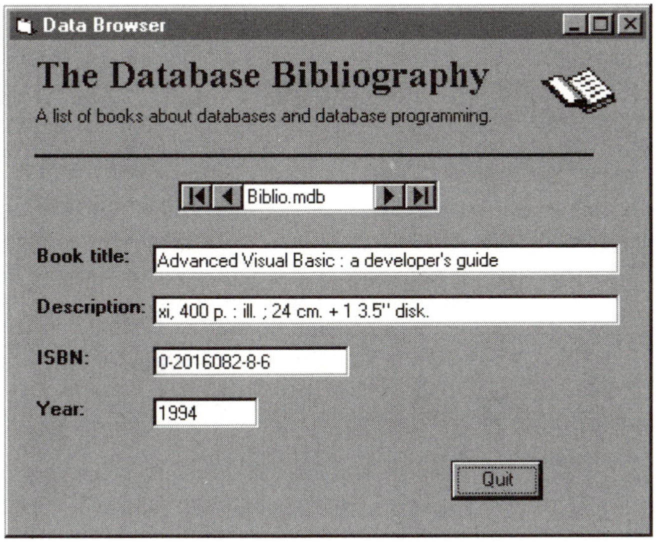

5 Click the inside right arrow to view the second record in the Titles table.

The record for the book *Building Database Applications in Visual Basic* appears on the form. Each time you scroll in the database, all three text boxes are updated.

6 Click the outside right arrow to view the last record in the Titles table.

The record for the book *Visual Basic - Multimedia Primer* appears.

7 Click the Quit button to stop the program.

The Data Browser program ends.

This program contains only one line of program code (the End statement), but it still gives you quite a bit of information. The nice thing about it is that it displays only the fields *you* want to see in the Biblio database. By using a data object and several data-bound text boxes, you can create an effective database application.

Using a Recordset Object

A Recordset object represents the data you're working with in the program.

In the Data Browser program, you used a data property named RecordsetType to identify your database information as a table. In Visual Basic, a *Recordset* is an object representing the part of the database you're working with in the program. The Recordset object includes special properties and methods that let you search for, sort, add, and delete records. In the following exercise, you'll use a Recordset object to search for book titles in the Biblio.mdb database.

Search for data in Biblio.mdb

Before you modify the program, you'll save it under a new name to protect the original.

1 On the File menu, click the Save File As command. Save the Data Browser form as **My Data Finder.frm**.

2 On the File menu, click the Save Project As command. Save the project as **My Data Finder.vbp**.

CommandButton control

3 Click the CommandButton control, and then create a command button object on the lower left side of the form.

4 Set the following properties for the command button object:

Object	Property	Setting
Command1	Caption	"Find"
	Name	cmdFind

5 Double-click the Find command button to open the cmdFind_Click event procedure in the Code window.

6 Type the following program statements in the event procedure:

The Seek method searches for a matching record.

```
prompt$ = "Enter the full (complete) book title."
'get the string to be used in the Title field search
SearchStr$ = InputBox(prompt$, "Book Search")
datBiblio.Recordset.Index = "Title"      'use Title table
datBiblio.Recordset.Seek "=", SearchStr$ 'and search
If datBiblio.Recordset.NoMatch Then      'if no match
    MsgBox ("Sorry, I couldn't find your book.")
    datBiblio.Recordset.MoveFirst        'go to first record
End If
```

This event procedure displays a search dialog box to get a search string from the user (SearchStr$) and uses the Seek method to search the database Title field from beginning to end until it finds a match or reaches the end of the list. If no match is found, a message is displayed and the first record in the Recordset appears. The following Recordset properties and methods are used in the event procedure:

Recordset property or method	Description
Index	A property used to define the database field that will be used for the search
Seek	A method used to search for the record. In addition to =, the relational operators >=, >, <=, and < can be used to compare the search string to text in the database
NoMatch	A property set to True if no match is found in the search
MoveFirst	A method that makes the first record in the Recordset the current record

Save Project button

7 Close the Code window, and click the Save Project button to save your changes to disk.

Now you'll run the program.

Run the My Data Finder program

Start button

The complete Data Finder program is available on disk in the Lesson 9 folder.

1 Click the Start button on the toolbar.

Information from the Titles table in the Biblio.mdb database appears in the text boxes, as before.

2 Click the Find button.

The Book Search dialog box appears, as shown in the following illustration:

3 Type **Using SQL** in the dialog box, and press ENTER.

The cmdFind_Click event procedure searches the Title field of the database and stops on the following record:

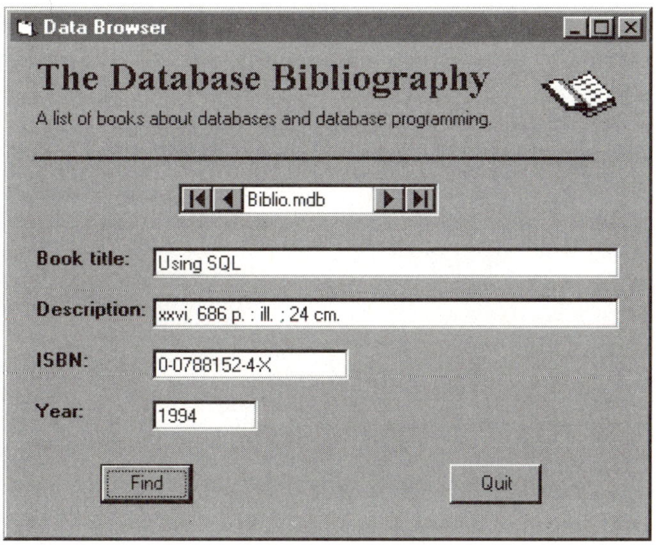

4 Click the Find button again, type **Pez**, and press ENTER.

The event procedure doesn't find a book named *Pez,* so the following message box appears:

5 Click OK to close the message box.

The current record changes to the first record in the database (the MoveFirst method at work).

6 Click the Quit button to end the program.

The program stops, and the programming environment returns.

Adding Records to the Biblio.mdb Database

To add a new record to a database, you set the data object's ReadOnly property to False in design mode, and then you use the AddNew method in an event procedure to open a new record in the database. When the blank record appears on the form, the user fills in the necessary fields, and when finished, moves to a different record in the database. The easiest way for the user to move to a different record is to click one of the buttons on the data object. When the user moves to a different record, the new record is inserted into the database in alphabetical order.

The following exercise demonstrates how the ReadOnly property and the AddNew method can be used to insert new records in a database. An InputBox function gives the user some visual feedback during the process.

Let users add records to the database

Before you modify the program, you'll save it under a new name to protect the original.

1 On the File menu, click the Save File As command. Save the My Data Finder form as **My Add Records.frm**. Use the Save Project As command to save the project as **My Add Records.vbp**.

Properties button

2 Click the datBiblio object (the data object) on the form, and then click the Properties button on the toolbar.

3 Change the datBiblio object's ReadOnly property to False.

The ReadOnly property determines how the Biblio.mdb database will be opened. Setting this property to False lets the user make changes to the database and insert new records.

CommandButton control

4 Click the CommandButton control, and then create a command button object to the right of the Find button on the form.

5 Set the following properties for the command button object:

Object	Property	Setting
Command1	Caption	"Add"
	Name	cmdAdd

Your form should look similar to the following illustration:

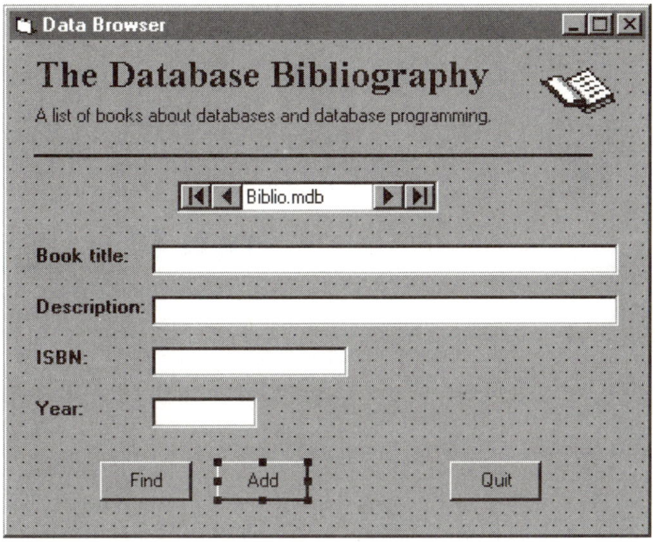

6 Double-click the Add button to open the cmdAdd_Click event procedure in the Code window.

7 Type the following program statements in the event procedure:

The AddNew method adds a new record to the database.

```
prompt$ = "Enter new record, and click left arrow button."
reply = MsgBox(prompt$, vbOKCancel, "Add Record")
If reply = vbOK Then                   'if the user clicks OK
    txtTitle.SetFocus                  'move cursor to Title box
    datBiblio.Recordset.AddNew         'and get new record
    'set PubID field to 14             (this field is required
    datBiblio.Recordset.PubID = 14     'by Biblio.mdb)
End If
```

The procedure first displays a dialog box containing data entry instructions for the user. The MsgBox function uses the vbOKCancel argument (a numeric constant defined by Visual Basic) to display a dialog box that has OK and Cancel buttons. If the user clicks OK, a new record is created by using the AddNew method. If the user clicks Cancel, the operation is skipped. The event procedure also uses the SetFocus method to place the cursor in the Title text box. The SetFocus method can be used to activate any object that can receive the focus.

The last statement in the If decision structure uses program code to set the PubID field in the Biblio.mdb database. Each new record requires this field, and because your database browser didn't contain it, you had to enter the PubID manually. The value 14 means that the book will be published by Microsoft Press.

Save Project button

8 Close the Code window, and then click the Save Project button on the toolbar to save your changes.

Now you'll use the Add button to add a record to the database.

Run the My Add Records program

Start button

The complete Add Records program is available on disk in the Lesson 9 folder.

1 Click the Start button on the toolbar.

Information from the Titles table in the Biblio.mdb database appears in the text boxes.

2 Click the Add button.

The Add Record dialog box appears, as shown in the following illustration:

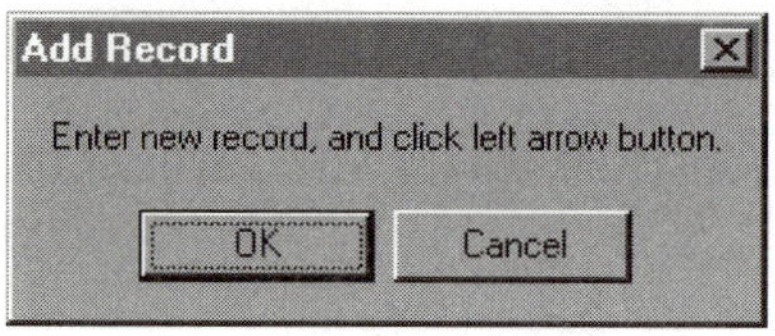

3 Click the OK button.

A new, blank record appears on the form. Enter the information shown in the following illustration for the new record, pressing TAB between fields:

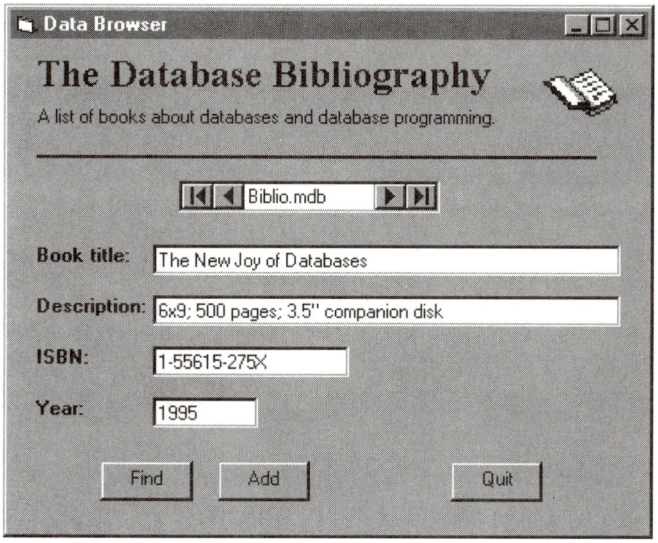

4 When you've finished entering the fictitious record, click the outside left arrow button on the data object.

The record for *The New Joy of Databases* is inserted in the database as the last record. The first record in the database is then displayed on the form.

5 Click the Find button, type **The New Joy of Databases**, and press ENTER.

The record for *The New Joy of Databases* appears on the form.

6 Click the inside left arrow button on the data object.

The record for *The Microsoft Visual Basic Workshop* appears on the form. You can use the Add button to add any number of records to the Biblio.mdb database.

7 Click the Quit button to end the program.

The program stops, and the programming environment returns.

Deleting Records from the Biblio.mdb Database

To delete a record from a database, you display the record you want to delete and then you use the Delete method with the Recordset object to remove the record. Before you open the database in the program, you must set the data object's ReadOnly property to False. (You also did this before using the AddNew method earlier.) After you delete the record, you should display a new record in the database because the data object doesn't do this automatically. Usually the best technique is to use the MoveFirst method to display the first record in the database.

The following exercise shows how you can use Visual Basic to delete records from the Biblio.mdb database. Pay particular attention to the use of the MsgBox function in the program. Because the data object doesn't provide an "undo" feature, it is important that the program verify the user's intentions before it permanently deletes a record from the database.

WARNING The Delete method permanently deletes a record from the database. Don't give your users access to this method unless you want them to be able to delete records.

Let users delete records from the database

Before you modify the My Add Records program, you'll save it under a new name to protect the original.

1 On the File menu, click the Save File As command. Save the My Add Records form as **My Delete Records.frm**. Use the Save Project As command to save the project as **My Delete Records.vbp**.

Properties button

2 Click the datBiblio object (the data object) on the form, and then click the Properties button on the toolbar.

3 Verify that the datBiblio object's ReadOnly property is set to False.

CommandButton control

4 Click the CommandButton control, and then create a command button object to the right of the Add button on the form.

5 Set the following properties for the command button object:

Object	Property	Setting
Command1	Caption	"Delete"
	Name	cmdDelete

Your form should look like the following illustration:

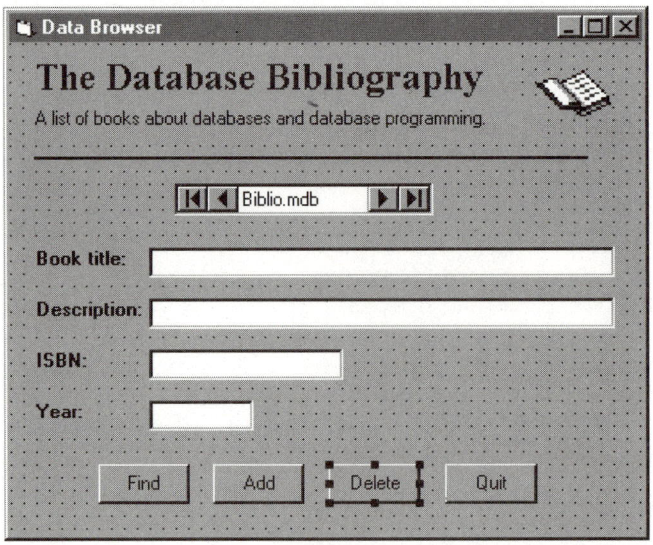

6 Double-click the Delete command button to open the cmdDelete_Click event procedure in the Code window.

7 Type the following program statements in the event procedure:

```
prompt$ = "Do you really want to delete this record?"
reply = MsgBox(prompt$, vbOKCancel, "Delete Record")
If reply = vbOK Then                  'if the user clicks OK
    datBiblio.Recordset.Delete        'delete current record
    datBiblio.Recordset.MoveFirst 'move to first record
End If
```

The Delete method deletes a record from the database.

This procedure first displays a dialog box asking the user if he or she wants to delete the current record. Again, the MsgBox function is used with the vbOKCancel argument to let the user back out of the delete operation if he or she decides not to go through with it. If the user clicks OK, the current record is deleted by using the Delete method and the first record is displayed by using the MoveFirst method. If the user clicks Cancel, the delete operation is skipped.

8 Close the Code window, and then click the Save Project button to save your changes.

Save Project button

Now you'll use the Delete button to delete the record for *The New Joy of Databases* from the database.

Run the My Delete Records program

Start button

The complete Delete Records program is available on disk in the Lesson 9 folder.

1 Click the Start button on the toolbar.

Information from the Titles table in the Biblio.mdb database appears in the text boxes.

2 Use the Find button to display the record for *The New Joy of Databases.*

The record you added in the last exercise appears on the form.

WARNING The following steps will delete this record from the Biblio.mdb database.

---

3 Click the Delete button on the form.

The Delete Record dialog box appears, as shown in the following illustration:

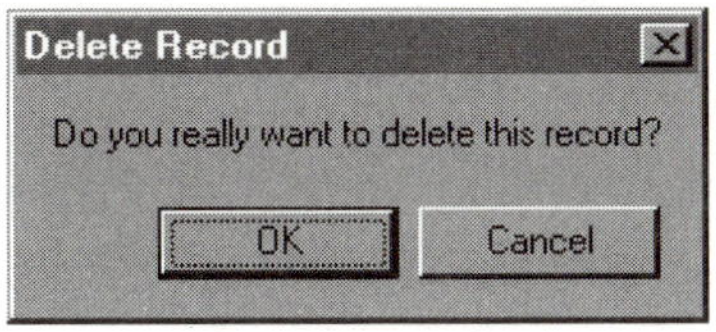

4 Click the OK button to delete the record.

The record for *The New Joy of Databases* is deleted from the database.

5 Click the Quit button to end the program.

You've finished working with the data object in this lesson. To learn more about writing database applications, read Chapters 22 and 23 in the Visual Basic *Programmer's Guide.* The Biblio.mdb database is used as a demonstration file in those chapters also. If you have Visual Basic Professional Edition, you can read the *Guide to Data Access Objects* included in the Visual Basic Professional Edition documentation set for detailed information about the Microsoft Jet database engine.

One Step Further: Making a Backup Copy of a File

The FileCopy statement makes a backup copy of a file.

If you're like most people, the information you keep in databases is very important, and you'd be in bad shape if something happened to it. For this reason, you should always make a backup copy of each database you use before making changes to it. If anything goes wrong when you're working with the copy, you can simply replace the copy with the original database. Your backup routine might include using a backup program, Windows Explorer, or a special backup feature in your database program. As an additional safeguard, you can create a backup copy of one or more files from within a Visual Basic program by using the FileCopy statement. FileCopy makes a separate copy of the file (as Windows Explorer's Edit Copy command does) when you use the statement with the following syntax:

```
FileCopy sourcepath destinationpath
```

where *sourcepath* is the pathname of the file you want to copy and *destinationpath* is the pathname of the file you want to create.

NOTE FileCopy does not work if the file specified by *sourcepath* is currently open.

In the following exercise, you'll add a backup feature to the My Delete Records program by placing a FileCopy statement in the Form_Load event procedure.

Use FileCopy to make a backup of Biblio.mdb

First you'll save the My Delete Records program under a new name to protect the original. If My Delete Records isn't open, load Delete Records.vbp from disk and display its form.

1 On the File menu, click the Save File As command. Save the My Delete Records form as **My Backup Copy.frm**. Use the Save Project As command to save the project as **My Backup Copy.vbp**.

2 Click View Form and then double-click the form (not an object) to open the Form_Load event procedure in the Code window.

Placing the FileCopy statement in the startup procedure gets the user to back up the database before making any changes to it.

3 Type the following program statements in the Form_Load event procedure:

The FileCopy statement makes a copy of the database.

```
prompt$ = "Would you like to create a backup copy of the database?"
reply = MsgBox(prompt$, vbOKCancel, datBiblio.DatabaseName)
If reply = vbOK Then     'copy the database if the user clicks OK
    FileNm$ = InputBox$("Enter the pathname for the backup copy.")
    If FileNm$ <> "" Then FileCopy datBiblio.DatabaseName, FileNm$
End If
```

This routine displays a message box when the program starts, asking the user if he or she would like to make a backup copy of the database. The MsgBox function is used with the vbOKCancel argument to give the user a chance to cancel. This time the DatabaseName property is also used in the MsgBox function to display the name of the database in the dialog box title bar. If the user clicks OK, another message box gets the pathname of the backup file and the FileCopy statement copies the file.

Save Project button

4 Close the Code window, and then click the Save Project button to save your changes.

Now you'll run the program to see how the backup feature works.

Run the My Backup Copy program

Start button

1 Click the Start button on the toolbar.

The following dialog box appears on the screen, asking whether you want to make a backup copy of the database:

The complete Backup Copy program is available on disk in the Lesson 9 folder.

2 Click OK to make a backup copy.

A dialog box appears asking for the pathname of your backup file.

3 Type **c:\vb\practice\lesson 9\my biblio.mdb**, and click OK.

Visual Basic copies the Biblio.mdb database to the Lesson 9 practice directory and gives it the name My biblio.mdb. Now if you make any mistakes in the Biblio.mdb file, you have a backup.

4 Click the Quit button to end the program.

If you want to continue to the next lesson

➤ Keep Visual Basic running, and turn to Lesson 10.

If you want to quit Visual Basic for now

➤ On the File menu, click Exit.

If you see a Save dialog box, click Yes.

Lesson Summary

To	Do this	Button
Open a text file	Use the Open...For Input statement. For example: `Open CmnDialog1.FileName For Input As #1`	
Get a line of input from a text file	Use the Line Input statement. For example: `Line Input #1, LineOfText$`	

Check for the end of a file	Use the EOF function. For example:
	`Do Until EOF(1)`
	`    Line Input #1, LineOfText$`
	`    Text$ = Text$ & LineOfText$ & Wrap$`
	`Loop`	

To	Do this	Button
Close an open file	Use the Close statement. For example: `Close #1`	

Display a text file	Use the Line Input statement to copy text from an open file to a string variable, and then assign the string variable to a text box object. For example:
	`Do Until EOF(1)`
	`    Line Input #1, LineOfText$`
	`    Text$ = Text$ & LineOfText$ & Wrap$`
	`Loop`
	`txtDisplay.Text = Text$`

Display an Open dialog box	Use the ShowOpen method of the common dialog object. For example: `CmnDialog1.ShowOpen`	
Create a new text file	Use the Open...For Output statement. For example: `Open CmdDialog1.FileName For Output As #1`	
Display a Save As dialog box	Use the ShowSave method of the common dialog object. For example: `CmnDialog1.ShowSave`	
Save text to a file	Use the Print # statement. For example: `Print #1, txtNote.Text`	
Open a database	Use the Data control to create a data object on a form, and then set its DatabaseName property to the name of the database. Specify the database type by using the Connect property, and specify the record type by using the RecordsetType property.	
Open a database in read only mode	Set the ReadOnly property of the data object to True.	
Display a data field in a text box object	Set the DataField and DataSource properties in the text box.	

To	Do this	Button

Search for data in a database	Prompt the user for a search string, and then use the Index, Seek, NoMatch, and MoveFirst properties of the Recordset object in an event procedure. For example:
	`SrchStr$ = InputBox(prmpt$, "Book Search")`
	`datBiblio.Recordset.Index = "Title"`
	`datBiblio.Recordset.Seek "=", SearchStr$`
	`If datBiblio.Recordset.NoMatch Then`
	`    MsgBox ("Book not found.")`
	`End If`	

Add a record to the database	Use the AddNew method of the Recordset object. For example: `datBiblio.Recordset.AddNew`	
Add a field to a database record by using program code	Specify the field name as a property of the Recordset object. Be sure to specify the correct data format. For example: `datBiblio.Recordset.PubID - 14`	
Delete a database record	Use the Delete method of the Recordset object. For example: `datBiblio.Recordset.Delete`	
Display the first record of a database	Use the MoveFirst method of the Recordset object. For example: `datBiblio.Recordset.MoveFirst`	
Copy a file	Use the FileCopy statement. For example: `FileCopy datBiblio.DatabaseName, FileNm$`	
Give an object the focus	Use the object's SetFocus method. For example: `txtTitle.SetFocus`	

For online information about	On the Visual Basic Help Menu, click Search For Help On, and then
Working with text files	Type **files: input and output**
Working with databases	Type **data control**
Recordset properties and methods	Type **Recordset object**

For more information on	**In the Visual Basic *Programmer's Guide,* see**
Working with text files	Chapter 19, "Processing Files"
The CommonDialog control	Chapter 11, "Dialogs"
Using the Data control	Chapter 22, "Accessing Databases with the Data Control"
Using objects to display data	Chapter 23, "Using the Data-Bound Controls"

Preview of the Next Lesson

In the next lesson, "Controlling Microsoft Office Applications by Using OLE," you'll learn how to launch Windows-based applications from inside Visual Basic and how to use the Object Browser to incorporate application objects from applications such as Microsoft Word and Microsoft Excel into your programs.

Lesson

10

Controlling Microsoft Office Applications by Using OLE

Estimated time
45 min.

In this lesson you will learn how to:

- Create an Enterprise Information System by using the OLE control.
- Establish active links to files that were created in Windows-based applications.
- Use the Object Browser to examine application objects.
- Use OLE Automation to control Excel and Word.

In Lesson 2, you learned how to use the OLE control to launch Microsoft Windows–based applications in your programs. If you found that topic interesting, you're in for a lot of fun in this lesson. Microsoft Visual Basic was specifically designed to be the "glue" that joins the data and features of a variety of Windows-based applications quickly and efficiently. In this lesson, you'll learn how to build an Enterprise Information System (EIS) by using the OLE control and data from several Microsoft Office applications. You'll also learn how to use the Object Browser to examine the application objects in Windows-based programs, and you'll use OLE Automation to incorporate features of Microsoft Excel and Microsoft Word into your projects.

Creating an Enterprise Information System

An Enterprise Information System (EIS) is a front-end application that provides important business information via a consistent and easy-to-use interface. Enterprise Information Systems are often built by management information service (MIS) departments or database specialists because these people are experienced with retrieving and formatting data from specialized database programs such as Oracle and SQL Server. The users of EIS applications are typically employees who have little or no experience in database management—company decision makers who need immediate access to the facts and figures for their organization. In this section, you will create a simple Enterprise Information System that will display records from a Microsoft Access database, employee photographs edited in Paint, and sales data from an Excel worksheet and chart. To create the Enterprise Information System, you'll use the Visual Basic OLE control and several Office applications.

Uses for an Enterprise Information System

The best Enterprise Information Systems combine the data and features of a variety of applications to create powerful business management tools. I created the following list of sample EIS applications to help you think about how you might use the Visual Basic OLE control and existing Office documents to create custom solutions for your business or organization. I'll discuss many of the techniques necessary to create a functional Enterprise Information System in this lesson.

Order entry system Users could display data entry forms and incoming orders by using Excel and could create sales reports by using Word.

Human resource manager Users could manage employee records in an Access database and personnel reviews stored in Word documents, and could edit photographs by using Paint.

Financial analysis tool Users could analyze company records and ledgers stored in Excel files and investment information downloaded from online services.

Inventory management system Sales and fulfillment personnel could examine inventory information stored in Oracle or SQL Server databases to help them make manufacturing and pricing decisions.

Executive information system Senior management could have electronic mailing services through Microsoft Mail, access to the company newsletter stored in Word documents, and the ability to run customized database queries in Access.

Project management system Users could manage schedule information by using Microsoft Project, track marketing projections by using Excel, create customized status reports by using Word, and prepare electronic presentations by using Microsoft PowerPoint.

Using the OLE Control

You use the OLE control to insert objects that support OLE into your Visual Basic programs. (OLE is the Microsoft technology that, among other things, allows your application to link to and embed another application's objects.) The OLE objects you have access to depend on the Windows applications you have installed on your system. Each application that supports OLE is identified, with the objects it supports, in the Windows registry (a system-wide database that Windows uses to keep track of such information). You choose OLE objects by using the Insert Object dialog box that appears when you first use the OLE control. Examples of OLE objects include Excel worksheets, Excel charts, Word documents, and Microsoft ClipArt images. OLE objects can be new, empty application documents or existing files loaded from disk.

In the following exercise, you'll use a data object, an image object, two OLE objects, and several labels and text boxes to create an Enterprise Information System that tracks up-and-coming recording artists in the Seattle area. This sample EIS application will display a photograph, records from an Access database, and data from an Excel worksheet and chart. When you've finished, your application will look similar to the following:

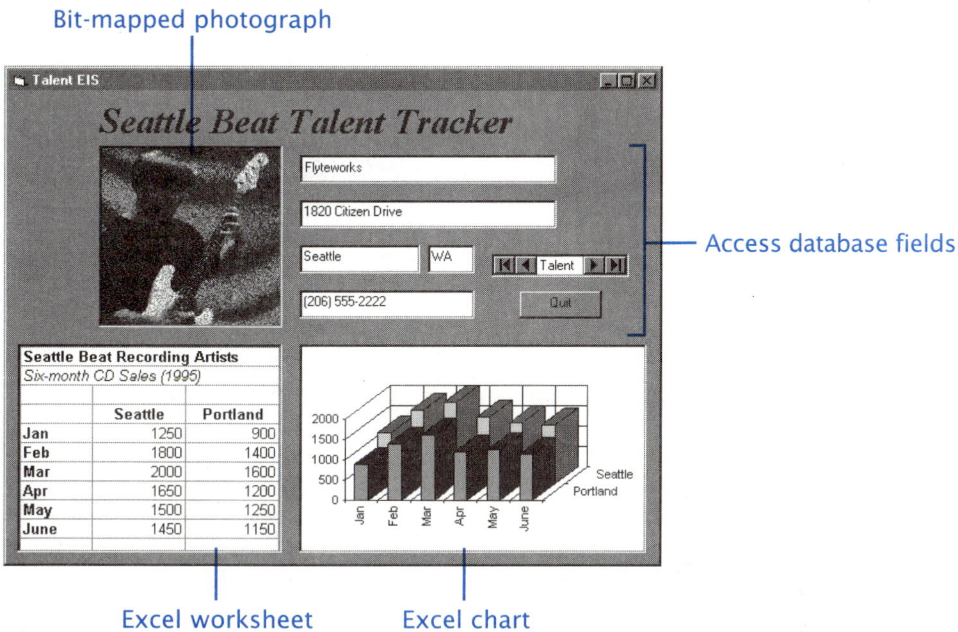

Build the Talent EIS application

1 Start Visual Basic.

If Visual Basic is already running, click New Project on the File menu. The application you will build is bigger than the default form, so you need to enlarge the form.

2 Increase the height and width of the form by using the mouse to drag the lower right corner of the form down and to the right.

Sizing pointer

While you are resizing the form, the mouse pointer changes to the sizing pointer.

3 Use the Label control to create a large label in the top center of the form.

Label control

This object will contain the title of the program. Look at the illustration above for the placement and size of all the objects in this exercise.

Image control

4 Use the Image control to create an image object below the label, on the left side of the form.

This object will display a photograph that has been scanned by an electronic scanner and saved as a .bmp file.

TextBox control

5 Use the TextBox control to create five text box objects to the right of the image object.

These text boxes will be linked to an Access database that contains the names, addresses, and phone numbers of musicians in the talent database of a fictitious company named Seattle Beat.

Data control

6 Use the Data control to add a data object to the right of the lower text box objects.

The data object will be used to scroll through the records of the talent database.

CommandButton control

7 Use the CommandButton control to add a command button below the data object.

This command button will be used to quit the program.

8 Set the following properties for the objects on your form. You'll find the talent database and a scanned .bmp file in the C:\Vb\Practice\Lesson 10 folder.

Object	Property	Setting
Form1	Caption	"Talent EIS"
Label1	Caption	"Seattle Beat Talent Tracker"
	Font	Times New Roman, Bold Italic, 24-point
	ForeColor	Dark red
Image1	BorderStyle	1 - Fixed Single
	Stretch	True
	Picture	C:\Vb\Practice\Lesson 10\Flyteworks.bmp
Data1	Caption	"Talent"
	Connect	Access
	DatabaseName	C:\Vb\Practice\Lesson 10\Talent.mdb
	ReadOnly	True
	RecordSource	Artists
Text1	DataSource	Data1
	DataField	Name
	Text	(Empty)
Text2	DataSource	Data1
	DataField	Address
	Text	(Empty)

Object	Property	Setting
Text3	DataSource	Data1
	DataField	City
	Text	(Empty)
Text4	DataSource	Data1
	DataField	State
	Text	(Empty)
Text5	DataSource	Data1
	DataField	WorkPhone
	Text	(Empty)
Command1	Caption	"Quit"

9 Double-click the Quit command button, and type **End** in the Command1_Click event procedure.

This program statement will close your application when the Quit button is clicked.

10 Use the Save File As command to save your form as **My Talent EIS.frm**, and then use the Save Project As command to save your project as **My Talent EIS.vbp**. Save your EIS application in the Lesson 10 folder.

Now you're ready to incorporate an Excel worksheet and chart into your application by using the OLE control.

Insert application objects

In the following steps, you'll use the OLE control to link your EIS application to an Excel worksheet and chart.

OLE control

1 Click the OLE control, and then draw a large rectangle in the bottom left corner of the EIS application form.

After you draw the rectangle and release the mouse button, the Insert Object dialog box appears, as shown in the following illustration:

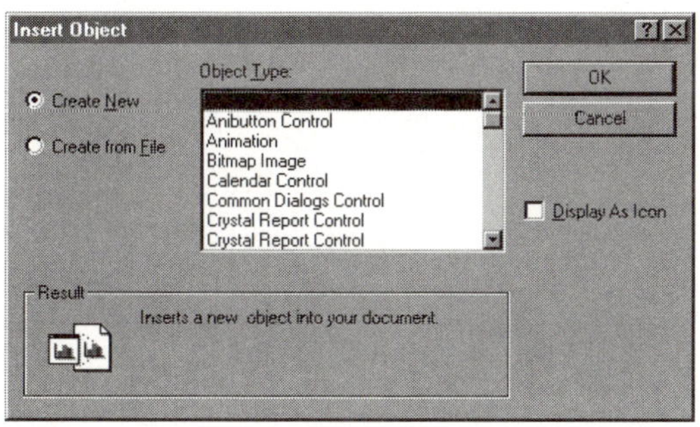

The Insert Object dialog box lists objects that are recorded in your system registry.

The Insert Object dialog box presents a list of the objects you can link to or embed in your application. A *linked object* contains data that is managed by the application that created it and is stored in an application file apart from your Visual Basic application. An *embedded object* contains data that is stored inside your Visual Basic application. Other applications can have access to linked objects—for example, other users in your office might routinely modify the same Excel sales worksheet you have linked to a Visual Basic application—but only one application (in this case, the My Talent EIS application) can have access to an embedded object.

2 Click the Create From File option button in the Insert Object dialog box.

An object pathname appears in the dialog box. You select Create From File when you want to add an existing file to your program.

3 Select the Link check box to create a linked object in your application.

When the Link check box is selected, a picture of the file you choose will be loaded into the OLE object. Since the file will be a linked object, it will continue to exist outside your Visual Basic application, and changes made to the file will be reflected in your program when you run it.

4 Click the Browse button to search for the Excel file you want to link to your program.

5 In the Browse dialog box, navigate to the Lesson 10 folder, and then click the Sales_95 Excel worksheet and click Insert. When the Insert Object dialog box reappears, click OK to establish a link to the Sales_95 file.

After a moment, a picture of the Excel worksheet appears in the OLE object. (If all the worksheet data is not visible, resize the OLE object.) Your form should look similar to the following:

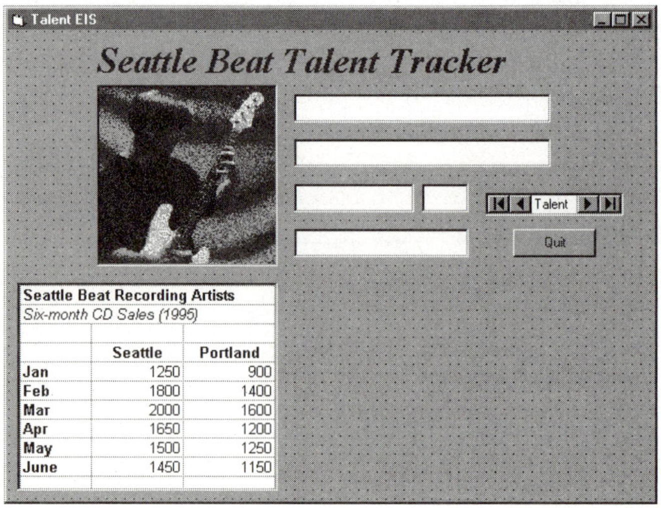

This worksheet shows the sales generated by local recording artists at the Seattle Beat company over a six-month time period. Since the OLE object has been linked to the Excel worksheet, employees at Seattle Beat can update the Sales_95.xls worksheet, and the changes will be reflected in the Talent EIS. Having access to current sales information might help the staff at Seattle Beat spot important regional sales trends.

Now you'll copy a sales chart from the Sales_95 worksheet and paste in into a new OLE object.

NOTE The following steps require that you have Excel 5 for Windows or Excel 7 for Windows 95 installed on your system.

OLE control

To insert part of a file into an OLE object, use the Paste Special command.

6 Click the OLE control, and then draw a rectangle in the bottom right corner of the form.

The Insert Object dialog box appears after you release the mouse button.

7 Click Cancel to close the Insert Object dialog box.

This time you'll place only a portion of the worksheet file—an Excel sales chart—into the OLE object. To include a specific part of a file, you must copy it from the application that created the data and then paste it into the OLE object by using the Paste Special command.

8 Start Excel, and open the worksheet Sales_95.xls, which is located in the Lesson 10 folder.

Your screen should look similar to the following:

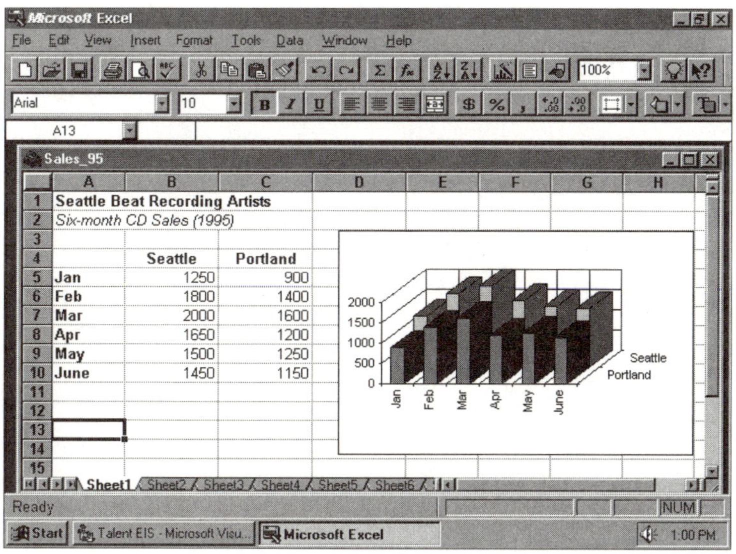

The right mouse button gives you access to the Paste Special command.

9 Click the sales chart, and click the Copy command on the Edit menu.

A copy of the sales chart is placed on the Windows Clipboard.

10 Close Excel, and maximize the Visual Basic programming environment.

11 Position the mouse pointer over the empty OLE object on the form, and click the right mouse button.

A context-sensitive pop-up menu appears next to the OLE object.

12 Click the Paste Special command on the pop-up menu to insert the Excel chart into the OLE object.

The Paste Special dialog box appears, as shown in the following illustration:

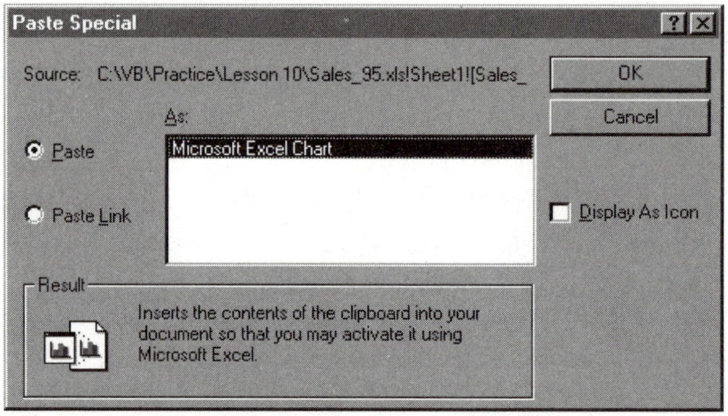

13 Click the Paste Link option button in the dialog box to indicate that you want to paste a link to the Excel chart into the OLE object.

When the chart is linked to the My Talent EIS program, changes made to the chart within Excel will be reflected in the Talent EIS.

14 Click OK in the Paste Special dialog box to link the sales chart.

The sales chart appears in the OLE object, as shown in the following illustration:

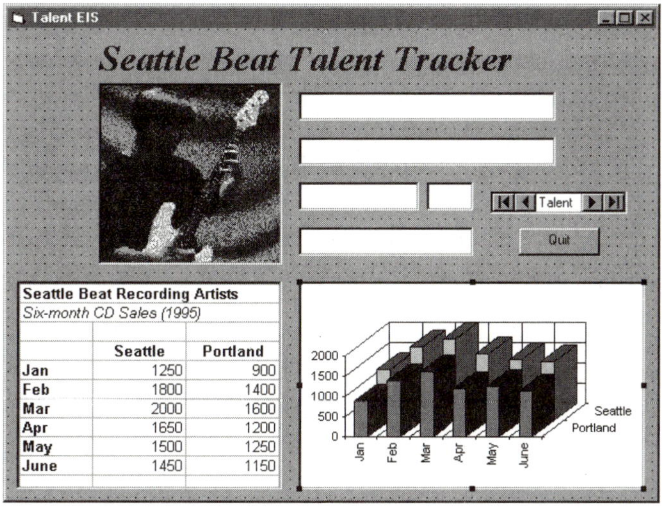

Your last step is to insert two lines of program code that will update the links to your Excel files when the EIS application starts.

15 Double-click the form to open the Form_Load event procedure in the Code window, and then type the following statements in the event procedure:

```
OLE1.Update
OLE2.Update
```

These statements use the Update method to load any changes made to the linked Excel files into your Visual Basic application. Adding these statements will make the program a little slower to load, but they are necessary if the linked files are used by others in your business.

Save Project button

16 Click the Save Project button to save your completed Enterprise Information System to disk.

Now run the Enterprise Information System to examine how it presents information from different sources.

The complete Talent EIS program is located on disk in the \Vb\Practice\Lesson 10 folder.

Run the Enterprise Information System

1 Click the Start button to run the program.

The Enterprise Information System loads data from three sources and displays it on the screen, as shown in the illustration on the following page.

Start button

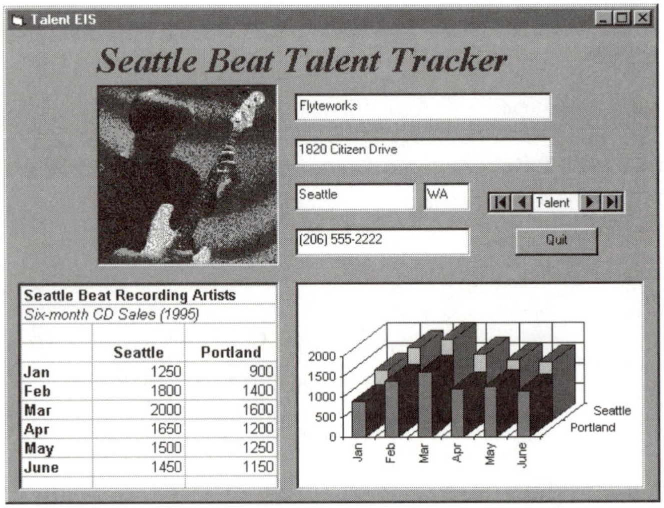

2 Click the inside right arrow in the data object to browse through the list of Seattle-area bands in the database.

Different names, addresses, and phone numbers appear in the text boxes as you click the data object. In this example, I included only one photograph, so the picture stays the same for each recording artist. If you were to connect to a database containing a photograph field, however, you could display a series of bit maps in the image box by setting the image object's DataField property to the photograph field in the database.

3 Double-click the six-month sales worksheet on the form.

Visual Basic starts Excel—the application that created the sales worksheet—and loads the Sales_95.xls worksheet. Since the object you inserted is linked to the worksheet, Visual Basic allows you to make changes to the original worksheet and save them to the original worksheet file.

NOTE If you don't want users to have the ability to start Excel and make changes to the linked file, set the Enabled property of the OLE object to False.

---

4 Move the cursor to cell C7 in the sales worksheet, type **0** (zero), and press ENTER.

The number of compact discs sold in Portland in March is changed from 1600 to 0.

5 On the Excel File menu, click Exit, and then click Yes to save your changes.

The original sales worksheet is updated, and Excel closes. The Enterprise Information System reappears with a new sales figure in the worksheet. However, the sales chart in the EIS has *not* been updated with the new March sales number. Visual Basic updates the contents of an OLE object only if you activate the link by double-clicking the OLE object to open the linked object or if you refresh the link by using the Update method in program code. Otherwise, Visual Basic will preserve the data as it was originally loaded so that your users can work without "disappearing data." If you would like to have Visual Basic respond to object changes as they occur, you can place the Update method in a special OLE event procedure called OLE1_Updated, which is executed every time an OLE object is changed. As you can see, Visual Basic lets you control how often linked data is refreshed.

6 Click Quit to close the My Talent EIS application.

You've finished working with the OLE control for now.

NOTE For more information about creating Enterprise Information Systems by using the OLE control, see Chapter 8, "Using the OLE Control," in the Visual Basic *Programmer's Guide*.

Programming Application Objects by Using OLE Automation

In the previous section, you learned how to incorporate objects from Windows-based applications into your Visual Basic programs. In this section, you'll learn how to use a technology called OLE Automation to incorporate the functionality of Windows-based applications into your code. Windows-based applications that fully support OLE Automation make available, or *expose,* their application features as a collection of objects with associated properties and methods. The Windows-based applications that expose their objects are called *object* or *server* applications, and the programs that use the objects are called *controlling* or *client* applications. OLE Automation is an industry standard that allows communication between the two applications, as shown in the following illustration:

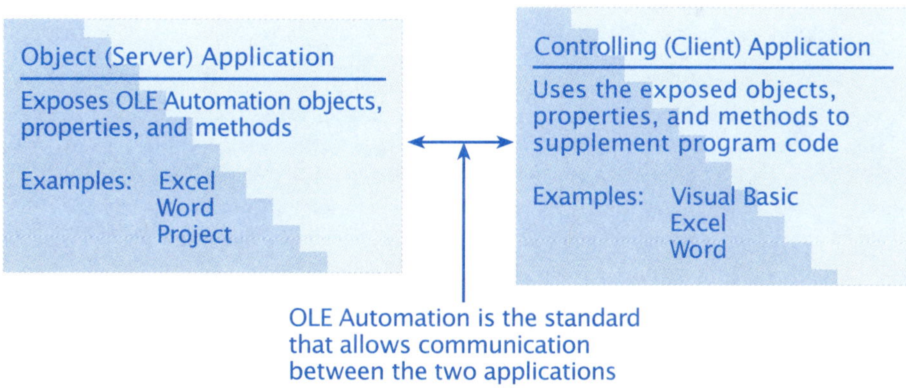

Using OLE Automation in Visual Basic

In Visual Basic 4, Microsoft has added the ability to create both object and controlling applications that support OLE Automation. Creating object applications that expose their functionality requires that you have Visual Basic Professional Edition and is beyond the scope of this book. Creating controlling applications that use the features of object applications is a straightforward process in both the Professional Edition and the Standard Edition of Visual Basic. In the next few sections, you will learn how to write a Visual Basic application that uses an Excel object to check the spelling in a text box. As you'll see, the objects, properties, and methods exposed by an object application typically correspond to the menu commands and dialog box options provided by the object application.

NOTE Excel, Word, Access, and Project are all capable of exposing their functionality through OLE Automation. Since the features and objects provided by each of these applications are unique, you'll need to review the product documentation or online Help for each program before you incorporate their functionality into your code. If you have one or more of these applications installed on your system now, the Visual Basic Object Browser will let you explore the objects, properties, and methods available to you.

The Visual Basic Object Browser

The Object Browser lets you view objects on your system.

The Visual Basic Object Browser is a viewing utility that has two uses: it can display the objects, properties, and methods used by the program you're working on in the Visual Basic programming environment or it can display the objects, properties, and methods available to you from object applications installed on your system. In the following exercise, you'll use the Object Browser to view the OLE Automation objects exposed by Excel.

NOTE To complete the following steps you'll need Excel 7 for Windows 95 or Excel 5 for Windows installed on your system. The Microsoft Excel 5.0 Object Library is the library that both versions of Excel use to expose their OLE Automation objects. In Excel 7 for Windows 95, however, the object library contains one new object and numerous new properties and methods for existing objects. If you don't have either version of Excel, use the Object Browser to examine other application objects on your system.

Use the Object Browser to view Excel objects

1 On the File menu, click the New Project command.

The My Talent EIS application closes, and a new form appears. You'll add a reference to the Excel object library to this new project.

The References dialog box lets you add references to object libraries to your project.

2 On the Tools menu, click the References command.

The References dialog box appears, which lets you include in your project references to any object libraries that are available on your system. Adding references to your project won't make your compiled program any bigger, but the more references you have, the longer it will take Visual Basic to compile the program. Therefore, Visual Basic adds references to OLE Automation object libraries only if you ask it to.

3 Select the check box next to the reference titled Microsoft Excel 5.0 Object Library.

You might have to scroll through the list to find the library. (The references are listed in alphabetic order.) Your screen should look like the following:

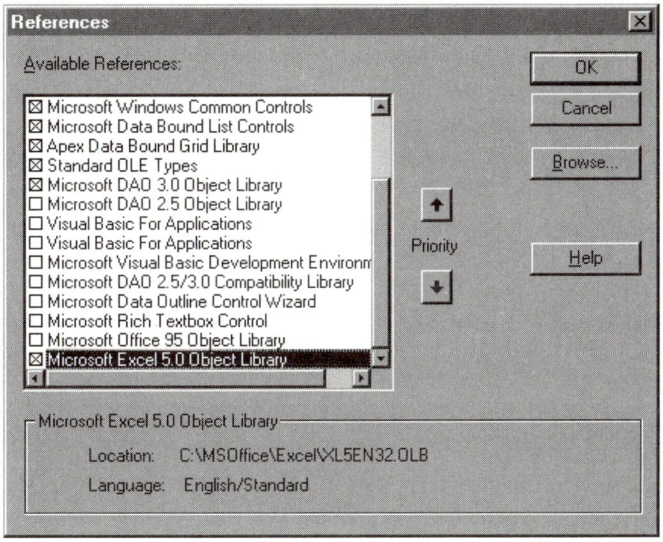

4 Click OK to close the dialog box and add the reference to your project.

Now you're ready to use the Object Browser.

5 On the View menu, click the Object Browser command.

The Object Browser appears, as shown in the following illustration:

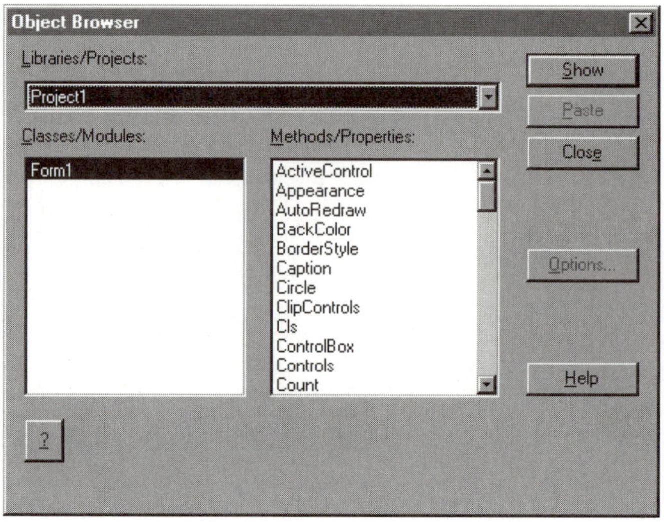

The Object Browser contains a Libraries/Projects drop-down list box, which you can use to display the object libraries included in your project. It also contains a Classes/Modules list box, which you can use to select an object to examine. When you select an object in the Classes/Modules list box, the methods and properties included in the object are listed in the Methods/Properties list box.

6 Open the Libraries/Projects drop-down list box, and then click Microsoft Excel 5.0 Object Library.

   A list of the OLE Automation objects exposed by Excel fills the Classes/Modules list box.

7 Scroll to the bottom of the list in the Classes/Modules list box, and then click the Worksheet object.

   A list of the methods and properties associated with the Worksheet object appears in the Methods/Properties list box. These are the commands Excel provides for manipulating information in worksheets.

8 Click the CheckSpelling method in the Methods/Properties list box.

   The syntax for the CheckSpelling method appears at the bottom of the Object Browser. This method invokes Excel's spelling checker, a feature available to you from within Visual Basic. The method syntax shows you the options available if you want to customize the command. Your screen should look like the following:

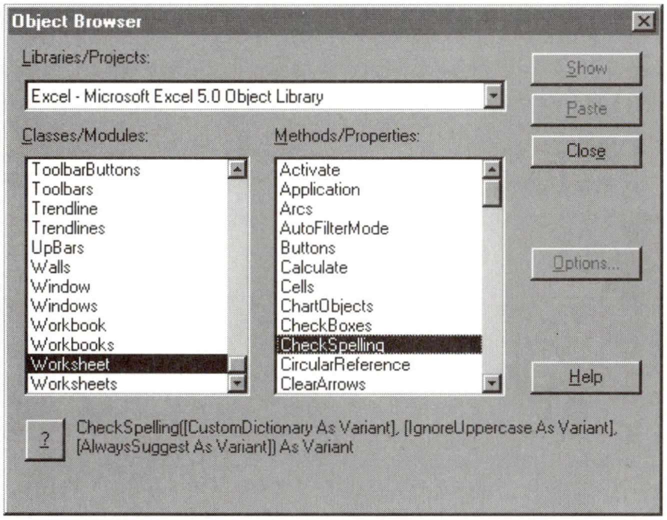

9 Click the question-mark button next to the CheckSpelling syntax statement in the Object Browser.

A Help file for the CheckSpelling method opens in the programming environment, as shown in the following illustration:

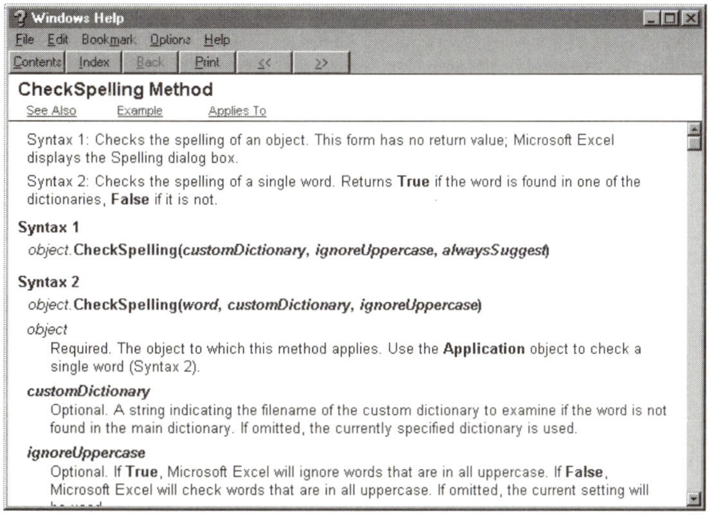

The object library Help system describes the properties and methods exposed by an object application.

This Help file gives you detailed information about how to use the properties and methods in the Excel object library. Many object applications provide this information along with their object libraries so that OLE Automation programmers can take full advantage of the programmable features the application provides. Using the object library Help system is a great way to learn more about OLE Automation programming.

10 Review the article on the CheckSpelling method, and then close the Help file.

11 Click the Close button in the Object Browser.

You've finished exploring OLE Automation objects for the time being. Now it's time to put the Excel CheckSpelling method to work.

Using the Excel CheckSpelling Method

To use the Excel CheckSpelling method in a Visual Basic program, you need to complete the following programming steps. Since the techniques apply to most application objects, you'll be able to use these guidelines to incorporate the functionality of most applications that support OLE Automation into your programs.

Step 1 Add references to the necessary object libraries to your project by using the References command.

Step 2 Write your Visual Basic program. In the event procedure in which you plan to use OLE Automation, create an object variable by using the Dim statement and then load an OLE Automation object into the object variable by using the CreateObject function:

```
Dim X As Object                     'use X as variable name
Set X = CreateObject("Excel.Sheet")
```

Step 3 Use the methods and properties of the OLE Automation object in the event procedure, consulting the Help files in the Object Browser or the object application documentation for the proper syntax:

```
X.Cells(1, 1).Value = Text1.Text    'copy text box data to cell 1,1
X.Visible = True                    'make Excel visible
X.CheckSpelling                     'call CheckSpelling method
```

Step 4 When you've finished using the object application, quit the application and release the object variable to conserve memory:

```
X.Application.Quit                  'quit Excel
Set X = Nothing                     'release object variable
```

In the following exercise, you'll create an application that uses the Excel spelling checker to verify the spelling in a Visual Basic text box. The program will be built entirely in Visual Basic, using the functionality of Excel remotely through OLE Automation.

NOTE In the following exercise, it is assumed that you have Excel 7 for Windows 95 installed on your system. If you have Excel 5 for Windows instead, you can use its version of the Microsoft Excel 5.0 Object Library and you can use the Excel 5 spelling checker.

Create a personal spelling checker

1 On the Tools menu, click the References command. Verify that the reference Microsoft Excel 5.0 Object Library has a check mark next to it, and then click OK.

The Microsoft Excel 5.0 Object Library gives you access to the objects, methods, and properties exposed by the Excel object application. This is the object library reference you added earlier in this lesson.

NOTE Object library references must be added to each new project by using the References command.

Now you'll create the form for the spelling checker and add the program code.

2 Decrease the height of the form until it appears as a smaller rectangular window.

Label control

3 Use the Label control to create a long label across the top of the form.

The label will contain the instructions for the program.

TextBox control

4 Use the TextBox control to create a wide text box, four lines deep, in the middle of the form.

The text box will hold the text that the user wants to check.

CommandButton control

5 Use the CommandButton control to add two command buttons below the text box object.

The first command button will be used to start Excel and to use the CheckSpelling method to check the spelling of the text in the text box. The second command button will be used to exit the program.

6 Set the following properties for the objects in the program:

Object	Property	Setting
Form1	Caption	"Personal Spelling Checker"
Label1	Caption	"Enter one or more words in the text box, and then click Check Spelling."
Text1	MultiLine ScrollBars Text	True 2 - Vertical (Empty)
Command1	Caption	"Check Spelling"
Command2	Caption	"Done"

After you set the properties, your form should look like the following illustration:

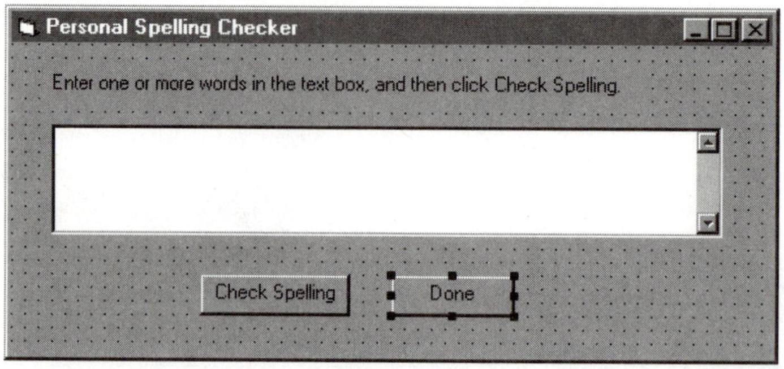

7 Double-click the Check Spelling command button to open the Command1_Click event procedure. Type the following code in the event procedure:

```
Dim X As Object                'create an object variable for Excel
Set X = CreateObject("Excel.Sheet")

X.Cells(1, 1).Value = Text1.Text 'copy text box to cell 1,1
X.Visible = True               'make dialog boxes visible
X.CheckSpelling                'use CheckSpelling method
Text1.Text = X.Cells(1, 1). Value 'copy corrected text to VB
X.Application.Quit             'quit Excel

Set X = Nothing                'release object variable
```

These statements create an Excel OLE Automation object in the event procedure, start Excel, set two of the Excel object's properties, call two of the Excel object's methods, and then release the memory used by the object. Excel starts automatically when the first reference to the object variable is made. The Excel Cells' Value property is then used to copy the contents of the text box to cell A1 in a new Excel worksheet. Since Excel starts invisibly, the Visible method is used to make the spelling checker visible when it runs. (To make the entire Excel application visible, you would use the statement X.Application.Visible = True.)

When the CheckSpelling method is executed, Excel runs the spelling checker and checks the contents of the worksheet for spelling errors. The Excel Spelling dialog box appears if a spelling mistake is found, and it gives the user a chance to make a correction. Excel checks each of the words in the text box, even if the text box contains more than one line of text. When the check is finished, the corrected words are copied back into the Visual Basic text box and the Excel application is closed. The Set statement at the end of the Command 1_Click event procedure releases the object variable's memory.

8 Close the Command1_Click event procedure, and double-click the Done command button.

9 Type **End** in the event procedure, and close the Code window.

You've finished building the Personal Spelling Checker program.

10 Use the Save File As command to save the form to disk under the name **My Spelling Checker.frm**. Use the Save Project As command to save the project to disk under the name **My Spelling Checker.vbp**. (Use the Lesson 10 folder for both files.)

Now run the My Spelling Checker program to see how OLE Automation works.

Run the My Spelling Checker program

Start button

The complete Spelling Checker program is located on disk in the Lesson 10 folder.

1 Click the Start button on the toolbar.

The program runs in the programming environment, as shown here:

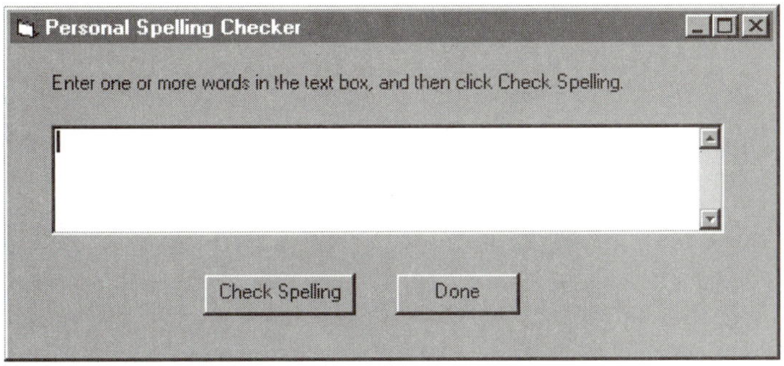

2 Type **workingg with objectss** in the text box.

Be sure to intentionally misspell the words *working* and *objects*.

3 Click the Check Spelling button.

Visual Basic creates an OLE Automation object and starts Excel. After a moment, the Excel Spelling dialog box appears, identifying the first word not in its dictionary. Your screen should look like the following:

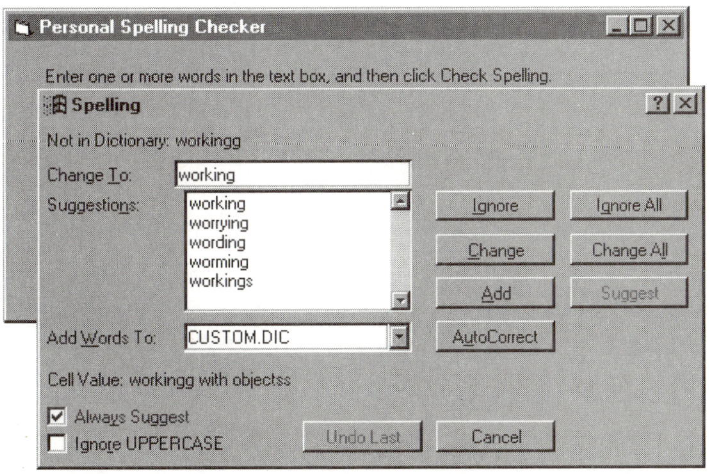

4. Click Change to fix the first mistake, and when Excel highlights the second spelling error, click Change again to fix it.

   The Spelling dialog box closes, and after a moment the words in the text box are corrected.

5. Click Done to close the program.

Congratulations! Through OLE Automation, you just used a handy feature of Excel to fix your typing mistakes for you. It's just the beginning of what you can do with Visual Basic and OLE.

One Step Further: Controlling Microsoft Word Objects

If you have Word installed on your computer, you can use OLE Automation to control Word's features through Visual Basic. Word exposes its functionality to controlling applications through an object named Word.Basic, and Word presents its commands and arguments as methods in Visual Basic program code. The following exercise shows you how to use Word to check the grammar of sentences you type in a Visual Basic text box. For more information about using Word commands via OLE Automation, read Word's macro language documentation or consult the Microsoft Office Developer's Kit (ODK), which is included with Visual Basic Professional Edition.

Create a personal grammar checker

To create the My Grammar Checker program, you'll modify the My Spelling Checker program to use an object from Word.

1. Use the Save File As command to save the My Spelling Checker form as **My Grammar Checker.frm**. Use the Save Project As command to save the My Spelling Checker project as **My Grammar Checker.vbp**. (Save the files in the Lesson 10 folder.)

2. Change the following properties in the renamed program:

Object	Property	Setting
Form1	Caption	"Personal Grammar Checker"
Label1	Caption	"Enter one or more words in the text box, and then click Check Grammar."
Command1	Caption	"Check Grammar"

3. Double-click the Check Grammar button to open the Command1_Click event procedure in the Code window.

   The contents of the old event procedure appear in the Code window.

4 Delete the text of the event procedure (the code between the Private Sub and End Sub statements), and then type the following program code:

```
Dim X As Object      'create Word object variable
Set X = CreateObject("Word.Basic")

X.FileNew            'open a new document
X.Insert Text1.Text  'copy text box to document
X.ToolsGrammar       'run grammar checker
X.FileClose 2        'close document without saving

Set X = Nothing      'release object variable
```

These Word commands are similar to the Excel commands you just deleted, but a few keywords and methods have been changed to meet the syntax requirements of the WordBasic macro language, which is built into Word. The four methods used are actual commands from WordBasic, and the arguments following the Insert and FileClose methods follow WordBasic's syntax requirements.

NOTE You can learn more about WordBasic commands and arguments by checking Word's macro language documentation.

Save Project button

Start button

The complete Grammar Checker program is located on disk in the Lesson 10 folder.

5 Close the Code window, and click the Save Project button on the toolbar.

Visual Basic saves your new OLE Automation code to disk.

6 Click the Start button on the toolbar to run My Grammar Checker.

The My Grammar Checker program appears, as shown in the following illustration:

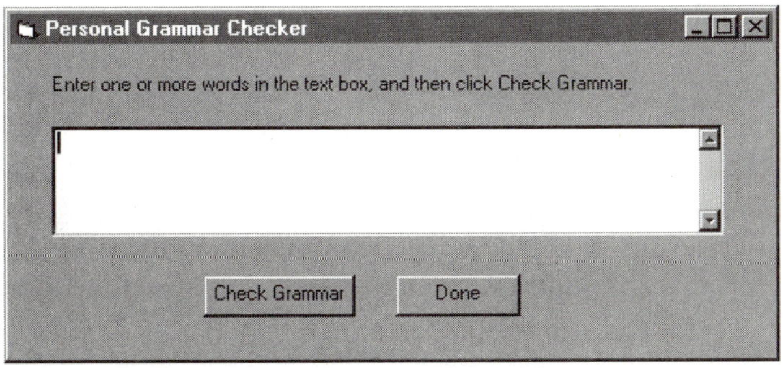

7 Type the following sentence into the text box: **She sat at the window watching the evening invade the avenue.**

8 Click the Check Grammar button to check the structure and readability of the sentence by using Word's grammar checker.

Visual Basic starts Word and checks the sentence's grammar. After a moment, a dialog box appears listing the results, as shown in the following illustration:

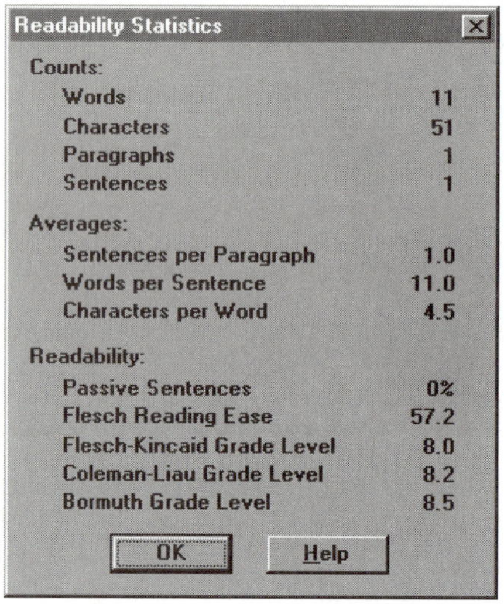

9 When you've finished reviewing the facts and figures, click OK to close the grammar checker.

Word is closed, and your Visual Basic program reappears. You've finished with My Grammar Checker.

10 Click the Done button to close the program.

The My Grammar Checker program closes, and the programming environment reappears.

If you want to continue to the Review & Practice section

➤ Keep Visual Basic running, and turn to the Part 4 Review & Practice section.

If you want to quit Visual Basic for now

➤ On the File menu, click Exit.

If you see a Save dialog box, click Yes.

Lesson Summary

To	Do this	Button
Insert an application object into your program	Use the OLE control to create a placeholder for the application object on the form, and then double-click the object in the Insert Object dialog box.	
Create a linked application object	Select the Link check box in the Insert Object dialog box.	
Create an embedded application object	Use the Insert Object dialog box without the Link check box selected. (Objects inserted by using the Insert Object dialog box are embedded—they reside in the Visual Basic application—by default.)	
Insert part of an application file into an OLE object	Select the data you want in the application, position the mouse pointer on the OLE object in Visual Basic, click the right mouse button, and then click the Paste Special command.	
Update the links to the OLE1 object when the program starts	Place the statement `OLE1.Update` in the Form_Load event procedure.	
View application objects that support OLE Automation	On the View menu, click the Object Browser command. Select the objects you want to examine in the Libraries/Projects drop-down list box.	

Create an object variable in a program	Use the Dim and Set statements. For example:
	`Dim X As Object`
	`Set X = CreateObject("Excel.Sheet")`	

Access application commands by using OLE Automation	Create an object variable, and then reference the methods or properties of the object. For example:
	`X.CheckSpelling`
	`X.Application.Quit`	

Release the memory used by an object variable	Use the Set statement and the keyword Nothing with the variable name. For example: `Set X = Nothing`	

For online information about	On the Visual Basic Help menu, click Search For Help On, and then
The OLE control	Type **OLE Control** and press ENTER
The Object Browser	Type **Object Browser** and press ENTER. Double-click the Object Browser topic
Programming application objects	Type **OLE Automation** and press ENTER. Double-click the OLE Automation topic

For more information on	In the Visual Basic *Programmer's Guide,* see
Adding application data to your programs	Chapter 8, "Using the OLE Container Control"
Using OLE Automation	Chapter 9, "Programming Other Applications' Objects"

Part

4

Review & Practice

Estimated time

30 min.

You will review and practice how to:

- Display records from a Microsoft Access database on your form.
- Use the Excel spelling checker to check for misspellings.
- Modify a database field and save your changes.

You can practice the skills you learned in Part 4 by solving the programming problem in this Review & Practice section. You will use a data object, a label object, two command button objects, and several text box objects to create a database viewer that lets you examine the records in a music review database and check for misspellings in a text field used for review comments.

Scenario

In Lesson 10 you used a Microsoft Access database named Talent to create an Enterprise Information System (EIS) that showed the names, addresses, and phone numbers of recording artists in the Seattle area. This EIS let executives in the Seattle Beat company track the sales and vital statistics of recording artists represented by their organization. In the programming problem in this Review & Practice section, you'll use the same database to create a front-end application for a music reviewer who wants to make notes about the artists she evaluates at live performances. This front-end will feature a field in the Talent database named Comments, a 255-character text window devoted to comments about the recording artists listed in the database.

As a bonus, you've decided to give the music reviewer the ability to check her spelling in the Comments field before she moves on to a new record. (The clubs where she listens to music are usually packed and have a two-drink minimum, so she doesn't want to worry about her typing.) Since Access doesn't provide a spelling checker utility, you'll use OLE Automation to incorporate Microsoft Excel's spelling checker into your application. Your front-end will use a data object to connect to the Talent database, and it will use several text boxes to display the fields your reviewer will want to see. The program should also contain a Check Spelling button that runs Excel's spelling checker utility to correct any spelling mistakes in the current Comments field, and it should contain a Quit button to end the program.

If you like, you can try solving this programming problem before looking at the following practice steps. Solving the problem on your own will give you some "real world" programming experience using Microsoft Visual Basic and will give you a chance to express your own tastes and interests. You can also solve the problem by following the steps below and reviewing the related sections in Part 4 when you have a detailed question. The solution to the problem is available in the \Vb\Practice\Review folder, in a project file named Problem 4.vbp.

Step 1: Design the User Interface

The first step in building your program is designing the user interface. To do this you'll open a new project and add the objects necessary to run your database front-end. You'll add a label object to display the program's title, five text boxes to hold database fields, a data object to make the database connection, and two command buttons to control the program.

1. Start Visual Basic. (If Visual Basic is already running, open a new project.)
2. Use the Label control to create a label named Music Review Notepad on the top of the form.
3. Use the TextBox control to create text boxes that will hold the Name, Address, City, State, and Comments fields from the Talent database.
4. Use the Data control to create a data object to the right of the text boxes.
5. Use the CommandButton control to create a button named Check Spelling and a button named Quit, below the data object.
6. Set the following properties for objects on the form:

Object	Property	Setting
Form1	Caption	"Music Review"
Label1	Caption	"Music Review Notepad"
	Font	Times New Roman, Bold, 18-point
	ForeColor	Dark blue
Data1	Caption	"Talent"
	DatabaseName	C:\Vb\Practice\Lesson 10\Talent.mdb
	RecordSource	Artists

Object	Property	Setting
Text1	DataSource	Data1
	DataField	Name
	Text	(Empty)
Text2	DataSource	Data1
	DataField	Address
	Text	(Empty)
Text3	DataSource	Data1
	DataField	City
	Text	(Empty)
Text4	DataSource	Data1
	DataField	State
	Text	(Empty)
Text5	DataSource	Data1
	DataField	Comments
	MultiLine	True
	Text	(Empty)
	ScrollBars	2 - Vertical
Command1	Caption	"Check Spelling"
Command2	Caption	"Quit"

Your completed form should look similar to the following:

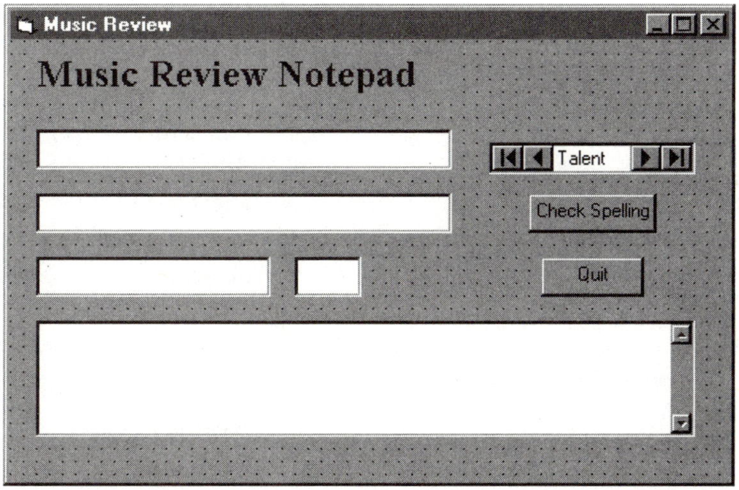

7 Use the Save File As command to save your form to disk under the name **My Problem 4.frm**. Use the Save Project As command to save your project to disk under the name **My Problem 4.vbp**. (Save the form and the project in the \Vb\Practice\Review folder.)

For more information on	See
Working with databases	Lesson 9

Step 2: Write the OLE Automation Code

Next you'll write the program code for the Check Spelling button, the object that uses OLE Automation to check the spelling of the Comments field by using Excel. Before you write the program code, use the References command to include the Excel object library in your project.

NOTE To complete the following steps you'll need Excel 7 for Windows 95 or Excel 5 for Windows installed on your system. The Microsoft Excel 5.0 Object Library has the same name in both versions of Excel. In Excel 7 for Windows 95, however, the object library contains one new object and numerous new properties and methods for existing objects.

1. On the Tools menu, click the References command.
2. Ensure that there's an "x" in the check box next to the Microsoft Excel 5.0 Object Library to include it in your project, and then click OK.
3. Double-click the Check Spelling button on the form.
4. Enter the following program code to use Excel's CheckSpelling method in your program:

```
Dim X As Object 'create object variable for Excel
Set X = CreateObject("Excel.Sheet")

X.Cells(1, 1).Value = Text5.Text   'copy Comments field to cell 1,1
X.Visible = True                   'make dialog boxes visible
X.CheckSpelling                    'call CheckSpelling method
Text5.Text = X.Cells(1, 1).Value   'copy corrected text to VB
X.Application.Quit                 'quit Excel

Set X = Nothing                    'release object variable
```

5. Close the Code window, and double-click the Quit button.
6. Type **End** between the Private Sub and End Sub statements, and then close the Code window.
7. Click the Save Project button on the toolbar to save your changes.

For more information on	See
Adding object library references to your project	Lesson 10
Using OLE Automation objects, properties, and methods	Lesson 10

Step 3: Run the Program

After the program is finished, you'll need to run it in the programming environment and verify that the database and spelling features work correctly. When you've finished testing the program, you can compile it as an executable file if you plan to use it in the future.

1. Click the Start button on the toolbar.
2. Verify that the information in the five text boxes matches the fields in the Talent database.
3. Click the Check Spelling button to the evaluate the spelling in the first database record's Comments field.

   After a moment, Excel's spelling checker should appear, as shown in the following illustration:

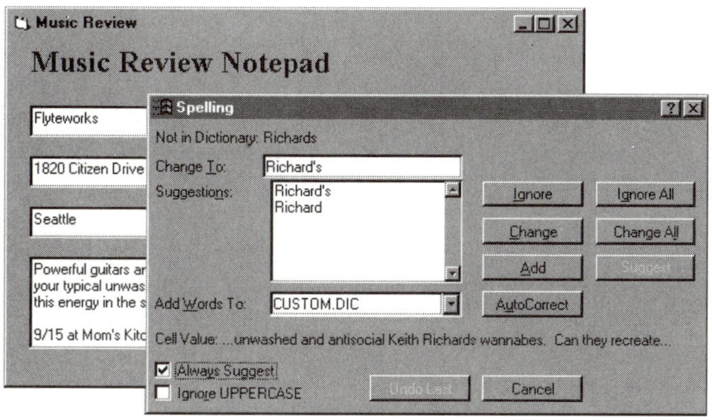

4. Correct any misspelled words in the field, and then verify that the event procedure updates the spelling on your form when the spelling checker closes. When you scroll to the next record in the database, your spelling correction will be written to the Talent database.
5. Scroll through the remaining database records, and verify that the data object is operating properly. Try entering some new data in the Comments field, and check your spelling.
6. When you've finished testing the music review front-end, click the Quit button.

For more information on	See
Running a database front-end	Lesson 9
Using Excel's CheckSpelling method	Lesson 10

Index

Special Characters

A

B

C

D

G

N

T

X–Z

About the author

Michael Halvorson is coauthor (with David Rygmyr) of *Learn Basic Now, Learn Basic for the Apple Macintosh Now,* and *Running MS-DOS QBasic*, all published by Microsoft Press. He worked for Microsoft Corporation from 1985 to 1993, where he was employed as a technical editor, an acquisitions editor, and a localization manager. He received a B.A. in computer science from Pacific Lutheran University in 1985, and he is currently a graduate student in early modern European history at the University of Washington.

Michael welcomes comments and questions about *Microsoft Visual Basic 4 Step by Step* via electronic mail. He can be reached at mikehal@carson.u.washington.edu.

The manuscript for this book was prepared and submitted to Microsoft Press in electronic form. Text files were prepared using Microsoft Word 2.0 for Windows. Pages were composed by Microsoft Press using Aldus PageMaker 5.0 for Windows, with text in Stone Informal and display type in Lucida Sans Bold. Composed pages were delivered to the printer as electronic prepress files.

Cover Designer
Rebecca Johnson

Cover Illustrator
Dean Fleming

Interior Graphic Designer
Kim Eggleston

Interior Graphic Artist
Michael Victor

Principal Compositors
Peggy Herman &
Elisabeth Thébaud

Principal Proofreader/Copy Editor
Sally Anderson

Indexer
Julie Kawabata

Unleash the power of Microsoft Visual Basic with HARDCORE VISUAL BASIC!

Available October 1995!

Visual Basic wizard Bruce McKinney shows how to blast through the so-called limits of Visual Basic and reach the powerful object-oriented development tool that lurks within. The result is applications with better performance and more functionality.

HARDCORE VISUAL BASIC provides developers and programmers with detailed coverage of such topics as:

- **Exploring the Spirit of Basic** — Language purification, the Basic Hungarian naming convention, efficient code versus correct code, and Basic wrappers for un-Basic hacks
- **Taking Control of Windows** — Calling the Windows API, understanding C in Basic, and mastering messages and processes
- **Programming Objects, Basic Style** — Classes and objects, the form class, collecting objects, and creating new controls by delegating to classes
- **Painting Pictures** — The Basic way of drawing, painting, and animating
- **Reusing Code** — Modular packages for sorting, shuffling, searching, and parsing; reusable Search, Replace, About, and Color Select forms; classes for editing, animating, managing the keyboard, handling menus, and sharing memory between programs
- **Programming in Different Environments** — Code for MS-DOS®, Windows 3.1, Windows 95, Windows NT™, and OLE

If you want to push Visual Basic to the max, HARDCORE VISUAL BASIC is your guide—it's essential for any serious Visual Basic programmer's library.

Valuable Information Included on CD!

- Thousands of lines of code that illustrate advanced programming techniques with the Windows API and the new object-oriented features of Visual Basic 4
- The Windows API type library and other useful tools such as Property Shop, Bug Wizard, Time It, and the VBUTIL dynamic-link library

"Hardcore Visual Basic is a book for people who like Basic but don't like limits. It's for people who won't take no for an answer. If you're willing to go the extra mile for better performance and more functionality, you'll have fun with this book."

—Bruce McKinney

Microsoft Press® books are available wherever quality books are sold and through CompuServe's Electronic Mall—**GO MSP**. Call **1-800-MSPRESS** for more information or to place a credit card order.* Please refer to **BBK** when placing your order. Prices subject to change.
*In Canada, contact Macmillan Canada, Attn: Microsoft Press Dept., 164 Commander Blvd., Agincourt, Ontario, Canada M1S 3C7, or call 1-800-667-1115. Outside the U.S. and Canada, write to International Coordinator, Microsoft Press, One Microsoft Way, Redmond, WA 98052-6399, or fax +1-206-936-7329.

ISBN 1-55615-667-7
672 pages, one CD-ROM
$39.95 ($53.95 Canada)

Microsoft Press

IMPORTANT — READ CAREFULLY BEFORE OPENING SOFTWARE PACKET(S).
By opening the sealed packet(s) containing the software, you indicate your acceptance of the following Microsoft License Agreement.

Microsoft License Agreement

MICROSOFT LICENSE AGREEMENT
(Single User Products)

This is a legal agreement between you (either an individual or an entity) and Microsoft Corporation. By opening the sealed software packet(s) you are agreeing to be bound by the terms of this agreement. If you do not agree to the terms of this agreement, promptly return the book, including the unopened software packet(s), to the place you obtained it for a full refund.

MICROSOFT SOFTWARE LICENSE

1. GRANT OF LICENSE. Microsoft grants to you the right to use one copy of the Microsoft software program included with this book (the "SOFTWARE") on a single terminal connected to a single computer. The SOFTWARE is in "use" on a computer when it is loaded into temporary memory (i.e., RAM) or installed into permanent memory (e.g., hard disk, CD-ROM, or other storage device) of that computer. You may not network the SOFTWARE or otherwise use it on more than one computer or computer terminal at the same time.

2. COPYRIGHT. The SOFTWARE is owned by Microsoft or its suppliers and is protected by United States copyright laws and international treaty provisions. Therefore, you must treat the SOFTWARE like any other copyrighted material (e.g., a book or musical recording) except that you may either (a) make one copy of the SOFTWARE solely for backup or archival purposes, or (b) transfer the SOFTWARE to a single hard disk provided you keep the original solely for backup or archival purposes. You may not copy the written materials accompanying the SOFTWARE.

3. OTHER RESTRICTIONS. You may not rent or lease the SOFTWARE, but you may transfer the SOFTWARE and accompanying written materials on a permanent basis provided you retain no copies and the recipient agrees to the terms of this Agreement. You may not reverse engineer, decompile, or disassemble the SOFTWARE. If the SOFTWARE is an update or has been updated, any transfer must include the most recent update and all prior versions.

4. DUAL MEDIA SOFTWARE. If the SOFTWARE package contains both 3.5" and 5.25" disks, then you may use only the disks appropriate for your single-user computer. You may not use the other disks on another computer or loan, rent, lease, or transfer them to another user except as part of the permanent transfer (as provided above) of all SOFTWARE and written materials.

5. LANGUAGE SOFTWARE. If the SOFTWARE is a Microsoft language product, then you have a royalty-free right to reproduce and distribute executable files created using the SOFTWARE. If the language product is a Basic or COBOL product, then Microsoft grants you a royalty-free right to reproduce and distribute the run-time modules of the SOFTWARE provided that you: (a) distribute the run-time modules only in conjunction with and as a part of your software product; (b) do not use Microsoft's name, logo, or trademarks to market your software product; (c) include a valid copyright notice on your software product; and (d) agree to indemnify, hold harmless, and defend Microsoft and its suppliers from and against any claims or lawsuits, including attorneys' fees, that arise or result from the use or distribution of your software product. The "run-time modules" are those files in the SOFTWARE that are identified in the accompanying written materials as required during execution of your software program. The run-time modules are limited to run-time files, install files, and ISAM and REBUILD files. If required in the SOFTWARE documentation, you agree to display the designated patent notices on the packaging and in the README file of your software product.

LIMITED WARRANTY

LIMITED WARRANTY. Microsoft warrants that (a) the SOFTWARE will perform substantially in accordance with the accompanying written materials for a period of ninety (90) days from the date of receipt, and (b) any hardware accompanying the SOFTWARE will be free from defects in materials and workmanship under normal use and service for a period of one (1) year from the date of receipt. Any implied warranties on the SOFTWARE and hardware are limited to ninety (90) days and one (1) year, respectively. Some states/countries do not allow limitations on duration of an implied warranty, so the above limitation may not apply to you.

CUSTOMER REMEDIES. Microsoft's and its suppliers' entire liability and your exclusive remedy shall be, at Microsoft's option, either (a) return of the price paid, or (b) repair or replacement of the SOFTWARE or hardware that does not meet Microsoft's Limited Warranty and which is returned to Microsoft with a copy of your receipt. This Limited Warranty is void if failure of the SOFTWARE or hardware has resulted from accident, abuse, or misapplication. Any replacement SOFTWARE or hardware will be warranted for the remainder of the original warranty period or thirty (30) days, whichever is longer. Outside the United States, these remedies are not available without proof of purchase from an authorized non-U.S. source.

NO OTHER WARRANTIES. Microsoft and its suppliers disclaim all other warranties, either express or implied, including, but not limited to implied warranties of merchantability and fitness for a particular purpose, with regard to the SOFTWARE, the accompanying written materials, and any accompanying hardware. This limited warranty gives you specific legal rights. You may have others which vary from state/country to state/country.

NO LIABILITY FOR CONSEQUENTIAL DAMAGES. In no event shall Microsoft or its suppliers be liable for any damages whatsoever (including without limitation, damages for loss of business profits, business interruption, loss of business information, or any other pecuniary loss) arising out of the use of or inability to use this Microsoft product, even if Microsoft has been advised of the possibility of such damages. Because some states/countries do not allow the exclusion or limitation of liability for consequential or incidental damages, the above limitation may not apply to you.

U.S. GOVERNMENT RESTRICTED RIGHTS

The SOFTWARE and documentation are provided with RESTRICTED RIGHTS. Use, duplication, or disclosure by the Government is subject to restrictions as set forth in subparagraph (c)(1)(ii) of The Rights in Technical Data and Computer Software clause at DFARS 252.227-7013 or subparagraphs (c)(1) and (2) of the Commercial Computer Software — Restricted Rights 48 CFR 52.227-19, as applicable. Manufacturer is Microsoft Corporation, One Microsoft Way, Redmond, WA 98052-6399.

This Agreement is governed by the laws of the State of Washington.

Should you have any questions concerning this Agreement, or if you desire to contact Microsoft for any reason, please write: Microsoft Sales and Service, One Microsoft Way, Redmond, WA 98052-6399.

097-000-681

The **Step by Step** *Practice Files Disk*

The enclosed 3.5-inch disk contains timesaving, ready-to-use practice files that complement the lessons in this book. To use the practice files, you'll need Visual Basic version 4 and the Windows 95 operating system or version 3.51 or later of the Windows NT operating system.

Each *Step by Step* lesson uses practice files from the disk. Before you begin the *Step by Step* lessons, read the "Getting Ready" section of the book for easy instructions on how to install the files on your computer's hard disk. As you work through each lesson, be sure to follow the instructions for renaming the practice files so that you can go through a lesson more than once if you need to.

Please take a few moments to read the License Agreement on the previous page before using the enclosed disk.

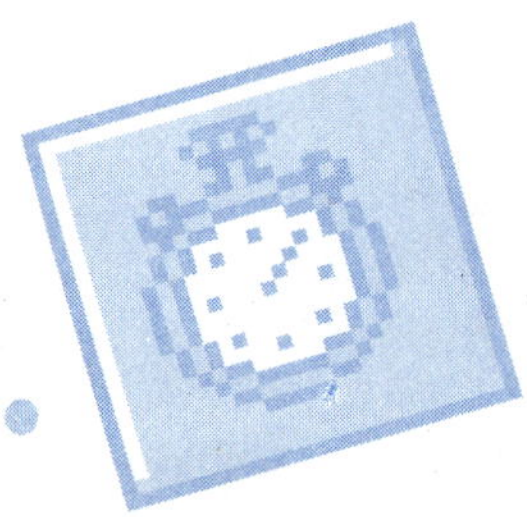